THE PARLIAMENTARY SYSTEM

By the same author:

Falling Over Backwards
Will the Iron Fence Save a Tree
Hollowed by Termites?
Governance, and the sclerosis that has set in
Courts and their Judgments
Harvesting Our Souls
Eminent Historians
Worshipping False Gods
The World of Fatwas
Missionaries in India
A Secular Agenda
Indian Controversies
'The Only Fatherland'
The State as Charade
These Lethal, Inexorable Laws
Individuals, Institutions, Processes
Religion in Politics
Mrs. Gandhi's Second Reign
Institutions in the Janata Phase
Symptoms of Fascism
Hinduism: Essence and Consequence

The Parliamentary System

What we have made of it
What we can make of it

ARUN SHOURIE

ASA

Rupa • Co

In memory of my parents
concerned about others, to the very end

for Malti Shukla
our anchor

for Adit
our life

from Anita and me

Contents

1. Introduction   9

Structures

2. Is this system a law of nature?   17
3. The system we have   21
4. Myths about the present system   24
5. Just one among many possible systems   84
6. The alternative   94

The Sovereignty-mongers

7. The 'alert and quick-acting' sovereign   115
8. Sovereignty in full spate   149
9. Some important lessons   173

Notions

10. Lessons from liberals, for liberals   195
11. Romanticising 'the people'   220

A few readings   255

Index   259

Acknowledgements   265

1.

Introduction

Today in India, two races are afoot. The first is the race between a creative society, a society that shows much energy and is surging upwards on the one hand and, on the other, the scaffolding of the State which is being hollowed by termites. The second is the race between those who are making the new India—primarily, the entrepreneurs and middle-class professionals—and the political class that is stoking the old India—for instance, by pumping in the poison of caste—to keep itself in business.

If things are just left to proceed at will, the outcome may go either way: a dynamic economy and those forging it may be so hobbled by the worsening of governance that they may put enough pressure on the political class to mend its ways, to improve governance; or governance may deteriorate to such an extent that Bihar and U.P. are generalized and economic growth is once again pulled down.

Why is it that, to take the obvious contrast, in industry new leaders are emerging by the year, leaders who are doing better and more innovative things; but in public life second-raters are giving way to third-raters, politicians are giving way to politicians-dependent-on-criminals, and the latter to criminals-who-have-become-politicians?

Why is it that while our entrepreneurs are venturing into newer and newer fields, that while they are registering conquests in more and more distant countries, that while they are thinking and planning farther and farther into the future and transforming their operations today so that they may outdo the world in the distant future; why is it that while in one sphere we see these features, in the other sphere, our politicians are stoking ever narrower sections; why is their horizon becoming shorter and shorter?

This brief book is about features in the structure of the 'parliamentary system'—actually, that should be 'in the structure of *what we have made of* the parliamentary system'—which hurtle us into the kind of politics that we see today, which steer power into the hands of the sorts of politicians we see today. And about the structure that we may adopt as an alternative.

Of course, there is no structure which cannot be perverted. And it has been well said that agitations to change constitutional arrangements often are 'exercises in escapism'—that instead of rectifying conduct, we expend time debating and devising and decreeing some other set-up, only to find, decades later, that conduct has remained the problem it was, and the new arrangement has become another problem. That is fair warning. But it is only half the truth.

One structure will induce conduct of one kind; another structure will make some other type of conduct more profitable. Our tax system of the 1950s and 1960s with its extortionate taxes ensured neither higher revenues nor equality. It fanned the black economy. As the rates have been lowered, compliance has improved. Similarly, under the license-quota *raj*, knowing the technology or the markets was not a fraction as important as knowing the Minister for Commerce and Industries, and the civil servants in the DGTD and the Office of the Controller of Imports and Exports—yes, *Exports* too: even to *export* something you had made and earn the foreign exchange the country so desperately needed, you needed permission which only these worthies could give. That structure induced one kind of effort; it brought one kind of entrepreneur to the top—the one whose core-competence lay in his ability to manipulate the State apparatus. As that structure has been dismantled, we see an entirely different kind of conduct among our entrepreneurs; we see an entirely new type of entrepreneur rise to the top.

Pluck, as an example, a proposal that figures later in the book. We lament the fact that today elections are greatly influenced by the money that a candidate can deploy; by the castes that he can work up. We dread the advantage that dons now have over ordinary candidates because they have a network of criminals that they can mobilize. Suppose we dispensed with elections altogether, and instead selected legislators by lottery. That 'X' can throw out more money; that he is from one caste rather than another; that he has a whole posse of criminals to do his work—none of these 'strengths' would improve his chances. The influence of money/caste/criminality would be erased.

So, structures do affect the outcome. They do affect conduct. And, therefore, the fact that there is no structure that cannot be perverted, should not deter us from exploring alternatives.

The conclusions that this brief review urges are:

❏ The key problem today is that the parliamentary system, anu uıe electoral system from which it springs are fragmenting the electorate on the one hand, and, on the other, are not yielding persons who have the competence, integrity and dedication to govern a billion people;

❏ Our legislatures, thus, are the root of the problems we face in governance today;

❏ Accordingly, we should find ways to reduce the role and influence of legislatures;

❏ Correspondingly, we should devise ways which improve the chances of getting a better type to man the Executive;

❏ Thereafter, we should tilt the balance away from legislatures towards the Executive;

❏ We should seek to secure accountability through institutions other than legislatures;

❏ In particular, we should strengthen the powers and role of the Judiciary.

Yet, the fact that the proposition *is* half the truth, that there is no structure which can work the cure by itself, is also important. The ills that the 'parliamentary system' as we know it has fomented, have been facilitated by and made worse by wrong *notions*. The cult of the 'common man'. The sense in which a legislator is a 'representative of the people'. The linear ascent: 'The *people* are sovereign'; 'Therefore, the *Parliament* is sovereign'; 'Therefore, *parliamentarians* are sovereign'; 'Therefore, the *majority* of parliamentarians is sovereign'; 'Therefore, *the one who controls the majority* of parliamentarians is sovereign'... Such notions are the staple of politicians: they are ever so handy whenever politicians need to push some inconvenience, like the Judiciary, aside. And as the quality of persons in public life has deteriorated, the politicians hurl these notions more and more often to aggrandize their power, and to squash all questioning of their conduct.

Having observed Parliament first hand for ten years; reading accounts of the condition to which discourse has fallen in the Assemblies of our states, I fear that the greatest present threat to governance, and the most imminent threat to our liberties is this string of notions—starting from 'The people are sovereign' and ascending to 'Therefore, Parliament is sovereign.' I have, therefore, devoted a good bit of the book to recalling one sequence of events—to recalling what was proclaimed in the name of the people, to what was claimed and then grabbed in the name of sovereignty of Parliament. As voices of that kind continue to be raised every other month in and out of our legislatures, I fear that sequence of events—though seemingly three decades old—is as current as can be.

There is another reason for recounting that sequence. In many ways the Emergency was a defining moment for our generation—it awakened and politicized the middle class. But two-thirds of our people—yes, two-thirds—were not even born then. Another sixth or seventh, though born, were too young to realize what was happening. And yet, unless such usurpations are kept fresh in our minds, we are liable to set ourselves up for the next forfeiture. For governance goes out of hand not as often by a sudden collapse as by gradual erosion. Liberties are lost not by sudden assault alone. They are eroded as people get accustomed to bits falling off. They are lost not just to the usurper in distant capitals but to the neighbourhood gangster.

Given this threat to governance, and its fountainheads—namely, legislatures and the claim on their behalf to being sovereign—the book argues that the doctrine of the Basic Structure—a doctrine that Mrs. Indira Gandhi and her acolytes had denounced as 'an invention of the judges'—is a dyke we need. Accordingly, I urge that, even as the power and role of legislatures is reduced and that of the Executive strengthened, this dyke, and the power that it accords to the Judiciary, should be reinforced. But even a brief review of some major pronouncements of the courts on the Basic Structure shows that the judges themselves have chiseled several fissures in the dyke. Hence, the book illustrates the sorts of pronouncements, often born of excessive trust, by which judges have weakened the dyke, and argues that it is not enough to grant more powers of review and oversight to the Judiciary. The judges must act the independence that has been given to them.

There are twin problems, of course. First, the decision to change the system lies in the hands of those who are the beneficiaries of the system as it is. Second, in an open society, the key to bringing pressure on them lies in a vigorous public discourse. But this too is dominated by them—look at the play that inane speeches of whoever happens to be in the government get in our media; look at the way organizations of industry have become mere event-managers for whoever happens to be in the government. And, then, for other reasons, reasons independent of the political structure, there is the dumbing down of the media. That has contributed as much to elevating these notions to the status of 'truths we hold as self-evident'.

But there are several factors that give ground for the hope that change can be brought about in spite of these problems. For one thing, governance is sinking to such depths that even the influentials are getting affected. For another, legitimacy, authority, power have passed out of the hands of beneficiaries of things as they are—the political class—into the hands of those who are set back by the deterioration; that is, it has passed into the hands of those who are making the new India.

So, the need for another structure is there. The opportunity for bringing it about is also there.

From these two facts flows the plea of this book. Excel in your specialization, of course. But step beyond that specialization. Don't just wait for a breakdown to do the job, as the breakdown in our external account did with regard to economic reforms. Spare time and effort for improving the general condition of governance. In a word, 'Give history a helping hand.'

Structures

2

Is this system a law of nature?

A management expert writes of an experiment. Take a frog, he says. Throw it into a pot of boiling water. It will be shocked. It will jump free out of the water. It will get scalded, no doubt, but it will survive. Now take a frog, and put it in a pot with water at room-temperature. Bring the water to a boil, gradually. The frog will get accustomed to higher and higher temperature. It will sink into a stupor, and will eventually get boiled to death.

We are that frog. We are getting accustomed to worse and worse conduct in public life, to the winding down of our institutions. Who could have thought even ten years ago that we would have as ministers in the Central government persons against whom cases involving the gravest corruption charges are proceeding in the courts or, indeed, even cases of murder? Haven't we got used to them? Were they to come to our school, would we not run around them? Do civil servants not do their bidding? Do incidents that used to happen in the Bihar and U.P. Assemblies and shock us, not happen now in Parliament, and do they shock us any longer? Have we not got used to killings by terrorists? Can you recall which was the last major assault by them? When? Have we not reconciled ourselves to the clogging in courts? To the fact that the bureaucrats will just keep going through the motions?

Therefore, the first question we must ask ourselves is: Is there a bottom, on reaching which, we will conclude, 'Yes, this arrangement is not working, it has to be replaced'?

Are criminal MPs and ministers, are the 13 years of Lalu's rule in Bihar, the price that we have to pay for being a democracy? That is, are they inevitable? Is what we are seeing, 'Democracy', or '*what we have made of Democracy*'? Is it '*Kleptocracy*' or '*Democracy*'? Is it 'Democracy' or *disarray?*

Next, we must ask ourselves whether a multitude can govern. Can a mob, can a pack govern? We romanticize the 'average man'. But is governing a billion people not too complex for him? Are his concerns—getting through the day, taking care of his immediate family, helping or warding off his immediate neighbours—appropriate for governing the totality?

Similarly, when it suits them, our politicians romanticize the present parliamentary system. 'He has a secret agenda,' they shout at anyone who urges that we look for an alternative constitutional system. 'He is a high-caste man, he is out to pull down the sacred Constitution just because it was framed by Dr. Ambedkar'—I have had to hear them allege. This, even though many of them do not so much as blink as they overturn provisions of the Constitution to crush judgements of the Supreme Court which do not suit their political convenience. As for the Constitution and its Framers, the process by which it evolved was far too complex for the authorship of the final document to be attributed to any one person. If one person has to be singled out, that would certainly be Sir B.N. Rau, the then Constitutional Advisor to the Constituent Assembly. In any case, Dr. Ambedkar repudiated not just the claim to having authored the document but the Constitution itself, and that in the strongest possible words. 'People always keep on saying "O, you are the maker of the Constitution." My answer is I was a hack. What I was asked to do, I did much against my will....,' he told the Rajya Sabha on 2 September 1953. 'Sir, my friends tell me that I have made the Constitution. But I am quite prepared to say that I shall be the first person to burn it out. I do not want it. It does not suit anybody...' In any event, the Framers, including Dr. Ambedkar, could never have visualized that the system they were putting in place would throw up the type of persons who now occupy seats in our legislatures and councils of ministers.

But the basic point is different. It goes beyond mere questions of authorship, and of whether changing the Constitution constitutes blasphemy. The point is, the present system is just a means, an instrument. It has to be judged by the results it produces.

The Framers of the Constitution had no doubt about this. Even as the Objectives Resolution was being considered, that is even at the very first step, Panditji told the Constituent Assembly, on 22 January 1947,

> A free India will see the bursting forth of the energy of a mighty nation. What it will do and what it will not, I do not know, but I do know that it will not consent to be bowed down... This House cannot bind down the next generation or the people who will duly succeed us...

Almost two years later, as the Constituent Assembly was deliberating over the Draft Constitution, Panditji returned to this theme, and told the members:

> The Constitution is after all some kind of legal body given to the ways of government and the life of the people. A Constitution if it is out of touch with the people's life, aims and aspirations, becomes rather empty: if it falls behind those aims, it drags the people down. It should be something ahead to keep people's eyes and minds made up to a certain high mark... Remember this that while we want this Constitution to be as solid and as permanent a structure as we can make it, ...there should be a certain flexibility. If you make anything rigid and permanent, you stop a nation's growth, the growth of a living, vital, organic people.

The Constitution had been working for just two years. In part to overcome some judgements of the Supreme Court, a Bill was introduced to amend it in 1951. Members complained: but it is just two years since we adopted the Constitution, it is wholly wrong to amend it so soon. Panditji was forthright:

> ...we have in India a strange habit of making gods of various things, adding them to our innumerable pantheon, and having given them our theoretical worship, doing exactly the reverse. If we want to kill a thing in this country, we deify it. That is the habit of this country largely. So if you wish to kill this Constitution, make it sacred and sacrosanct—certainly. If you want it to be a dead thing, not a growing thing, a static, unwieldy, unchanging thing, then by all means do so, realizing that that is the best way of stabbing it in the front and in the back... A Constitution which is unchanging and static, it does not matter how good it is, but as a Constitution it is past its use. It is in its old age already and gradually approaching its death. A Constitution to be living must be growing; must be adaptable; must be flexible; must be changeable... Therefore, it is a desirable and a good thing for people to realize that this very fine Constitution that we have fashioned after years of labour, is good in so far as it goes, but as society changes, as conditions change, we amend it in the

proper way. It is not like the unalterable law of the Medes and Persians that it cannot be changed, although the world around may change.

And again, when the Constitution was being amended for the fourth time, in 1955, Panditji reiterated,

After all, the Constitution is meant to facilitate the working of the government and the administrative and other structures of this country. It is meant to be not something that is static and which has a static form in a changing world, but something which has something dynamic in it, which takes cognizance of the dynamic nature of modern conditions, modern society.

And the fact is that, whenever they want to alter the provisions—to shield themselves, as Mrs. Indira Gandhi did in 1975; to advance their political calculations, as in the numerous amendments that have been made to overturn judgements of the Supreme Court on reservations—these very rulers invoke these very words! As do others—for instance, the National Commission to Review the Working of the Constitution. It is just that whenever anyone else proposes changes, they charge 'He has a secret agenda.' In any case, it lies ill in the mouth of persons who have altered the Constitution close to a hundred times to foreclose discussion of the matter by alleging secret agendas. In fact, that figure, 'close to a hundred times', *understates* what they have done to the Constitution. The number of *amendments* has been 94. But several of the amendments have altered, in some cases turned upside down, a number of Articles of the Constitution. A rough count indicates that Articles have been changed 332 times.

The system we have

A country of our size, a country facing problems as complex as the ones that face India, a country that, at the same time, has unlimited opportunities it can avail itself of provided its leaders steer it towards those horizons—such a country needs strong Executive leadership. In particular, it needs a strong Centre. And it needs a system that ensures efficient governance.

The essential elements of the present system, and the ones with which we will deal are as follows:

❏ Universal adult franchise: the eligible voter having the option to vote or not.
❏ Periodic elections: as these are held for several layers of institutions—Parliament, state Assemblies, corporations, down to *panchayats*—at most times, some election or the other is either being conducted or is round the corner.
❏ Single member constituencies with first-past-the-post winners.
❏ The Government is formed by the party that commands a majority in the House, or by the single largest conglomeration of parties—the conglomeration may be formed before or after the elections.
❏ The leader elected by that party or that conglomeration is the Prime Minister or Chief Minister.
❏ He selects ministers from within the legislature—he may select someone who is not a member of the legislature but the latter must become one within six months.
❏ The Government can be voted out even if there is no agreement on who is to be the next Prime Minister or what is to be the next Government.
❏ If a new Government cannot be formed, new elections are to be held.

This system is justified on several counts:

❑ It is said to yield governments with clear majorities, governments that are stable and in a position to take the difficult decisions that governing such a large and complex country like India requires.
❑ It is said to be representative—of the people as well as of their will.
❑ It is said to ensure participatory governance, that under it every party and leader is induced to round off his edges, that it brings contenders together, and thus harmonizes interests.
❑ It is said that as the Government that results from such a system will be necessarily broad-based and representative, it is stable, durable, and effective.
❑ It is said that while the system may take some time to yield a consensus, the solutions that emerge from it are more durable.
❑ It is said to ensure accountability—of each minister to the Prime Minister; through the principle of collective responsibility, of each minister to his colleagues; and of the political Executive collectively to Parliament.
❑ It is said to induce a two-party system, to discourage fragmentation of parties as well as of the electorate.

A telling analogy

In his important, posthumous work, *Power and Prosperity*,[1] Olson distinguished between a stationary and a roving bandit. The first and foremost objective of both is to preserve their power, to extend it. In the process, both rob those in their sphere. But there is an important difference, Olson pointed out. The prosperity of the stationary bandit—the mafia don controlling prostitution in an area—depends to an extent on the continuance and growth of that activity in his jurisdiction. He will, therefore, desist from extracting so much out of his subjects that they either migrate elsewhere or, unable to move elsewhere, just waste away and die. The roving bandit, a Chengez Khan so to say, has no such compunction. His prosperity does not

---

[1] Mancur Olson, *Power and Prosperity, Outgrowing Communist and Capitalist Dictatorships*, Basic Books, New York, 2000. Unless otherwise indicated, all portions italicised, have been italicised by me.

depend on tne continued prosperity of those who come under his sway. He loots them dry, and sweeps to the next settlement.

Our system has descended to such a level that large parts of the country are now not just under the sway of bandits; they are prey to roving bandits, not just stationary ones.

The first priority of the ruler/bandit is to stay in power. Ensuring prosperity for his people can only be an aim if doing so will make them support him to remain in power; he may go on impoverishing them if doing so makes them more helpless and therefore more dependent. The question, Olson explains, thus turns on how *encompassing* the interests of the bandit are.

The ordinary criminal, the pickpocket takes everything in your pocket. A mafia leader leaves enough so that you do not migrate to another town and shift your business there. He, in fact, provides you protection against exactions by other criminals in return for protection money within his territory. But the roving bandit takes all.

Hence, the pillage will be greater, the more rapidly governments change; the more unstable, the more fragmented they are.

'We are going to be out soon,' the rulers of the moment will reason, 'Hence, gobble up all you can.'

Notice that it is not just the shortness of the likely life of the government. The fragmentation of legislatures and, therefore, of governments comes to constitute an additional reason for concentrating on what one can rake in than on doing right by the country. As the survival of the government now depends on every little clutch of MPs, a minister from every party can loot. None of them need fear punishment. Indeed, in a textbook illustration of Roy Harrod's theorem about 'the importance of being unimportant', the ones who form the smaller groups can loot the most and with the greatest impunity, as predation by their members will affect the total the least! Those who are most incompetent, who are most unpopular will also loot with abandon as in their own eyes they are least likely to return. And so will the ones who are most secure, the ones whose return is not affected by their loot—recall the number of ministers and their controllers who are returned by their caste-followers irrespective of their performance, and think of what they do in office.

Myths about the present system

The standard argument for a first-past-the-post system over, say, that of Proportional Representation is that the former yields secure majorities, and, therefore, decisive governments. The latter is supposed to provide an incentive for progressive fragmentation of the electorate and of parties. Our experience—our unbroken experience extending now over thirty years—is the exact opposite. The first-past-the-post system has given the maximum inducement to splinter the electorate, and to go on fragmenting parties.

When this fragmentation first appeared and a coalition became necessary in 1967, political commentators romanticized it: 'India is coming into its own,' they said, 'Parliament is becoming truly representative of India's rich diversities.' Some still rationalize what has become of our legislatures and parties, but the rationalization is different: 'If the people are happy to elect Raja Bhaiyya,' I was told the other day by a senior police official, 'if they are happy to elect Shahabuddin and Ansari, if these persons are the ones who help them in time of need, who are we to object?' Such rationalizations, when they are not just cleverness, strike me as alibis. They exempt the person from doing anything—this is a democracy, after all; the people want such persons to represent them; who are we to interfere? That apart, I wouldn't be as confident attributing the victories of such persons to the people's happiness. But, even if the people were happy, I wouldn't take the matter as settled. We must judge an electoral and political system on an altogether different criterion. Is it putting into place persons who can actually legislate? Is it putting into office persons who can actually administer a country of a billion people?

The myth that the parliamentary system ensures accountability to Parliament

The descent to assured safety for looters punctures one of the major myths about the current system, that it ensures accountability.

The myth covers two assertions. Under the parliamentary system, the argument goes, the Executive is accountable to Parliament. Second, individual ministers are said to be under the constant vigil of Parliament in addition to the supervision of the Prime Minister, as well as of their colleagues; the principle of collective responsibility of the Council of Ministers ensures, so the theory goes, that others, in particular the Prime Minister, will not let any colleague get out of line lest they get hurt collectively.

The condition which our governments have reached shows that each of these presumptions is a myth.

Far from the Council of Ministers being accountable to and controlled by Parliament, it is the Council of Ministers precisely because *it* controls Parliament. And unless you can bring the government down, it cares little for what you say or do on the floor of Parliament. This is made evident day after day. Even on the most 'non-political' of issues, in the end members vote and speak strictly along party-lines. Recall the impeachment proceedings against Justice V. Ramaswamy. Recall the various debates on internal security, on Kashmir, on foreign policy, on the budget. Everyone speaks on party-lines; that feature by itself robs the 'debates' of significance and influence. When was it last that a budget proposal was altered because of reasoned discussion in Parliament? To say nothing of a negligent and inefficient minister, when was it last that Parliament was able to bring an out-and-out corrupt one to book?

That goes, *a fortiori*, for governments as a whole. And when they are pulled down, that has nothing to do with policies or issues or conduct. Recall the two constables on account of whom Chandrashekhar's Government was ostensibly pulled down; recall the plaintive wail of H.D. Deve Gowda when his Government was being pulled down, 'I ask only, "What wrong have I done?"' Governments are brought down because their prop has concluded that it will gain more through a new election than by keeping the government in office. Similarly, a government is kept going not because the props feel that it is pursuing the right policies—look at the denunciations that the Left-leaders hurl every other day at Manmohan Singh's Government: its policies are 'anti-people,' they shout; it has mortgaged our foreign policy to the US, they shout; but they keep the government in place. They do so because they have not yet been able to cobble together an alternative, and because they do not think that they can get a majority for some alternative combination through another election just yet. Confident that it is not going to be thrown out, the government of the day cares little for what is said in Parliament. Just brazen it out, is the settled 'policy', just shout them down. On the other side, certain that what it says is not going to have the least effect, the Opposition takes to shouting, disruption...

Nor is it just a question of governments and their props becoming wayward. The other side of the equation is as destructive. First the legislatures of states, and now Parliament are in such disarray that they cannot deliver accountability at all. Bills are passed without meaningful discussion, indeed, amidst ear-splitting *hulla*. Even budgets are passed amidst chaos. Hours and hours are spent on adjournments over the headline of the day, and then the 'legislators' are corralled to constitute a quorum and the Bill is declared to have been passed... And at the end of the Session, the presiding officer intones, 'This was a very productive Session... The House passed twenty-three Bills. Two hundred and seventy-five papers were laid on the Table of the House. Very productive debates were held on issues of national and international significance which, I am sure, will provide very useful guidance to the Government as it guides the country in its onward march to destiny...'

The reality is very different from the figures. C.V. Madhukar, who has begun studying the workings of Parliament diligently, points out that while, formally, Parliament has passed 58 or so Bills per year during the last six years, 'Over the past seven sessions of Parliament, the time spent on debating legislative issues was approximately 20 per cent in Lok Sabha and 23 per cent in Rajya Sabha. In fact, in the winter session of 2004, less than 15 per cent time was spent on legislation in Lok Sabha...' In fact, that vastly overstates the deliberative effort of members. Madhukar points out that in 2006, 'Over 40 per cent of the Bills were passed in Lok Sabha with less than one hour of debate. The situation is only marginally better in Rajya Sabha.' But even *this* vastly overstates the work that is done. For, while the House may be said to be formally debating a piece of legislation, the chamber may be embarrassingly empty. Madhukar recalls the case of the Contempt of Courts (Amendment) Bill that *The Indian Express* had reported earlier: there were all of 21 MPs in the Treasury Benches and nine in the Opposition Benches when this important Bill was passed by voice vote in the Lok Sabha...[1] Of course, passing laws is not the only function of legislatures. Discussing policy, discussing events and the government's response to them is as important. The record here is even more dismal. The Session usually begins with those in Opposition—that is, whichever side happens to be in Opposition at that time—demanding that issues 'X' and 'Y' be taken up immediately—farmers' suicides, price rise, the crisis in agriculture... The government insists that the business that has already been settled be adhered to. The House is adjourned a few times. Each side having 'given the right signal' to the section whose eye it wants to catch, all sides agree to have a discussion on the issue. The debate has but to start, and the issue is over. The House barely has a quorum... The singular exception in the last few years has been the Indo-US nuclear deal. It is the only issue I can recall on which Government had to reverse course as a result of what was said in the House of which I am a member, the Rajya Sabha.

In a word, these chambers are now not legislatures that hold governments to account, they are now halls in which the motions are gone through, in which put on melodramas are enacted.

The only sense in which the system ensures accountability is that the government can be thrown out at the next election. But that is just as true of the Presidential system as it is of the parliamentary system. It is as true of single-party governments as it is of coalitions.

The myth that a parliamentary system ensures representativeness
In contrast to the Proportional Representation system, the system we have, the first-past-the-post system, is supposed to give victory to

---

[1]C.V. Madhukar, 'House this for debate?,' *The Indian Express*, 3 January, 2007.

one party. It is supposed to induce the growth of a two-party system by penalizing smaller parties. It is supposed to encourage large parties to broad-base their appeal. It is supposed to give the people a greater say in the selection of candidates. Yet, in every particular, in India it is leading to the opposite.

In the Lok Sabha elections of 2004, 230 parties put up candidates. The Lok Sabha now has 39 parties. The Rajya Sabha has 30. The NDA Government consisted of 11 parties. The UPA Government consists of 14 parties. Continuity has been ensured, so to say, by some who were ministers in the NDA Government switching sides and continuing as ministers in the UPA Government—the DMK ministers, the ever-in-office Ram Vilas Paswan...

Legislators, and now governments are getting elected by progressively smaller proportions of the electorate: even in the early stages, the fact that Pandit Nehru and Mrs. Indira Gandhi got steamroller majorities with just 38 to 41 per cent votes used to trouble several thoughtful observers.

Glance at the proportion of votes by obtaining which members of the Lok Sabha got elected in 2004:

Votes Polled by Winners as % age of Voters

Groups	No. of Winners	% age	Cumulative percentage
Below 20%	0	0	
20% to 30%	16	3	3
31% to 40%	95	17	20
41% to 50%	214	39	60
51% to 60%	176	32	92
61% to 70%	36	7	99
Above 71%	6	1	100
Total	543	100	

Votes polled by Winners as %age of Electors

Groups	No. of Winners	% age	Cumulative percentage
Below 10%	2	0	
11% to 20%	93	17	17
21% to 30%	220	41	58
31% to 40%	186	34	92
41% to 50%	36	7	99
51% to 60%	4	1	100
61% to 70%	2	0	100
Above 71%	0	0	100
Total	543	100	

In a word, 99 per cent of the members got into the Lok Sabha by getting less than half the electors to vote for them. Almost 60 per cent got in with the endorsement of less than 30 per cent of electors in their constituencies. Even if we consider only the electors who actually turned out to vote, 60 per cent of the members got in on a minority vote. The unrepresentativeness of governments and legislators in the states is even greater:

Elections to state Assemblies: 2001-2005

Votes polled by winner as per cent of Voters	Below 20% % seats	Up to 30% % seats	Up to 40% % seats	Up to 50% % seats	Up to 60% % seats	Up to 70% % seats	70% & above % seats
Andhra Pradesh		1	8	34	89	100	
Assam	4	27	68	90	97	100	
Bihar	0	4	49	89	98	100	
Chhatisgarh		4	34	80	98	100	
Delhi	1	4	39	80	99	100	
Gujarat		1	7	42	88	96	100
Haryana		3	35	64	83	89	100
Himachal Pradesh		3	24	61	92	100	
Jharkhand	3	29	71	94	99	100	
Karnataka	0	6	34	75	99	100	
Kerala		1	41	96	100		
Madhya Pradesh		9	32	67	98	100	
Maharashtra		2	27	64	92	98	100
Orissa	3	19	60	97	99	100	
Punjab		3	2	73	97	99	100
Rajasthan		6	34	75	98	100	
Tamil Nadu			3	42	97	100	
Uttar Pradesh		26	78	96	99	99	100
Uttarakhand	1	29	81	96	100		
West Bengal			2	50	88	96	100

Elections to state Assemblies: 2001-2005

Votes polled by winner as per cent of Electors	Below 20%	Up to 30%	Up to 40%	Up to 50%	Up to 60%	Up to 70%	70% & above
	% seats	% seats	% seats	% seats	% seats	% seats	% seats
Andhra Pradesh	2	18	64	99	100		
Assam	2	29	73	95	98	99	100
Bihar	62	100					
Chhatisgarh	4	44	94	98	100		
Delhi	4	66	99	100			
Gujarat		1	31	89	99	100	
Haryana		3	41	87	98	99	100
Himachal Pradesh	2	27	75	99	100		
Jharkhand	49	95	99	100			
Karnataka	7	56	96	100			
Kerala	6	80	100	100			
Madhya Pradesh	9	43	93	100			
Maharashtra	7	53	86	97	100		
Orissa	3	37	96	100			
Punjab		5	50	99	100		
Rajasthan	7	55	94	100			
Tamil Nadu	1	42	98	100			
Uttar Pradesh	62	96	100	100			
Uttarakhand	70	97	100	100			
West Bengal		1	8	63	93	98	100

Notice:

❏ In Bihar, 100 per cent of the winners got into the Assembly even though 70 per cent of the electors had *not* endorse them: they got in though the voters who voted for them constituted less than 30 per cent of the electors in their respective constituencies. In Jharkhand, the figure was 95 per cent; in U.P., 96 per cent; in Uttarakhand, 97 per cent.

❏ Even if we focus only on electors who actually cast their votes, the per cent of winners who got in though they polled a minority of votes cast was in Bihar, 89 per cent; in Chhatisgarh, 80 per cent; in Jharkhand, 94 per cent; in U.P., 96 per cent; in Uttarakhand, 96 per cent. Even in several of the other states— Assam, Haryana, Karnataka, Madhya Pradesh, Punjab, Rajasthan—the figure ranged between 65 and 75 per cent.[1]

Pointing to this alarming feature, the Constitution Review Commission observed, 'In some cases those who would otherwise have forfeited their security deposit have been declared elected as they had obtained the highest number of votes amongst the candidates.'[2] Representativeness?

---

[1]This problem has come to afflict several countries that adhere to the first-past-the-post system. Thus, in UK, 'In 1951, the Government was elected on 40% of the support of the electorate and in the third triumphal election victory of Mr. Blair, it is just over 20%–35% of the votes cast, that is just over a third of the votes cast and only slightly over 1 in 5 of those competent to vote, have supported the Government.' Remarks of Professor John Spencer QC at the Royal Society of Arts meeting on 'Trouble at the top?', 5 October 2005, *www.theRSA.org*

[2]*Report of the National Commission to Review the Working of the Constitution*, Justice M.N. Venkatachaliah, and others, New Delhi, 2002. There is a related problem to which the Constitution Review Commission devoted a good bit of attention: the large number of independent candidates who stand or are put up to stand. Results of the 2004 Lok Sabha elections afford a glimpse of the issue. The total number of Lok Sabha seats is 543. The distribution of candidates shown on the next page explains itself:

Parties	Number of candidates	Number who forfeited deposits	(3) as % of (2)
National parties	135	541	40
State parties	801	440	54
Unregistered parties	898	867	96
Independents	2385	2370	99
Total	5435	4218	77

The Commission proposed measures to enhance the costs for non-serious candidates to enter the fray.

There is an allied myth. It is entirely fictitious to suppose that the individual member of Parliament can 'represent' the interests of his constituents in the sense that this has come to be understood in India—that is, that he can take care of their individual interests and problems. With almost twenty lakh people to a constituency, there just is no way that a member of the Lok Sabha, howsoever conscientious, will be able to ensure jobs for them and postings to the place of choice for their brothers-in-law. And yet that he must do so is not just the myth. It is the expectation; advocates of the present system, with its single-member geographical constituencies, believe that it is his duty to attend to the interests and problems of his constituents! The nadir of this kind of reasoning has been attained in the M.P. Local Area Development Scheme. Each M.P. is given Rs.10 crore per term in the Lok Sabha and Rs.12 crore per term in the Rajya Sabha. Ostensibly, this vast amount—Rs.1,600 crore a year in the case of Parliament alone—is given on the premise that the local administration is not responsive enough, and only the local M.P. has sufficient empathy for the people. This leads to blurring the boundaries between legislative and executive functions on the one hand, and to charges of corruption and neglect on the other. Members who assign funds for works in one village are accused by residents of the neighbouring village for neglecting them, and of doing so for collateral purposes.

The consequences of the feature, that members get elected by a minority of votes, are brought home even more vividly when we consider individual constituencies. Consider the figures shown on the next page relating to the 2004 elections to the Lok Sabha:

Uttar Pradesh, 2004: Lok Sabha
votes polled by winners as %age of electors

Constituency	% Votes.	Constituency	% Votes
Moradabad	16.1	Ghatampur (SC)	13.3
Aonla	13.4	Jalaun (SC)	14.9
Bareilly	17.3	Jhansi	15.6
Pilibhit	19.9	Hamirpur	18.6
Shahjahanpur	17.8	Banda	14.4
Kheri	15.6	Fatehpur	12.8
Shahabad	16.7	Chail (SC)	13.2
Sitapur	13.3	Allahabad	15.0
Misrikh (SC)	16.8	Phulpur	18.8
Hardoi (SC)	16.8	Mirzapur	12.4
Lucknow	19.8	Robertsganj (SC)	11.4
Mohanlal Ganj (SC)	11.6	Varanasi	13.9
Unnao	13.7	Chandauli	12.9
Pratapgarh	17.9	Saidpur (SC)	15.1
Sultanpur	17.9	Meerut	19.0
Faizabad	15.6	Bilhaur	16.3
Bara Banki (SC)	16.2	Kanpur	14.8
Kaiserganj	17.3	Farrukhabad	12.9
Bahraich	13.3	Firozabad (SC)	16.3
Gonda	18.1	Agra	17.0
Basti (SC)	11.0	Mathura	14.7
Domariaganj	15.0	Hathras (SC)	14.4
Khalilabad	16.8	Aligarh	12.5
Bansgaon (SC)	12.5	Khurja (SC)	14.7
Maharajganj	17.4	Hapur	13.0
Padrauna	13.8	Jaunpur	14.5
Deoria	15.1	Machhlishahar	16.1
Salempur	13.2	Lalganj (SC)	18.2
Ballia	18.9	Azamgarh	18.1
Ghosi	14.1		

Here is a series of constituencies from which persons won even though they had received the endorsement of just 10 to 20 per cent of the electors. Forty-seven per cent of our population is below the age of 19. As electors would be around 55 per cent of the population, these figures would suggest that the successful candidates had to persuade just 5 to 10 per cent of the population in their constituencies and they would be in!

This fact contains an all-important operational lesson, for candidates and their leaders: namely, just get a tenth or a fifth of the electorate; that is, 5 to 10 per cent of the population solidly behind you. This is the tactic that the Congress relied on for long. This is the secret of the 'strength' of Lalu Yadav, Mulayam Singh, Mayawati. This is what lies behind the 'invincibility' of the district-parties that play such a decisive role in forming and overturning governments in Tamil Nadu. This is the reason that the Muslims are courted by every party today. Frighten those tenth or fifth, cajole them, show them any *sabz-baag*, 'persuade' the ones who control them or can sway them—the *mullahs* giving the Friday sermons, the *sarpanchs*—and you are home. If your particular target-group is not sufficient by itself, form a 'grand social alliance'—the KHAM made notorious in Gujarat; Lalu Yadav's MY, Muslim-Yadav combination; the knitting together of district 'parties' in Tamil Nadu—and you will sweep the election.

So splintered is the electorate by now that there is hardly a 'national issue' on which it is exercised. And that lesson is not lost on even the national parties. Assume that a party that has a presence across the country is able to get 15 per cent of the total vote across the country. Of what avail would that be? It would not get a single seat. If, on the other hand, it concentrated on a few local issues; if it focused its resources on sowing hatred and fear in 15 per cent of the electorate in a particular part of the country, it would be certain to get its candidates into Parliament. Look at the 'success' of the Samajwadi Party, the Shiv Sena, the DMK and AIADMK, the Akalis, the BSP, the Communists themselves, and contrast that with the waning presence of the Congress and the BJP.

What could be a greater inducement to a leader to fragment the electorate? To address his appeal to narrower and narrower sections? To drill into them *divisive* notions—that they are different from the rest, that they are being discriminated against by the rest and that the rest are out to grab the little that is left with them?

The elections over, a party realizes that it has won. Other parties see that by teaming up with it, their members can become ministers and the like. It isn't that they have had any views in common, and, therefore, they come together to form a government—indeed, many of them, like the Communists and the Congress, have just fought *against* each other in the elections. Rather, seeing the opportunity

that has fallen in their lap, that of forming a government, they *look* for
an 'issue', an *excuse* by which to justify forming that government. In
this last round, the 'issue', the excuse has been the dire need to save
the country from 'communalism'!

This consummation is facilitated by instantaneous assertions by
committed commentators over TV networks. 'Voters have given a
mandate for...'

While the people are being prepared in those crucial hours by
such instant 'analysis', three/four well-practised hacks are rustled up
to draw up a 'Common Minimum Programme' so that opportunism
can be dressed up as principle: 'We have not come together for
power but to implement this programme...'

Weaker and weaker governments

With the electorate splintered, the legislature cannot but be equally
splintered: thus, as we noticed, even the Lok Sabha now has 39
parties. Mr. Vajpayee's Government could be put together only by
stitching up 11 parties. Dr. Manmohan Singh's Government has been
made possible only by cobbling together 14 and even then, it is
entirely at the mercy of four Communist parties that are outside the
United Progressive Alliance, so-called.

Not only is a coalition of such disparate groups inherently weak,
the singular interest of constituents other than the dominant one is to
ensure that the government *remains* weak. It is then that the
government, and, therefore, the dominant partner are most at their
mercy. All parties other than the dominant one thus are happier the
more tenuous the overall coalition, and, within the coalition, the
weaker is the dominant constituent. Look at the conduct of the
Communists since the day the UPA Government was sworn in. They
denounce it for anti-people policies, for making India's foreign
policy an instrument of American designs, but they keep it in office;
break their legs, and keep them there, that is their 'strategy'. All the
blame, much of it pasted by you, will pile up on them; all the credit
for 'taking up people's causes' will accrue to you!

A weak coalition in place, the dominant constituent of the coalition
rendered lame, every puny 'leader' is king. Who is to be a minister
from a party becomes the prerogative of the controller of *that* party,
not of the Prime Minister. And, once in government, the minister may
do well or ill, he may ruin the institutions under his charge, he may

rake in money brazenly to the knowledge of the Prime Minister and others, no one dare touch him. And he knows that: he feels accountable to *his* boss, the controller of the party to which he belongs, not to the Prime Minister. That the Cabinet system is built on 'collective responsibility' becomes just a phrase, a mythical phrase. Ministers belonging to the DMK attended the Cabinet meeting in which the Cabinet decided to disinvest government equity in the Neyveli Lignite Corporation. Their controller, M. Karunanidhi declared the decision to be unacceptable. The Central Government had to meekly take back its decision. On the other side, individual ministers announce far-reaching policies on matters of the greatest significance, from drug prices to reservations, without so much as a 'By your leave', and the entire Government has to meekly acquiesce. Dr. Manmohan Singh's helplessness—the subject of daily sneering—is only in part due to his innate diffidence. It isn't just that he has been nominated to the post, it isn't just that he must remember every minute the way Congressmen prostrated themselves before Mrs. Sonia Gandhi, and how not one mentioned him as a possible substitute for her. It is also that since then, even his colleagues in Government pay as little heed to him and his office. Every day he sounds more and more as if he were a consultant to the Government rather than as one who is directing it. The prime ministership is an institution? 'Collective responsibility' is at the heart of the Cabinet form of government?

Following a specific sequence will reveal where we have reached.

A recent example

Jharkhand is one of the best endowed regions of our country, richer in mineral wealth than most countries of the world. Yet its people are poor. The region was pushed lower down by Lalu Yadav's ruinous 13 years, as it was then part of composite Bihar. A new state was created in 2000. The hope was that doing so would liberate the people of this region from the disastrous politics of Bihar. What has been happening since then testifies to what has happened to these hopes in fact.

The last Assembly elections in undivided Bihar were held in February 2000. Out of a total 324 seats, 81 fell in the region which would soon become Jharkhand. As creation of a separate Jharkhand state had by that time become a distinct possibility, it was widely believed that the elections were being held not for just the Bihar Assembly, but for the future Jharkhand Assembly as well.

After the elections, the following party position emerged for the future Jharkhand Assembly:

BJP: 32	JDU: 3
JMM: 12	CPI: 3
Congress: 11	CPI (ML): 1
RJD: 9	MCC: 1
Samata: 5	Independents: 4

There are many arcane matters that need not detain us at the moment—for instance, the fact that 'MCC' here stands for the Marxist Co-ordination Committee which is not to be confused with 'MCC', an extremist organization that would, of course, regard participation in electoral politics to be a gross betrayal of 'The Revolution'.

But there is one detail for which we should spare attention—a few names, though nothing is likely to be heard of them even a few months hence.

There were four Independents. One of them, Sudesh Mahto of the All Jharkhand Student Union (AJSU), had nominally contested the election on the symbol of, of all things, the UDGP (the United Democratic Goans Party), but for all practical purposes was treated as an Independent. A lady, Joba Manjhi, was the widow of a local leader, Devendra Manjhi, who had been very popular in the West Singhbhum district. She also contested on the UDGP symbol, but she too was looked upon as an Independent, and clubbed together with them.

The third Independent was Samresh Singh. He had been elected to the Assembly of composite Bihar in the 1985 and 1990 elections on the BJP ticket. He had left the party because of differences with some senior leaders. In 2000, he won by a huge margin on his own.

The fourth Independent, Madhav Lal Singh, belongs to a very prominent family. He had also won in 1985 and 1990, but lost to a BJP candidate in 1995.

When the creation of a separate Jharkhand state became a certainty and the date for its formation (15 November 2000) was also announced, two rival alliances quickly formed to capture power.

Ultimately, the BJP-led alliance won the race. In the House of 82 (of which 81 were elected members, and one a nominated member), this alliance had the support of 45 MLAs.

The 45 were made up as follows: BJP, 32; Samata, 5; JDU, 3; Independents, 4; and the member who had been nominated against the quota for Anglo-Indians.

Babulal Marandi was first elected leader of the BJP Legislature Party and then leader of NDA. He was, at the time, a member of Parliament and a Union Minister of State. Later, he was elected to the Jharkhand Assembly in a by-election which, in turn, was caused by the death of the sitting CPI member. Thus, the strength of the BJP increased to 33 and that of the CPI was reduced to two.

Marandi was sworn in as Chief Minister on 15 November 2000.

The first Council of Ministers of the state consisted of 27 Ministers including the Chief Minister. There were 16 Cabinet Ministers (10 from BJP, 2 from Samata Party, one from JDU and three Independents), 8 Ministers of State (Independent Charge) and two Ministers of State.

All five MLAs from the Samata Party had to be accommodated in the Council of Ministers—two had to be given Cabinet rank, and three were made Ministers of State with Independent Charge. Out of the three JDU members, one was elected as Speaker, one was made the Minister for Energy, and one was made a Minister of State with Independent Charge.

Out of the four Independents, all, except one, Madhav Lal Singh, were made Cabinet Ministers.

The first whiff of trouble

Within months, signs of trouble erupted. As usual, the matter concerned not high policy, but a 'heavy' office: the chairmanship of the—bankrupted—Jharkhand State Electricity Board. The Energy Minister, Lal Chand Mahto, wanted to appoint one H.B. Lal as Chairman. The Chief Minister appointed another person, one Rajiv Ranjan. All sorts of caste arguments were invoked—the Energy Minister was a Kurmi, but, 'for some reason', was favouring a Kayastha; the man the Chief Minister had chosen was a Kurmi, and was, therefore, said to have the backing of a Central Minister, a leader of Kurmis. This was the beginning of the enmity between Mahto and Marandi.

Another Cabinet Minister, Madhu Singh, who had the Revenue and Land Reforms portfolio, wanted the Registration Department also under his belt. Marandi did not oblige. Other ministers had their lists of grievances. The Chief Minister somehow kept things under control.

Samresh Singh, yet another Independent who had to be made Minister, resigned. The Chief Minister did not accept the resignation. Things continued as before—that is, there were rumours and counter-rumours every second day. And much jostling.

By the beginning of 2003, it became apparent that serious trouble was brewing. Dissident ministers were becoming more and more aggressive.

Five ministers (four from the Samata Party and one from the JDU) formed an anti-Marandi group. The ministers were Lal Chand Mahto (JDU), the Energy Minister; Madhu Singh (Samata), the Revenue and Land Reform Minister; Ramesh Singh Munda (Samata), the Minister of State for Excise and Prohibition; Jaleshwar Mahto (Samata), the Minister of State for Public Health and Engineering Department; and Bachha Singh (Samata), the Minister of State for Urban Development.

One Samata Minister, Ram Chandra Keshri, was in the Marandi camp. Baidya Nath Ram, the Minister of State from the JDU quota, was supposed to be very close to the Speaker and remained neutral. Thus, the JDU and Samata parties were divided into two camps. At that time, Sharad Yadav was the President of JDU and George Fernandes was the National President of Samata Party.

By the end of February 2003, the final showdown—rather, the final showdown for this round—began.

21 February 2003: The five dissident ministers demand a change of leadership, making the usual charge: they are unhappy with Marandi's 'style of functioning'.

George Fernandes, the Samata President and Convener of the NDA, rejects the demand and asks his Party's ministers to obey the central directive.

26 February 2003: Rebel ministers defy the central leadership and issue an ultimatum to them to change the leader by 28 February.

28 February 2003: The BJP High Command asks Marandi to come to Delhi. The rebel ministers are also called by their respective central leaders.

1 March 2003: The BJP High Command declares that there will be no change in the leadership. The rebel ministers declare that they no longer consider Marandi as Chief Minister. They say they want some non-BJP man as the Chief Minister.

2 March 2003: Marandi calls on the rebel ministers. But the deadlock continues.

3 March 2003: The rebel ministers leave for Delhi.

4 March 2003: The JDU President, Sharad Yadav, arrives in Ranchi to 'assess the situation'.

5 March 2003: Sharad Yadav returns to New Delhi without meeting Marandi. He publicly criticizes the state Government—in which his party men are ministers.

6 March 2003: Central leaders of JDU and Samata ask Marandi to be more accommodating but reject the demand for changing the leadership.

8 March 2003: Bachcha Singh leaves the rebel camp and returns to Marandi's side. He says that he is obeying central leaders.

9 March 2003: George Fernandes and L.K. Advani once again reject the demand for changing the leadership. In Ranchi, four rebel ministers meet Shibu Soren, the leader of the JMM.

13 March 2003: After what always goes by the name of 'hectic political parleys' extending over four days, seven ministers resign *en bloc* from the Marandi Ministry. They are Lal Chand Mahto and Baidya Nath Ram of JDU; Madhu Singh, Ramesh Singh Munda and Jaleshwar Mahto of Samata Party; Samresh Singh and Joba Manjhi (both Independents).

The seven ministers leave the Treasury Benches in the Assembly and sit with the Opposition. The Opposition parties elect the Speaker, Namdhari, as their leader. In the Assembly, NDA members abuse Namdhari for his role and demand his resignation.

14 March 2003: The Governor, M. Rama Jois, asks Marandi to prove his majority in the Assembly.

16 March 2003: All Opposition members shift to a place near Ranchi for staying together. Sharad Yadav asks the BJP High Command to change the leader. Rajnath Singh, BJP Central Secretary and in charge of Jharkhand affairs, arrives in Ranchi.

17 March 2003: Marandi resigns. Arjun Munda is elected leader of the BJP legislative party. Rebel ministers return to the NDA fold.

Namdhari and Shibu Soren bitterly criticize rebel ministers for betraying them and taking them for a ride.

18 March 2003: Arjun Munda takes oath as Chief Minister with five ministers. Four of them are Independents: Samresh Singh, Sudesh Mahto, Joba Manjhi, Madhav Lal Singh; and one, P.N. Singh, is from the BJP.

25 March 2003: The Council of Ministers is expanded. All rebel ministers are elevated to Cabinet rank.

Assembly Elections 2005

After the creation of the separate Jharkhand state, the first Assembly elections are held in February 2005. Results are declared on 27 February. The party position turns out to be as follows:

BJP: 30	CPI (ML): 1
JMM: 17	NCP: 1
Congress: 9	Jharkhand Party: 1
RJD: 7	Independents: 5
JDU: 6	UGDP: 2
Forward Block: 2	

The five Independents include Sudesh Mahto and Chandra Prakash Choudhary of AJSU; Madhu Koda, Stephen Marandi and Hari Narayan Rai.

A word about each of them will give us a glimpse of the 'issue-based politics' that is always invoked.

❏ Sudesh Mahto: He was a product of the All Jharkhand Student movement. He was elected to the Assembly for the first time in 2000. He won again in 2005. He was the Road Construction Minister in the Marandi Government. After that fell, he became very powerful in the Munda government as Home Minister.

❏ Madhu Koda, a name we shall soon come across again, had been what goes by the name of a committed RSS/BJP man. He won in 2000 for the first time on a BJP ticket. The BJP denied him a ticket in 2005. He contested as an Independent and won. He became a Minister in the Marandi Government. And then in the Munda Government. And, then, as we shall see, the Chief Minister.

❏ Stephen Marandi was a member of Rajya Sabha at that time. He belonged to the JMM, and wanted to contest from his old seat,

Dumka. Shibu Soren refused to give him a ticket for that seat, and denied him a JMM ticket; hence, he contested as an Independent.

❑ Joba Manjhi: her husband, Devendra Manjhi, was a leading figure in the Jharkhand movement. He was murdered. She entered politics in his stead. She was elected to the Bihar Assembly in 1995 and 2000, and to the Jharkhand Assembly in 2005. She and Bandhu Tirkey contested on the symbol of that Goa party, the UDGP.

❑ Enos Ekka: till just three years ago, he was a small contractor. He won the 2005 Assembly elections on the ticket of the Jharkhand Party. He supported the NDA in 2005, and then switched over to the UPA in September 2006. As for his party, he was elected as a candidate of Jharkhand Party led by N.E. Horo; soon enough, he had formed his own faction.

As we can see from even these thumbnail sketches, each of these representatives of the people has all the hallmarks of an Independent character!

The elections gave neither alliance a clear majority. As a consequence, what goes by the name of 'a high voltage political drama' commenced as soon as the results were out.

28 February 2005: Arjun Munda is elected as leader of the NDA. At this time, the NDA consists of 36 MLAs—30 from the BJP and 6 from the JDU.

Demonstrations break out at the headquarters of the state BJP in support of Babulal Marandi.

1 March 2005: Both groups submit lists to the Governor, by now one Syed Sibte Rizvi. Each side claims support of 41 MLAs in a House of 81.

The Governor invites Shibu Soren to form the Government.

2 March 2005: Shibu Soren is sworn in as Chief Minister along with six Ministers—Stephen Marandi is Deputy Chief Minister; Girinath Singh and Annapurna Devi of RJD, Bandhu Tirkey and Joba Manjhi of UDGP, and Kamlesh Kumar Singh of NCP are Ministers. The Government is to last all of nine days.

The Governor asks Soren to prove by 21 March that he commands the confidence of a majority of the House.

The NDA protests. Why has Soren been given three weeks to buy and sell?

3 March 2005: The NDA parades 41 MLAs before the President at the Rashtrapati Bhavan. Thirty of them are from the BJP and six from JDU. Five Independents are also present—Sudesh Mahto, Chandra Prakash Choudhary, Madhu Koda, Enos Ekka, and Hari Narain Roy.

All these MLAs are shifted to Jaipur to keep them out of the reach of poachers.

7 March 2005: Arjun Munda takes his case to the Supreme Court.

9 March 2005: The Supreme Court asks Shibu Soren to prove his majority in the Assembly on 11 March. It directs the Soren Government *not* to nominate the Anglo-Indian representative in the Assembly till the Vote of Confidence has been completed.

. A day before the day on which the Confidence Vote has been scheduled, Kamlesh Singh 'falls ill'. He does not turn up for the Vote of Confidence. Soren's fate is sealed.

11 March 2005: The Confidence Motion cannot be moved in the Assembly because of the pandemonium that the members have caused. The Pro-tem Speaker, Pradip Balmuchu, adjourns the Assembly. The Governor at last receives a revelation. He issues a directive to Shibu Soren to resign. Soren resigns.

12 March 2005: Arjun Munda is sworn in as Chief Minister. All five Independents and Kamlesh Kumar Singh are inducted as full Cabinet Ministers. The latter's name is called out for taking the oath, he is not present as, it is said, he is in hospital.

Sudesh Mahto bargains hard. He thereby grabs the Home portfolio and several other 'heavy' ones. There is much pushing and pulling centred on Enos Ekka. His Jharkhand Party sends a letter to the Governor stating that it supports the UPA. Enos Ekka sends a letter to the Governor stating that he supports the NDA.

15 March 2005: Arjun Munda proves his majority in the Assembly. Namdhari is elected Speaker. At the time of the Vote of Confidence, Joba Manjhi does not reach the Assembly. She says that her car developed trouble. She is soon rewarded for this trauma.

16 March 2005: The state unit of the NCP merges with the BJP.

29 March 2005: The overworked Cabinet is expanded.

Pradip Yadav and Raghuvar Das of the BJP and Ramesh Singh Munda and Radha Krishna Kishore of the JDU join as Cabinet Ministers. Kamlesh Kumar Singh also takes oath. Arjun Munda has to give Independents the portfolios they demand.

Champions of Jaleshwar Mahto demonstrate for his induction.

10 April 2005: Radha Krishna Kishore resigns from the Cabinet.

19 April 2005: Jaleshwar Mahto of the JDU and Satya Nand Bhokta of the BJP join the Ministry as full Cabinet Ministers.

Five Independents who are Ministers form the 'G-5'. Kamlesh Singh is not among them. They are to put the Government into trouble every other week.

Petitions under the anti-defection law are filed with the Speaker against Stephen Marandi, Kamlesh Kumar Singh and Enos Ekka.

End of NDA Rule

On one pretext or another, the five Independents who constitute the 'G-5' make new demands every day.

By the end of July 2006, it is more than apparent that all is not well in the Munda Government. Reports coming from Delhi suggest that three Independent Ministers—Madhu Koda, Enos Ekka and Hari Narayan Rai—are in touch with the Congress and RJD leaders. But there is still one obstacle, the only principle that matters! Who shall be the leader? As the Constitution has placed a limit on the extent to which the Jharkhand Ministry can be enlarged—it cannot exceed 12—there is this additional problem: what loaves can be given to the ones who cannot be made ministers?

In the first week of August 2006, what is known as 'the flash point' comes. As usual it is over a matter of urgent public importance! Madhu Koda has accused a contractor, Shambhu Singh, of threatening him over the contract for constructing a road. The Chief Minister, Arjun Munda, sides with the contractor and gives him a clean chit. This triggers a series of events that soon enough leads to the fall of the Arjun Munda Government.

Three Independent Ministers are said to meet Sonia Gandhi in the first week of September.

4 September 2006: Kamlesh Kumar Singh, one of the dissident ministers, is going *via* Jamshedpur to Delhi to join other Independent ministers. On instructions of the Chief Minister, he is detained at Jamshedpur by the police. Kamlesh Singh is forced to stay at the Circuit House. Police claim that this has been done for security reasons.

5 September 2006: Madhu Koda, Enos Ekka, Hari Narayan Rai and Kamlesh Kumar Singh meet the Governor and tender their resignations from the Munda Ministry.

7 September 2006: The Governor calls the Chief Minister and asks him to prove by the 15th that he still has the confidence of the majority in the Assembly.

8 September 2006: Speaker Namdhari issues notices to Stephen Marandi, Kamlesh Kumar Singh and Enos Ekka regarding petitions that he had received against them under the anti-defection law— petitions that have been lying with him for some time.

9 September 2006: The three go to the Supreme Court praying for a stay of notices issued by the Speaker.

12 September 2006: The Supreme Court refuses to intervene.

14 September 2006: The Speaker, Namdhari, withholds judgement against the three. Arjun Munda resigns without moving the Confidence Motion.

18 September 2006: Madhu Koda, an Independent, is sworn in as Chief Minister. Kamlesh, Enos and Rai take oath as Cabinet Ministers.

20 September 2006: Koda proves his majority in the Assembly with 41 members supporting him. NDA members do not take part in the voting. Their demand is that first a permanent Speaker must be elected.

24 September 2006: Joba Manjhi, Sudhir Mahto, Nalin Soren and Bandhu Tirkey are sworn in as Cabinet Ministers. Sudhir Mahto is designated as Deputy Chief Minister.

9 October 2006: Stephen Marandi, Dulal Buiyan, Chandra Prakash Choudhary—the latter after breaking away from his Party—join the Ministry. Stephen Marandi insists that he be made Speaker. The Congress does not agree. Hence, he is made Deputy Chief Minister. The Government thus comes to have two Deputy Chief Ministers.

7 November 2006: Bhanu Pratap Shahi, an Independent MLA supporting the UPA who had earlier been expelled from the Forward Bloc, is not able to get bail in a criminal case. This technicality comes in the way of his being sworn in as a minister. But a word of honour is a word of honour. So, his father, Hemendra Pratap Dehati, an ex-MLA is inducted into the Ministry. This Government has eight Independents as ministers.

But distributing portfolios becomes a headache. In addition, the issue of Deputy Chief Ministership is far from closed. To put pressure in regard to these weighty matters, a 'G-3' is formed. It consists of Harinarayan Rai, Enos Ekka and Kamlesh Singh.

But within days, the 'G-3' falls apart. The great issue that tears it apart is the distribution of portfolios. Enos is still unhappy; he wants the 'heavy' Road Construction portfolio.

Then a highly public fight breaks out over another 'heavy' portfolio, the control over the Electricity Department. It is only after some 'commitment' that Stephen Marandi starts 'cooperating' with the Ministry.

Time for another 'G-3' to be formed. This one is formed to ensure that the portfolios are distributed 'fairly'. It consists of Stephen Marandi, Harinarayan Rai and Enos Ekka. Kamlesh Singh is not in it.

And then a meteor descends. The Government had been made possible by the cooperation of Shibu Soren. The Congress had manipulated things. Its hand-picked Governor, Sibte Rizvi, had disgraced his office and installed Soren as Chief Minister. Soren could not prove that he had the confidence of the majority. He had had to resign. But the Congress needed his support at the Centre to keep the forces of communalism at bay. He was inducted as a Cabinet Minister at the Centre, and given a 'heavy' portfolio. Before he had time to distinguish himself in any way other than the one for which he had first come to the attention of the country, a court issues a non-bailable warrant against him in connection with a case of murder, one in which a dozen or so Muslims were killed. He disappears, and thereby creates history—a Minister of the Government of India, absconding, untraceable to all the police and intelligence agencies of the country .. Eventually, he has to resign his ministership. But the Government in Delhi still needs his services to fight communalism. Hence, he is once again inducted as Minister in the Manmohan Singh Government. But, lo and behold, soon a court in Delhi convicts him in connection with the murder of his Personal Assistant...

The Koda Ministry goes into shock—for Soren is an indispensable prop. But value is not to be confused with price. Though he has had to resign from the Government, he continues as member of Parliament. He still commands the allegiance of some MLAs in Jharkhand. So, though in jail, he is being courted by all sides...

As 2007 dawns, newspapers are reporting that another war has broken out, over another great issue. There are 30-odd boards and public sector corporations. These are the *nagar vadhus;* everyone has his eyes on them, and what they can provide. The Chief Minister announces that he will dismiss all heads of these corporations, as they had been appointed by the previous Government. All parties get into the fray. With its resourceful leader, Shibu Soren, no longer able to put the mines to work, the JMM presses its claim for these *vadhus* even harder. After all, it has 17 MLAs; the other partners have fewer—the Congress has nine, the RJD has seven. Certain that moral strength as well as need are on its side, the JMM gives the Chief Minister a list of 15 boards and corporations that it just must get. The Congress and the RJD are up in arms, they must get their share...

Nor is a sequence of this kind atypical. Recall Bhajan Lal in 1979 waiting upon Mrs. Indira Gandhi with his entire Council of Ministers standing in line, hands folded. Mrs. Gandhi had just returned to office; all of them left the Janata Party *en bloc* and swore fealty to her. Did Gegong Apang do any different in Arunachal Pradesh recently? He and his entire ministry also walked across, in single file and to the man! Nor should one console oneself on the ground that these sorts of things happen in states, not in the Centre. That is how people used to console themselves about the collapse of standards and decorum in legislatures of Bihar and U.P. But what used to happen in them yesterday, happens in Parliament today. In any case, how were Charan Singh, Chandrashekhar, H.D. Deve Gowda and I.K. Gujral selected as Prime Ministers of the country? And how were they removed? Were the 'grounds' any more substantive than the ground—'style of functioning'—that is invoked in the states?

Incidentally, I do hope that some day someone will be pulled down for his 'style of *non*-functioning'.

Manifest pointers

❑ Such sequences are the stock-in-trade of what we have made of the 'parliamentary system'. Indeed, have they not become as typical as strikes by terrorists? Can we remember the last perversion of the Constitution any more than we can remember the last assault by the terrorists?

❑ Always remember, what happens in such states today happens at the Centre tomorrow. As we just noticed, the sequences by which Charan Singh, Chandrashekhar, I.K. Gujral, H.D. Deve Gowda were made—not Chief Ministers of some state but the Prime Ministers of India—and then pulled down, were hardly different. And the fact that serving ministers are facing criminal trials for corruption; that a minister is absconding; that a minister has been convicted of murder—these are not things that have happened in regard to some ministry of some distant state. They have happened in regard to ministers of the Government of India.

❑ Notice what has become of what are always referred to as 'high constitutional authorities', illustrated in this sequence by the office of the Governor.

❑ Notice that such Governors hardly ever act on their own. They are agents of, and do not take a step without the directions of the Central Government.

❑ What must have gone on 'behind the scenes' and 'under the tables' must have been much more colourful than the bare to-ing and fro-ing of these sovereign representatives of the people.

❑ Reflect on the great 'issues' that are invoked from time to time during such sequences. And on the subterfuges that pass for stratagems these days—the sudden sojourn in hospital, the car breakdown!

❑ Reflect on whether any of these persons became a minister because he or she had the executive competence to run ministries.

❑ Reflect on the consequences for administration of both, the type who become ministers, and their preoccupations while they are ministers.

❑ Reflect on how phantasmagorical are what pass for 'political parties' today: how, in several of these cases, the 'central leaders', the 'Party High Command' are in fact at the mercy of state and even local chieftains: with what impunity the central leaders are defied... And how the central leaders then try to make out that that defiance was all part of a pre-arranged drama.

❑ Reflect how the tussles among leaders of parties in far-away Delhi topple and paralyse governments in states and *vice versa...*

Small shifts, major dislocations

The Jharkhand sequence was facilitated in part by the fact that the Assembly was splintered—exactly as a number of other Assemblies and the Parliament itself are splintered. The consequences are compounded by two additional factors. Shares of parties in seats are often way out of proportion to their shares in votes. Second, small swings in the votes a party gets trigger large swings in the number of seats it secures. Scores of examples can be cited to illustrate the consequences. Our present purpose is a limited one: to weigh the advantages that are commonly claimed for the present first-past-the-post system. Just a few examples will be sufficient to show that these are mythical.

Andhra: The Andhra Assembly has 294 members. Glance at the share of the Telugu Desam Party and the Congress in votes, and at the relative number of seats that the two got in successive elections:

Year	Telugu Desam Party		Congress	
	% votes polled	Seats won	% votes polled	Seats won
2004	37.6	47	38.6	185
1999	43.9	180	40.6	91
1994	44.1	216	33.8	26
1989	36.5	74	47.1	181
1985	46.2	202	37.2	50

Notice:

❏ In 2004, there is not much difference between the shares in votes that the two parties poll. But the Congress bags *four times* the number of seats that accrue to the Telugu Desam.

❏ In 1999, the Telugu Desam's share in votes is about 3.5 per cent higher than that of the Congress. But it bags *double* the number of seats that the latter does.

❏ In 1989, the TDP gets 36.5 per cent of the votes and 74 seats. In 2004, it gets 37 per cent of the votes and just 46 seats.

❏ The percentage of voters who vote for the Congress *falls* by 2 per cent between 1999 and 2004. The number of seats it bags *doubles*—from 91 to 183.

Delhi: The Delhi Assembly has 70 seats. The Congress and the BJP have been the principal rivals. Here are their respective shares in votes and the number of seats they obtained:

Year	Congress		BJP	
	% votes polled	Seats won	% votes polled	Seats won
2003	48.1	47	35.2	20
1998	47.8	52	34.0	15
1993	34.5	14	42.8	49
1983	47.5	34	37.0	19

Notice how in 1983, 1998 as well as 2003, the Congress gets around 48 per cent of the votes. Its seats oscillate between 34 and 52.

Haryana: The Haryana Assembly has 90 seats. For the last two elections the Congress and the Indian National Lok Dal have been the main rivals.

Year	Congress		INLD	
	% votes polled	Seats won	% votes polled	Seats won
2005	42.5	67	26.7	9
2000	31.2	21	29.6	47

A three per cent fall in the share of votes slashes the number of seats of the INLD from 47 to 9.

In 2000, with less than 30 per cent of the votes, the INLD gets more than half the seats.

Kerala: The Kerala Assembly has 140 seats. The state is one of the classic examples of the electorate having been splintered, and the splinters remaining frozen. It is also a textbook example of another feature of our elections. Voters keep shuttling from one set of rulers to another, and that gives one the illusion that a real choice is being exercised. In fact, the set that replaces the one that is ousted, in practice turns out to be little different from the predecessor: witness the fact that, even though parties and coalitions have alternated in ruling the state, there has hardly been any net investment in the state, and the state has lived off exporting its problems—labour to the Gulf, and ideologies to the rest of India! The state also illustrates the secular pursuits of parties like the Muslim League. They ally with one pole in one election and another in a subsequent one so that, while the principal parties replace one another, legislators of the League are in government oftener than all their allies! They have the additional boon: as everyone knows that they are available at all times for switching, all sides bend backwards to woo them. Those who induct them also gain: inducting such an out-and-out communal party establishes the alliance to be secular!

Here are the share of votes polled by the principal rivals, and the seats they got in successive elections:

Year	Congress		CPM	
	% votes polled·	Seats won	% votes polled	Seats won
2006	24.1	24	30.4	61
2001	31.4	62	21.4	23
1996	30.4	37	21.6	40
1991	32.1	55	21.7	28
1987	24.8	33	22.8	38
1982	11.9	20	18.8	26
1980	11.3	21	19.4	35

Notice:

❑ Between 1987 and 2001, CPM's vote share hovered around 21 and 22 per cent. But the number of seats it secured oscillated between 23 and 40.

❑ As a mirror-image, in 1991, 1996 and 2001, Congress got 30 to 32 per cent of the votes. But its seats jumped between 37 and 62.

❑ In 1996, the Congress got 30.4 per cent of the votes, and secured 37 seats. In 2006, the CPM got 30.4 per cent of the votes, and bagged 61 seats.

❑ In 1996, the Congress got 30.4 per cent of the votes, and from these it secured 37 seats. The CPM got 21.6 per cent of the votes, but from these it got 40 seats.

Madhya Pradesh: The Assembly had 320 seats before the creation of Chhatisgarh. The principal rivals have been the BJP and the Congress.

Year	Congress		BJP	
	% votes polled	Seats won	% votes polled	Seats won
1998	40.6	172	39.3	119
1993	40.7	174	38.8	117
1990	33.4	56	39.1	220
1985	48.8	250	32.4	58
1980	47.5	246	30.3	60

Between 1990 and 1998, the BJP secured around 39 per cent of the votes. Its seats oscillated between 117 and 220. In 1993 and 1998, the share of the Congress and the BJP in votes was not all that different—both secured around 40 per cent—but their seats were 172/174 in one case and 119/117 in the other.

Maharashtra: In 1990, 1995 and 1999 respectively, the Shiv Sena secured 52, 73 and 69 seats. Its share in votes, on the other hand, did not change much: it was 15.9 per cent, 16.4 per cent and 17.3 per cent respectively.

Orissa: The Orissa Assembly has 147 seats. In recent years, the Biju Janata Dal, the Congress and the BJP have been the principal contenders.

Year	Congress		BJD		BJP	
	% votes polled	Seats won	% votes polled	Seats won	% votes polled	Seats won
2004	34.8	38	27.4	61	17.1	32
2000	33.8	26	29.4	68	18.2	38

Notice:

❏ In 2004, the Congress gets 34.8 per cent of the votes, and only 38 seats. With 27.4 per cent of the votes, the BJD secures 61 seats.

❏ In 2004, the share of the BJP in votes—17 per cent—is half that of the Congress—35 per cent. It gets 32 seats against the Congress' 38.

❏ Between 2000 and 2004, the share of the Congress in the votes changes from 33.8 per cent to 34.8 per cent. But the seats it has increase from 26 to 38.

❏ In 2000, the BJP, with 18 per cent of the votes, gets 38 seats. In 2004, the Congress gets 35 per cent of the votes and yet gets the same number of seats—38.

Rajasthan: The Rajasthan Assembly has 200 seats. The BJP and the Congress have been the principal rivals.

Year	Congress		BJP	
	% votes polled	Seats won	% votes polled	Seats won
2003	35.6	56	39.2	120
1998	44.9	153	33.2	33
1993	38.3	76	38.6	95
1990	33.6	50	25.2	85
1985	46.5	113	21.2	39

In 1993, both the principals get around 38 per cent of the votes. The Congress gets 76 seats in return, the BJP gets 95.

Notice how the shares in votes swing sharply from election to election. Voters turn from one party to the other in anger or despair. These swings are magnified in the swing in seats. A 6 per cent increase in the share in votes between 1998 and 2003, increases the BJP seats from 33 to 120, just as a 5 per cent drop in its share of votes between 1993 and 1998 had led its seats to drop from 95 to 33.

Tamil Nadu: Tamil Nadu constitutes a composite illustration of all the three features—the unrepresentativeness of governments; the violent swings that result from even small swings of votes; and, as the electorate is splintered and the splinters are frozen, the effect that stitching different local parties has on the final outcome.

The AIADMK and the DMK have been the main contestants for the 234 seats in the Assembly.

Tamil Nadu Assembly Elections

	1991	1996	2001	2006
Per cent share in votes cast				
DMK	22.5	42.1	30.9	26.5
ADK*	44.4			
AIADMK		21.5	31.4	32.6
Seats secured				
DMK	2	173	31	96
ADK*	164			
AIADMK		4	132	61

* Later AIADMK, All India Dravida Munnetra Kazhagam

Here then is an almost textbook illustration of Professor Finer's characterization of the first-past-the-post system as the system of '*dis*proportional representation'. Between the 2001 and 2006 elections, the share of the DMK in votes polled *falls* from 30.9 per cent to 26.5 per cent. The seats it secures *shoot up* from 31 to 96. AIADMK secures a higher proportion of votes cast, but its seats *plummet* from 132 to 61.

Notice also,

❑ In 2006, the DMK gets 26.5 per cent of the votes, and for that it is rewarded with 96 seats. The AIADMK gets 32.6 per cent of the votes, and yet only 61 seats.

❑ The AIADMK's share in the votes in 2006 at 32.6 per cent was *more than* its share in 2001 at 31.4 per cent. In the former, it got 61 seats; in the latter, 132.

❑ In 2001, both the parties got around 31 per cent of the votes. But the DMK got only 31 seats, against the AIADMK's 132.

Uttar Pradesh: In the 1991, 1993 and 1996 elections for the Assembly's 425 seats, the BJP's share in votes remained more or less constant—31.4 per cent, 33.3 per cent and 32.5 per cent respectively. Its seats were 221 in 1991, 177 in 1993, and 174 in 1996.

There are, of course, many explanations for such 'anomalies'. Clearly, the outcome will be influenced not just by the support that a party's candidate enjoys but also by the number and strength of his opponents. It will also be influenced by the nature and geographical spread of its supporters. Assume that 15 per cent of the population of the state prefers a party. It may get no seat at all as in each constituency its candidate may poll less than the candidate of some other party, a different one in each constituency. In the opposite case, assume that 15 per cent of the population of the state are its followers, but they are all concentrated in a few constituencies: it will win these seats handsomely but a large number of the votes it polls will be superfluous. In each constituency, they will be more than the votes that its candidates need to win that particular constituency, yet they will be no help to its candidates in constituencies in which even a few more votes could have seen them through. Similarly, there is the effect of alliances. Getting a Mayawati on your side can make a great difference as her votes are 'transferable', they go to the party she prescribes. And so on.

The point is not that the 'anomalies' cannot be explained. Rather that, whatever the explanation, the outcomes—and the illustrative examples given above can be multiplied many times over—call into question the claims that are so often made on behalf of the present system, that the governments that emerge from it are representative, that the legislatures that emerge are representative, to say nothing of the claims that are *not* made—that this system is the best possible way of selecting rulers for a billion people, for instance.

Insecure governments

This feature, of small swings triggering wide swings in seats, afflicts the Centre as much. Glance at the share of the two principal parties— the Congress and the BJP—in votes polled and seats secured in the Lok Sabha elections.

Votes and seats secured by the Congress

Year of General Election	Percentage of votes polled by the Congress	Number of seats obtained by the Congress
1971	43.7	352
1977	34.5	154
1980	42.7	353
1984	48.1	405
1989	39.5	197
1991	36.5	232
1996	28.8	140
1998	25.8	141
1999	28.3	114
2004	26.7	145

Notice, first, that in 1984, the Congress was able to get 405 of the 540 Lok Sabha seats—that is, almost three-quarters of the total—with 48 per cent of the votes. Second, notice the changes in the number of seats the Party has secured and how they compare with its share in votes. In 1991, its share in votes cast *fell* by 3 percentage points; its seats *increased* from 197 to 232. In 1998, its share in votes again *fell* by 3 percentage points. Its seats *increased* by one. In the 1999 election, on the other hand, its share in votes increased by 2.5 percentage points. The seats it had *fell* precipitously—from 141 to 114. In 2004, its share in votes reached the lowest ebb ever. It fell even in comparison with 1999—from 28.3 per cent to 26.5 per cent. The number of seats it garnered, *increased* from 114 to 145. And it became the core of the new coalition that today rules at the Centre!

The BJP's numbers illustrate the same phenomenon—as a sort of mirror image.

Votes and seats secured by the BJP

Year of General Election	Percentage of votes polled by BJP	Number of seats obtained by BJP
1984	7.4	2
1989	11.5	86
1991	20.1	121
1996	20.3	161
1998	25.6	182
1999	23.6	182
2004	22.2	138

Till its share in votes crosses the 10 per cent mark, BJP's share in seats remains well below its share in votes. As for changes, BJP's figures are the reverse of the Congress. While its share in votes remains about the same between 1991 and 1996, its seats leap from 121 to 161. Conversely, while its share in votes falls by 2 percentage points between the 1998 and 1999 elections, its seats remain at 182. In the 2004 elections, its share in votes falls, but by just 0.6 per cent. But the number of seats it gets falls sharply—from 182 to 138: that is, a 0.6 per cent fall in the share in votes triggers a fall in the share in seats from a third of the Lok Sabha to a quarter. This becomes one of the principal reasons why a new coalition comes to acquire office at the Centre.

A leading investment banker draws attention to another feature— one whose consequences can spell intensified problems for governance in the near future. Look at the total number of seats that the Congress and BJP command *together*. From 352 in 1991, this figure fell to 301 in 1996. It rose to 323 in 1998—only to fall to 296 in 1999, and to 283 in 2004. The magic figure that has to be exceeded to form a government at the Centre is 272. If the two keep eating up only each other's seats, he says, and keep losing ground, it will soon be possible to form a coalition at the Centre without either of them.

These features—the electorate splintered; the splinters frozen; small swings in votes having such pronounced consequences for the share in seats—lead the politician to the same operational lessons: somehow exacerbate divisions; somehow swing a small fraction of the electorate; somehow stitch up the small groups and sections. Performance? 'Arithmetic is the answer to performance,' a 'strategist' explained to me.

And you don't have to stitch those small segments together across the country or the state: just focus on the small segments in just a few constituencies—the marginal constituencies, namely, the ones in which you lost by a small number in the preceding election. Is it any wonder that the Election Commission's report on the 2004 elections to the Lok Sabha lists 230 'parties'? Is it any surprise that, with the U.P. elections round the corner, *The Indian Express* found that 150 'parties' had mushroomed?

This feature does not affect just the fortunes of political parties and individual leaders. The reason Mrs. Indira Gandhi was able to push her dictatorial changes of the Constitution through Parliament was that in the 1971 elections, having got just 43.7 per cent of the vote, she had got a two-thirds majority in the Lok Sabha.

Once you are in, you are as well placed as the next man to become anything; it is almost a lottery. You can even become Prime Minister or Deputy Prime Minister. Recall Charan Singh, Chandrashekhar, Deve Gowda, V.P. Singh, Devi Lal. They had little influence outside two or three districts around their birthplace, and yet they became Prime Ministers and Deputy Prime Ministers. The sway of some of the others did not cover even a district or two! Some way to select the person who should steer the fortunes of a billion people! And as I write, a mere puff from Sonia Gandhi—just one puff, the second one would not be necessary—would bring down Manmohan Singh. A single puff, and the Prime Minister of a billion people, the Prime Minister of the aspiring 'super-power' is out!!

More and more irresponsible policies

The effect of these features on policies and programmes is even more magnified than on the outcome of seats, etc. To begin with, parties today are not wedded to any ideology or even to any particular ideas, and of course not to any ideal. When there are coalitions, it is not that the constituents had some common ideas and, therefore, got together. The current 'United Progressive Front' is a perfect illustration of the state of affairs. Parties fought against each other in the 2004 Lok Sabha elections; to their astonishment, they won, or rather a combination could be put together that could be shown to have won. Having 'won' in this sense, a 'Common Minimum Programme' was typed up, and this became the excuse for stepping into office!

But that is just the beginning. The more splintered the electorate is, the smaller need a pressure group be to get politicians to bend to it. First SCs/STs were the ones to which parties had to pander, then Muslims, then OBCs, then every sub-caste among each of these groups. Nor is the pandering confined to caste groups and religious groups. The number of traders who would have to pay more if Delhi's Rent Control Law is modernized must be a minuscule portion of Delhi's electorate. Yet, they have been able to bend the entire political class to prevent for a decade the Act which has been passed from being notified! The builders who have constructed the—huge, illegal—buildings in Delhi that have been the target of successive demolition drives must be a tiny fraction of Delhi's population. Yet, they are able to bend the entire political class, and have it overturn a law so that the Supreme Court's orders are thwarted. Never is the political class as unanimous as it is when doing the wrong thing. Recall the unanimity with which the Constitution has been amended out of shape to overturn judgements of the Supreme Court on reservations. Often, while legislating such changes, even a formal vote has not been necessary, a 'voice vote' has sufficed. Recall the denunciations of the Judiciary when it removed the protection that had kept politicians safe hitherto—the protection that they could not be prosecuted without prior sanction of the politicians themselves.

Politicians are even more prone to pander to sundry groups and bend than figures about the numerical strength of the groups may suggest, and that for two reasons.

First, as we have seen, in a splintered electorate a shift of even two/three per cent of the votes spells the difference between sweeping victory and being swept away. As a result, on the one hand, to win that marginal vote of that marginal section, a party espouses extreme policies; policies that its leaders readily acknowledge are ruinous for the country. On the other, any one leader within a government, any party in the political spectrum, any faction within a party, can propose or announce a policy, and no one can resist going along: look at the sequence that ensued when, frightened of Devi Lal's announcement that he would hold a rally, V.P. Singh lunged for Mandal; look at the sequence that ensued when, hearing that he was being shunted out as a Governor, Arjun Singh announced reservations for OBCs in private, unaided educational institutions. To the oft-repeated assertion that governments are kept to responsible conduct by the fear of electoral defeat, the counter certainly rings true in our case: 'Indeed, the argument can be stood on its head by suggesting that insofar as fear of electoral consequences does influence the behaviour of governments, it is usually by way of making them responsive to demands from those supporters whose displeasure they most fear. And far from meaning responsible government in the sense of government carried on with a keen sense of being responsible for the consequences of decisions taken, this becomes the very epitome of *irresponsible* government.'[1] Political leaders are most reluctant to take any step that might cause offence to the lower bureaucracy, the police, primary school teachers, for instance, as these groups can have a devastating effect at the time of elections.

Second, politicians know as little as psephologists and journalists about who will react how to which measure. I remember Arif Mohammed Khan describing to me the Cabinet meeting at which V.P. Singh's Government lunged for the Mandal Commission's ruinous proposals. He recalled one Minister telling V.P. Singh, 'Sir *ise laagoo kar dijeeye, bees saal ke liye koi hamen sarkar se hila nahin sakegaa.*' Many will remember the weight that was placed on the 'Nagpur Sandesh' of the then President of BJP. It is out of the same expectations of likely reactions that the NDA Government put through the two circulars and constitutional amendments to overturn aspects of Supreme Court judgement on reservations: 'This will send an excellent signal to the SC/ST voters.' Later, a prominent participant observed, 'We did not get one extra vote from SCs/STs.

---

[1]*Adversary Politics and Electoral Reform*, S.E. Finer (ed.), Anthony Wigram, London, 1975, p.78.

On the other hand, we lost at least 10 per cent votes of government servants in New Delhi.' Not only are the principals in the dark about what the precise effect will be of such steps, at each juncture there are enough persons around to egg the leader on, 'Sir, massive response among Muslims... SCs/STs...' In my reckoning, the benefit actually accrues to the one who has espoused the extreme position: when some concession is made to the SCs, the SCs give the credit to Mayawati...

Having been pandered to, having seen how political parties will genuflect to them, many of these sections have become truculent. By now it is an article of belief with them that *you* must submit to their demands, that *you* must make the sacrifices that the submission entails, that they will *not* heed your needs, that they will *not* countenance any restriction in return. After all, the whole message that is conveyed while stoking a section is that it is being exploited, that it is the victim. How can the inference that flows from the message not register with it? The message that there is no reason for it to heed the consequences that it's grabbing will inflict on the system as a whole?

The consequences for the polity are magnified by another fact. So many of our 'independent' organizations—trade unions, students' organizations, NGOs—are but limbs of political parties. Once a political party capitulates, it is not just other political parties that capitulate; much of what is romanticized as 'civil society' capitulates.

What the country needs is thwarted for the same reason: as few can 'prove' why something has happened, opponents can blame whatever they have been blocking. 'Reforms are what got us,' many said as the NDA lost in 2004. 'It was that damned "India Shining" campaign,' they said. Not one of them had discovered the error in these till the results were out. As my colleague, Yashwant Sinha was to inquire, how could it be that reforms led to the rout of the BJP and Chauthala's party in Haryana but caused its victory next-door, in Rajasthan? How could it be that they were such a hit in Gujarat, Madhya Pradesh and Chhatisgarh, and caused a defeat in adjacent Maharashtra? How could reforms have secured the largest ever number of seats for the BJP in Karnataka and caused Chandrababu Naidu's rout in neighbouring Andhra? The overall outcome was the arithmetical aggregation of separate state results. And the latter were the result of (i) who allied with whom; and (ii) the condition of the parties as organizations.

The first factor is illustrated by what happened in Tamil Nadu. Karunanidhi had given no cause for offence to the NDA leadership in Delhi. He was not just allowed to drift away, two or three local 'leaders' were allowed to go on traducing him personally till he got convinced that the seniors of the NDA had decided to jettison him, come the next elections. This single blunder made a difference of almost 30 seats to the final tally—16 seats that would have accrued to the NDA combination, went to the rival alliance that was cobbled together after the election results were announced.

The second factor is illustrated by what erupted in several of the parties *after* they had lost the elections: the faction-fights that broke out; the splits that occurred; the back-biting that broke out, the stories that several 'leaders' began planting against each other after the loss of government. These eruptions were not sudden. They reflected what had been the real condition of the parties as organizations *before the elections*. The fact of being in government had obscured that condition. With the lid of office lifted, all could see what their real condition was. This condition is what enabled opponents to win. But reforms were the casualty.

Doubly so. Those who won got convinced that reforms had caused the NDA to lose. So, they froze into possums. And the parties that had constituted the NDA got convinced that reforms had done them in, so they also completely distanced themselves from reforms in the ensuing period.

Soon, there is a race to outdo the other in espousing populist measures. The Employment Guarantee Scheme of the UPA Government was itself a populist lunge. If it were to be implemented sincerely, it would cost the Exchequer 40,000–50,000 crore at the least. It would compound corruption at the grassroots. But who could resist it? To the plea that we must oppose such irresponsible schemes, that we owed a responsibility to the country, the counter invariably is, 'By being responsible, we lost the Government. They made irresponsible demand after irresponsible demand, they made false accusation after false accusation. And, see, *they* are in Government. Forget responsibility. Let *them* be responsible for a change. We should criticize the Bill on the ground that it does not go far enough. Why does it say Government will give a job to only one person in a family? Why only to families in rural areas? Why at only Rs. 60 per day? Why only for a few days? Any one, whether in rural or urban areas, who needs a job, must be provided a job. He must be given a job at the minimum wage that has been prescribed by law, not the measly Rs. 60. He must be given a job for as long as he cannot find another one.' And it is this sort of a view that will invariably prevail. You just have to glance through the debates on any populist measure to see that this is so.

In a word, the operating premise is, 'Carrying on government is the job of those who are in Government. Our job is to oppose, to shout at, to block whatever is proposed, our job is to demand more. After all, if the Government succeeds in implementing these measures, it will have that much more to commend itself at the next elections.'

Now, it is not enough to say of populist policies, 'But the excesses of these fellows will be corrected at the next elections when the people will vote such an irresponsible Government out.' For one thing, by then the damage would have been done. For another, once introduced, such policies and schemes are next to impossible to weed out. Recall how many committees have recommended that subsidies be cut, that they are not reaching the targeted beneficiaries, that they are distorting investment decisions. Recall how many Finance Ministers have said that they will prune these. Even better, notice how it has become literally impossible to reverse the avalanche of reservations. If under this fragmented system, governments had been strong enough to repeal these policies and schemes, they would not have introduced them in the first place.

The myth that the parliamentary system harmonizes interests;
that, while it may be slow to produce solutions,
the solutions that emerge are durable

Under the present system, every section is induced to take account of the interests of others, to round off its edges, we are told. Yes, it sometimes takes longer for us to arrive at a consensus about what should be done, we are consoled, but once that consensus is reached, it is more durable.

Neither assertion is borne out by our record. To start with, far from rounding off edges, leaders and parties have learnt that it is by sharpening their appeal, and honing it to ever narrower sections that they win. This is implicit in the figures we noticed earlier: when candidates win by polling 25–40 per cent of the votes cast, and when just 60 per cent of eligible voters cast their votes, the way for a candidate to win is to enflame 15–25 per cent of the voters, and that means enflame 10 to 15 per cent of the people in a constituency and convince them that they are different from the others. The way for a candidate and his leader is to frighten them that the others are out to get them, and that he and his party are the only available saviours. Look at the appeals that Lalu Yadav, Mulayam Singh, Mayawati address to their followers. Anyone who can enflame such small groups, anyone who can stitch 'alliances' of one or two such groups, wins. Recall the 'KHAM' strategy that the Congress pursued in Gujarat—the 'alliance' of Kshatriyas, Harijans, Adivasis, Muslims. Recall the 'MY' strategy that Lalu Yadav and Mulayam Singh have pursued in their respective regions—the 'alliance' of Muslims and Yadavs. Recall the spell that Mayawati exercises over the Scheduled Caste voters in U.P. Recall what has happened in Tamil Nadu. The state is often held up as a textbook example of the success of 'progressive' measures like caste-based reservations. In fact, by now its entire politics, and the civil services too are completely caste-ridden. The followers of political parties are from one caste or the other. Vanniyars are with this party, Thevars mainly with that other party... Several of these parties have strictly local influence. And the leader, who can stitch together these district parties, wins. Indeed, she or he doesn't just win, she or he sweeps. In the last election, Jayalalitha was able to stitch the district parties together. She swept to power, the numerous cases of malfeasance notwithstanding. She provided an efficient Government. But this time round, her rival, Karunanidhi was able to stitch the same parties together. He swept to office.

Are the policies that are eventually adopted through such politics more durable? Does such politics bring people together? Does it harmonize interests?

Durable? Quite the contrary. In India today, there really *is* a consensus in practice. Every political party that comes to power, every political party wherever it *is* in power, attempts to do the same things. No one knows what else may be done that would make things better—look at the CPM in West Bengal. And yet it is next to impossible to get any of those things through. And for a manifest reason. When a party is in opposition, it feels compelled to oppose everything that whoever is in government is doing, even when that is not just a further development of, but a literal and faithful continuation of what it was doing when it was in office. As a result, when it comes to power, it has to repudiate the policies that were being followed. Recall the way privatization has been repudiated by the Manmohan Singh Government; the way the protracted effort to free the Government from the Administered Price Mechanism in the petroleum sector has been reversed, with disastrous consequences for the sector; recall the way reforms relating to banks, to the financial sector have been cast aside...

A typical case: We need uranium for our nuclear reactors. We have large quantities of it under the ground. New deposits were found in Andhra. Mrs. Indira Gandhi announced the discovery and proclaimed it to be a breakthrough for the country *in 1983*. Twenty four years later, we are still not able to exploit them. Three years ago, the then Chief Minister of Andhra, Chandrababu Naidu was trying to help the Uranium Corporation inch forward with the project. The then Leader of the Opposition, Y.S. Rajasekhara Reddy, stoutly opposed it. He wrote an article in the *Times [of India] News Network*. Here is what it said:

UCIL claims need review
The Times of India
Y S Rajasekhara Reddy, Times News Network
August 21, 2003
Attention is now focused on uranium mining across 500 acres surrounding Lambapur in Nalgonda district. The Uranium Corporation of India (UCIL) has been given permission to mine and process uranium, the most radioactive substance.
India needs its own uranium for its defence programme and to generate 4,000 MW of nuclear power by 2008 and 10,000 MW by 2010. This is imperative as all developed countries have decided not to sell India any uranium.
This Rs 500-cr project is frightening. On the one hand, it is 6 kms from the Rajiv Gandhi Tiger Sanctuary. The mining area is 4 kms from the Nagarjuna Sagar dam and the processing plant is 4 kms from the Akkampally Balancing Reservoir,

being developed as the permanent water source for the twin cites. Both are at least 300 metres above the water bodies. The UCIL will be mining an astonishing 1,250 tonnes of uranium every day, for at least the next 20 years.

This means that there will be huge amounts of radioactive waste. Uranium has a half-life period of 80,000 years, when it is at its hazardous worst. The UCIL is mining uranium in three places in Jharkhand. And the total disaster it has created at one of the mines at Jaduguda raises doubts about UCIL's credentials to be responsible. This was evident on Tuesday too when they shamelessly attempted to hijack the environmental hearing at Lambapur.

My Congress colleague M. Sashidhar Reddy organised a round table conference of political leaders, scientists, environmentalists and NGOs on August 16. He showed participants a video of Jaduguda. The fruits there have abnormal seed. People are developing illnesses resistant to known forms of cure. The deformities among children I cannot describe for fear of hurting readers' sensibilities. Yet, the UCIL is claiming that there would be no danger. This despite questions on how the waste would be dealt with, the quality of radioactive tailings and the relevance of tailing ponds. They rule out underground water contamination, claiming they will function on a zero discharge concept.

It would be foolish and criminal to take this at face value. It is precisely for this reason that the Meghalaya CM last month constituted a high-level committee to go into the full details of a similar uranium project at Domiasiat, again taken up by UCIL.

Our CM is absolutely silent even a week after PCC president D. Srinivas demanded an all-party meeting to discuss the issue.

The past has taught us that Chandrababu Naidu is like the deaf who don't listen, but invent well. Today, he is forewarned.

And what is the position today? Reddy is now Chief Minister, and Naidu leads the Opposition. Reddy is pushing hard and trying to help the Uranium Corporation commence the mining. Every other political party—in particular, the Telugu Desam led by Naidu—is blocking him, and denouncing him for being insensitive to the health and well-being of the people. As evidence, they are circulating Reddy's article of three years ago!

Are interests harmonized? Quite the contrary. The present system makes adversarial politics inevitable. Summarizing what Professor S.E. Finer set out in *Adversary Politics and Electoral Reform*, Professor Wade says, 'On any given issue each party's point of compromise will be near the mid-point of its own spectrum, i.e. far to the right or the left of the true mid-point of parliamentary opinion as a whole. The true centre, that is the left wing of the right combined with the right wing of the left, is never mobilized at all. Yet this central body of opinion probably corresponds best to the wishes of the electorate as a whole. It is because the extremists pull each party's point of compromise well to the right or well to the left of centre that we get the succession of reversal of policies which, as anyone can see, have been so damaging. The system is calculated to produce the maximum antagonism and instability and the minimum consensus and consistency.'[1]

Is that not an almost literal description of the mutual rhetoric of the Congress and the BJP? And notice the irony of it all: the greater the homogenization of the political class—that is, the closer that, say, the Congress and BJP get in their views about foreign policy, economic reforms and the like—the shriller will each party be in insisting that its positions are different!

This inherent feature is compounded by what our parties have made of politics. On each question, each political party stakes a position that will polarize the country; each segment of political spectrum takes a view that will deepen divisions—subsidies, change in PSUs, even Kashmir, the response to Pakistan, the fight against Naxalites, the fight against Islamic terrorism, what should be done in regard to Bangladeshi infiltrators... To garner or hold on to some clutch of a constituency; to send 'the right signal' to that constituency—workers in governmental units, Muslims, backward castes; to differentiate itself from the others, parties feel compelled to take positions irrespective of the consequences these will inflict on the country. One of the most distressing consequences can be seen on any day in the Houses of Parliament: even in the face of a devastating blow—another round of blasts in Mumbai, another blow in Kashmir—members swiftly descend to throwing mud at each other; debates have but to begin and they are addressing not the issue but the sectional constituencies outside the House...

This perpetual, dogged 'differentiating one's product' itself has

---

[1]H.W.R. Wade, *Constitutional Fundamentals*, The Hamlyn Lectures, Thirty-second series, Stevens, London, 1980, p.12; and *Adversary Politics and Electoral Reform*, S.E. Finer (ed.), Anthony Wigram, London, 1975, in particular pp.12–16.

several consequences. First, it propels the parties into grievance-mongering: injustice, suffering, disaster are always around; a party takes these up; the more it takes them up, the more people come to it with fresh instances; when it has exhausted the mishaps that were brought to it, the party goes looking for them; when it can't find them, it invents some... On the one side, the air is filled with grievances. On the other, each section gets convinced that it is being exploited, that its grievances are being neglected. From that, it is but a short leap to the inference that the grievances and interests are being neglected because the community is Muslim/Hindu/SC/ST/Mizo/Naga/Manipuri/Kashmiri/poor... And from that it is an even shorter step to the conclusion that the interests are being ignored because the community is not militant enough...

By this process, parties and groups come to define themselves as 'I am *not* the other'—that is the way the two main political parties, the Congress and the BJP, parties many of whose policy-positions are in fact very close to one another, define themselves today. And then there is the fact that we now have a generation of political parties and leaders who believe in nothing. All this makes cooperation impossible. Reflecting on the experience of countries like Bangladesh and India, a thoughtful officer suggests that the only solution is to *force* cooperation, that is, to pass a law that, after the elections, the two principal parties *shall* form a coalition and jointly form the government. All we will have to ensure is that there is no Liaquat Ali Khan who uses his portfolio to paralyse the resulting government...

Society splinters into packs, each insisting that, unless you concede *its* demand, it will not let the whole proceed. Each group becomes a 'single-issue fundamentalist'. None of them heeds that the only way for the arrangement to endure, the arrangement that allows each of them the opportunity to pursue its demands, is that, save what is required for the security of the country, more than any specific issue, they must be committed to the system of resolving issues, to implementing decisions.

Again, this is compounded by the fact that the horizon of political parties and their controllers is the here and now, while the new policies will take years to take effect. Cut subsidies today and the beneficial effects will be visible five years from now and then, too, they will probably be so diffuse that you will not be able to pinpoint the beneficiaries. For instance, which group will it be possible to identify as having benefited because the fiscal deficit was contained by reducing subsidies? But those who will lose are very visible, and they lose here and now, including the really well-organized, vocal beneficiaries: for instance, the traders, the firms and politicians who sell the subsidized grain and sugar and kerosene in the black markets.

What has become of our political parties

Eventually, all this corrodes the building-blocks of the parliamentary system themselves—the political parties. For long there was only one national political party, the Congress. As it began losing its base, it lunged for appeasing castes, notably the Scheduled Castes, and minorities, especially the Sikhs in Punjab *via* Bhindranwale, the Christians in the Northeast promising them 'a Christian Government', and most persistently the Muslims. Addressing the Scheduled Castes as *castes*, paved the way for Kanshi Ram and Mayawati. Using Bhindranwale resulted in the instrument consuming the wielders. Appealing to 'backwards' cleared the way for Lalu Yadav, Mulayam Singh and the rest. Appeasing the Muslims fanned the most extreme among them. The discerning among these groups quickly saw the opportunity: the leading political party was seeing them *as a group;* it was trying to win them over *as a group.* Hence, the more they could organize themselves *as a group*, the more the Congress would bend to them.

Two inferences followed. Members of these communities were exhorted to constitute themselves into voting blocks: we are a minority in the country as a whole, but in individual localities we can tilt the balance; all we have to do is to vote consciously, purposively, as a block. The more the political parties see that we are voting as a block, the more they will bend to our will. Recall the maps that Syed Shahabuddin published in issues of *Muslim India* exhibiting the constituencies in which Muslims *as Muslims* could determine the electoral outcome. Soon enough, this heightened awareness of 'power lies in separateness' led to 'strategic voting', of Muslims voting as Muslims to defeat the candidates they set out to defeat.

The second effect has been equally consequential. In each case, while the initial advantage from appeasement, from addressing members of the group as a group, went to the Congress, ultimately the benefit accrued to some leader from within the group who adopted an out-and-out casteist or communal line. Bhindranwale was, of course, the epitome of this phenomenon. But, in essence, Kanshi Ram, Mayawati, Lalu Yadav, Mulayam Singh—all have been the outcomes, the entirely predictable outcomes of the stratagem of the dominant party. And the process does not end at the initial list of groups which have been addressed as groups. When one party panders to the Scheduled Castes, naturally another leader or party thinks of some other group which he can get behind him; recall V.P. Singh's lunge for 'Other Backward Castes'.

What the Congress adopted, other parties envied, and soon, imitated.

While each of the national parties was complimenting itself— 'See, we are now getting unprecedented response among sections that were entirely beyond our reach earlier'—in fact, the base was shifting to the out-and-out casteist and communal leaders.

To see what this progression portends, recall the closing speech that Dr. Ambedkar delivered as the Constituent Assembly met for its last session. He had been explaining how the Constitution had come to be put together, piece by piece, how so many had contributed to its evolution; he had been countering some of the criticisms that were already being levelled. And then he said,

Here I could have ended. But my mind is so full of the future of our country that I feel I ought to take this occasion to give expression to some of my reflections thereon. On 26th January 1950, India will be an independent country [*Cheers*]. What would happen to her independence? Will she maintain her independence or will she lose it again? This is the first thought that comes to my mind. It is not that India was never an independent country. The point is that she once lost the independence she had. Will she lose it a second time? It is this thought which makes me most anxious for the future. What perturbs me greatly is the fact that not only India has once before lost her independence, but she lost it by the infidelity and treachery of some of her own people. In the invasion of Sindh by Mahommed-Bin-Kasim, the military commanders of King Dahar accepted bribes from the agents of Mahommed-Bin-Kasim and refused to fight on the side of their king. It was Jaichand who invited Mahommed Gohri to invade India and fight against Prithvi Raj and promised him the help of himself and the Solanki kings. When Shivaji was fighting for the liberation of Hindus, the other Maratha noblemen and the

Rajput Kings were fighting the battle on the side of Moghul Emperors. When the British were trying to destroy the Sikh Rulers, Gulab Singh, their principal commander sat silent and did not help to save the Sikh kingdom. In 1857, when a large part of India had declared a war of independence against the British, the Sikhs stood and watched the event as silent spectators.

Will history repeat itself? It is this thought which fills me with anxiety. This anxiety is deepened by the realization of the fact that in addition to our old enemies in the form of castes and creeds we are going to have many political parties with diverse and opposing political creeds. Will Indians place the country above their creed or will they place creed above country? I do not know. But this much is certain that if the parties place creed above country, our independence will be put in jeopardy a second time and probably be lost for ever...

He added an exhortation, of course: 'This eventuality we must all resolutely guard against. We must be determined to defend our independence with the last drop of our blood...' And this exhortation too was greeted with acclamation: '*Cheers*', states the Record.[1]

But in view of what we see around us today, what strikes us? That our political parties are living up to Dr. Ambedkar's exhortation? Or to his foreboding?

Today, both national parties are not only cabined in their geographical ambit. They are organizationally weak. The only difference between them as regards their condition as organizations is that in the Congress at the top there is an ultimate arbiter, Sonia Gandhi. As she is the one visible leader, as she is the ultimate arbiter, as all authority within the Party flows from her, as all others in the Congress rise or fall on rumoured proximity to her, the illusion is created that the Party is unified. But that is no less a *non sequitur* than would be the premise that, as the Queen still sits in Buckingham Palace, the British Empire is still around.

Pressed by the consequences of having pandered to Muslims one day, the Scheduled Castes the next, the national parties soon had to lean on, and seek alliances with those who set themselves up as the extreme, out-and-out champions of these groups: Mayawati in U.P.,

---

[1] *Constituent Assembly of India Debates*, 25 November, 1949, Book VI, Volume X, pp.977–78.

and then with her mortal enemy, Mulayam Singh, Lalu Yadav in Bihar, Shibu Soren in Jharkhand, the AIADMK and then, its mortal enemy, the DMK in Tamil Nadu... The result has been predictable. These leaders and their 'parties' have gained, the national parties have lost more and more of their base.

We, therefore, are now left with two weak, and progressively weakening national parties, and a motley assortment of caste and regional parties. The only way that the two national parties can keep the ground from slipping further, is to cooperate with each other. But that option is foreclosed by the other feature that such a system imposes, the feature we noted earlier, namely, that it makes adversarial politics inevitable. As by now, each party is defining itself as 'Not the other', the one entity with whom neither can cooperate is the only one, cooperation with which will both serve the immediate needs of the country as well as stem the party's weakening.

But that is the one thing that it cannot do, and less and less so with each passing month. Recall that politics of the kind we have now has splintered the electorate. The splinters have been set up in contradistinction to each other. Each is made to fear the other. As a consequence, each party hones its appeal to some *part* of this electorate. And the way to do so, the way that it finds effective, is to proclaim that the *other* party is a party of the other group, the devourer. Having staked its fortunes on the Muslim vote, having shouted from the house-tops that the BJP is nothing but a 'communal Hindu party', how can the Congress cooperate with the BJP? Each has stoked some particular section to such a pitch of apprehension and suspicion, each has demonized the other to such a degree that to now cooperate with the other would be to 'betray' the cause. Things have reached so ridiculous an extent that today, the Congress leaders, realizing though they do that the reforms and Bills which they have introduced in regard to pensions, insurance, banks and the like are urgently needed, are unwilling to seek the cooperation of the BJP even in regard to these, eminently 'secular' matters! They realize that these need to be urgently implemented. They realize that help of the BJP alone can see them through. But, having demonized the latter, how are they to be seen to be getting anything through with the help of the demon? And, to double the irony, the personal relations among many of the leaders remain not just cordial, they remain close and intimate.

So, the only parties with which each of the national parties can cooperate are the out-and-out casteist and regional parties. But, with the exception of the Communists, almost all of these are now just groupings around individuals and their families.

There is an individual.

He or she has a gang, a coterie around him.

Followers who deify that individual, those who knit some braids to some member of that family or coterie, become subalterns.

Even as the mass who have been beguiled into supporting the leader and his/her 'party' gain little, the leader and his coterie prosper. Study the evidence produced in the 'disproportionate assets' cases of some of these leaders.

The followers do gain dominance. As long as their leader is in power, they are able to boss it over the populace and loot in their locality—for instance, usurp houses they come to fancy. This is hailed by progressive commentators as these castes, etc. acquiring 'self-respect'.

But the ruler is as suspicious of his followers as he is of those controlling other groups. He moves to knit networks of control over his followers. Through these networks, he becomes independent of the community at large. For instance, he suborns the bureaucracy: they are to be *his* functionaries, not of the State; their postings and transfers depend on whether they are useful to *him*, not on whether they are carrying out their duties well or ill. And he is deliberately brazen about this. He makes sure that every civil servant, every policeman sees that this is the order of things.

The patterns established, he can, of course, rake in what he wants. He can fix anyone who comes in his way. He uses his flock to put himself above the law—'I am being hounded only because I am a *dalit.*'

The loot is gathered in the name of the followers, often *from* the followers: 'Why do you go to temples and make offerings?,' one of them asked her followers. 'I am your living *devi*. Bring your offerings to me.'

The control over the coffers in turn makes the leader independent of her or his followers. The only saving grace is that families fall apart over the funds, and the fact that, beyond a point, they are using the 'party' to acquire funds, to save themselves from the law, undermines their legitimacy, and eventually that of the party.

Soon, the convenience of the leader is elevated into ideology. These leaders and their henchmen raise their loot into legitimate recompense: 'You fellows have exploited our people for centuries,' they and their academic apologists, proclaim, 'Now taste a bit of your own medicine.' They raise their incompetence into the norm—standards are elitist, they proclaim; they are a conspiracy to keep the downtrodden out of the offices of State. They proclaim their vulgarity to be authenticity—the 'masses' are coming into their own, they and, even more insistently our progressives-by-proxy, the intellectuals, proclaim. Intimidation becomes argument, indeed it becomes reason. The fact that they can and will have you assaulted, becomes proof.

None of this has been fortuitous. It is not the doing of some evil leader.

And we should reflect where this sequence will have carried us twenty years from now.

Multi-tiered incompetence

With standards having been traduced as elitist, with merit and efficiency having been denounced as a conspiracy of the haves to keep the deprived down, it can be no surprise that today, even to suggest that a person should not get a job because he is not competent to do the duties that go with the job, is to invite abuse. Neither ministers nor civil servants are selected and placed in a post because they have been specially trained for it. Indeed, for the entire Executive and Legislative branches of the State, the basic premise is that no one need have any special background or preparation. And this at every level, in every sphere.

The last consideration that a party manager has today in selecting a candidate is that he is competent to weigh legislative proposals, that he has the knowledge and judgement to weigh policy alternatives. Winnability is all, and that depends on his being from the right caste, on his being able to field sufficient muscle and money. Going by what prevails in our legislatures these days, next to winnability, the ability that controllers of parties have to value most is not knowledge of issues, not even the ability to put forth a reasoned argument in a sober way, certainly not integrity. It is the ability to shout and put up a show of anger and outrage. Seldom does even a veteran—that is, one who has been in the legislature for years—have any experience other than having spent years in the legislature. Rare indeed would be the case where a member of a legislature would have run an organization, that is, he would have had *executive* experience. And yet, suddenly, he may well land up in charge of a ministry, a large organization that requires intimate knowledge of issues that fall within its purview as well as extensive executive competence and experience. The consequence has been remarked upon again and again over the years. Addressing students of the Madras University at their Convocation twenty years ago, Mr. N.A. Palkhivala observed,

> When at this Convocation you see degrees conferred upon engineers, doctors, surgeons, lawyers and other professionals, you cannot fail to be struck by the grim irony of the situation where the one job for which you need no training or qualification whatsoever is the job of legislating for and governing the largest democracy on earth. You need years of training to attend to a boiler or to mind a machine, to supervise a shop floor or to build a bridge, to argue a case in a law court or to operate upon a human body. But to steer the lives and destinies of more than 650 million of your fellow-men, you are not required to have any education or equipment at all![1]

This systemic bias for incompetence has a dual consequence—both in the type that we get in the legislatures and, therefore, in governments, and in the type that we *don't* get. For this 'selection process', so to say, has dissuaded the middle and entrepreneurial classes, the very ones who are making the new India, from even attempting to enter the political arena.

The political Executive is selected from this lot. Is a person whose entire perspective is that of a locality-politician with its personal rivalries, its 'caste equations' likely to have the world-view to fashion the foreign or defence policy of the country? Will he be in

---

[1] N.A. Palkhivala, 'Constitutional changes and the Presidential System,' Convocation Address, University of Madras, September 1979, in *We, The People*, The Strand Bookstall, Bombay, 1984, p.239.

tune with the new imperatives—technologies, everchanging balances—to steer the country's economic reforms? And there is another problem, one that goes beyond the individual. Today, no party has a sufficient number of legislators who are competent enough to run the number of ministries into which the government has been splintered. In fact, there is no combination of political parties that can field enough competent persons to govern the country.

Even the head of the Executive, the Prime Minister, is selected more or less by lottery. Recall how Charan Singh, Chandrashekhar, H.D. Deve Gowda, I.K. Gujral, and now Manmohan Singh ended up as Prime Ministers. And in selecting his ministers, competence is way down on the list of considerations which the Prime Minister has to keep in mind. Indeed, now the choice of who from RJD or DMK shall become a minister has to be left to the controllers of *that* party. So, if only to make his own case less of an exception, Lalu Yadav were to nominate only those from among his MPs who have criminal cases pending against them to be ministers, they are the ones who will be ministers.

Nor should we focus only on the Central Government. To visualize the effect this has on governance, we must bear in mind that this pattern is repeated again and again *at every level*. We can scarcely imagine the consequences this pattern is already having for national security in regions as vast and as close to Delhi as U.P.

And what happens to the Executive is replicated in every other institution. These ministers and civil servants choose persons for every other post, including posts in those mythical institutions, ones that are taken to be 'autonomous.' Ministers appoint judges, they appoint vice chancellors, they transfer police officers down to the station house officer in your neighbourhood *thana*. They don't just appoint them. They determine who shall remain in which post. Thus, while civil servants are selected initially through a competitive examination, after that their posting, their career depends on the political Executive. That Executive, and its insistence that the bidding of each legislator from his party be carried out, determines not just the fate of the individual officer, it sets the ethos of the entire service.

Take *any* institution. Today the whole thing depends on who is manning it at that moment. This simple fact shows the low level, almost the non-existent level of *institutionalization* of these institutions. The institutions are just signboards, buildings. In the end, they are just instruments of the political class. If an institution acts independently today, it does so only by accident. The Executive appoints a particular person to the institution thinking that he would be cooperative and docile; he turns out to be independent. But the lesson which the political Executive draws from the person's independent conduct is not that the institution to which he has been appointed must be respected, but that the selection of that particular individual for that post was a 'blunder', a blunder which must not be repeated when the post next falls vacant.

The results are manifest all around us in the collapse of standards in higher education, the embarrassing quality of judgements, police registering cases against opponents of the ruler of the moment, and *not* registering them if someone belonging to the Chief Minister's caste or party or faction is involved...

And things get worse with each round. 'What explains the condition to which we have descended today?' Dr. P.V. Indiresen asked me once. As I was still groping for the answer, he said, 'No, no. Indiresen's Law.' 'Indiresen's Law?' I wondered. 'You mean you don't know Indiresen's Law? Second rate persons select third rate persons. You do that for thirty years and you get to where we have reached.'

Contrast this way of selecting rulers of a billion people with the care that Lee Kwan Yew expended in selecting those who would legislate on behalf of Singaporeans, and even more so in selecting those who would hold Executive positions in government. Recall his methodical search for persons with 'helicopter qualities'. This is also one of the principal differences between China and India, Tarun Khanna, the Harvard Professor who has devoted much time to studying China, points out: at every level of governance, especially at the provincial and local levels, the quality of China's personnel— ministers, mayors, officials—is so much higher than that of their counterparts in India.

Of course, the effects of this descent or, to put it the other way, of the ascent of such leaders and their henchmen are not limited to mere governance. Standards gone; moral norms rent; others emboldened both by their conduct and by the fact that they can never be brought to book—after all, the magistrates and judges too are their appointees or the appointees of persons like them—their systematic campaign to tarnish the few who remain honest so that the people conclude, '*Saale, saare chor hain*'; reason, evidence scoffed away... Society is left with no lever by which to restrain such leaders, or to retrieve ground.

As they lose legitimacy, the leaders and parties turn to criminals and armed gangs to stay in power.

Recalling what the N.N. Vohra Committee had reported on the basis of mountains of inputs from our intelligence agencies, the Commission to Review the Working of the Constitution had observed,

> The entry of criminals in politics is a matter of great concern. The Vohra Committee appointed by the Government had stated in strong terms that the nexus between crime syndicates and political personalities was very deep. According to the Central Bureau of Investigation (CBI) report to the Vohra Committee: 'all over India, crime syndicates have become a law unto themselves... Even in the smaller towns and rural areas, muscle-men have become the order of the day. Hired assassins have become part of these organizations. The nexus between the criminal gangs, police, bureaucracy and politicians has come out clearly in various parts of the country.' The Committee quoted other agencies to state that the mafia network is 'virtually running a parallel government, pushing the State apparatus into irrelevance.' The report also says 'in certain States like Bihar, Haryana and Uttar Pradesh, these gangs enjoy the patronage of local politicians cutting across party lines and the protection of the functionaries. Some political leaders become the leaders of these gangs/armed *senas* and over the years get themselves elected to local bodies, State assemblies and the national Parliament.'

The N.N. Vohra Committee had been set up to nail the nexus between criminals, politicians and the administration. It had received piles and piles of detailed, specific information. Vohra, then Home Secretary, and a well-known and distinguished civil servant, included details and specific information in his report. He presented the report personally to the Home Minister in September, 1993. He retired in May 1994. The report was shoved into the *almirahs* of the Home Ministry, and carefully locked! No one knew even that it had been completed and given to the Minister. The *tandoor*-murder took place: a political functionary of sorts chopped his lady-friend to pieces, and burnt the pieces in a *tandoor*, right in New Delhi, not far from Parliament. The monsoon session of Parliament was on soon. A member charged the Government: the police is protecting the murderer because of the nexus that has developed between police and... What is new about the nexus?, Rajesh Pilot, then Minister of State for Home, shot back. There is a full report about the nexus... Everyone was on his feet. Where is the report? Why has it been suppressed? You are shielding criminals... Overnight, a summary was printed, and presented to Parliament. It was a meaningless fragment—every detail had been excised. No wonder, the cancer has gone on spreading.

And it feeds itself. At first, political parties take occasional help from criminals and armed groups, say, at the time of elections. Then they begin turning to them for regular exactions, the two sets becoming business partners, so to say. Soon enough, the criminal wonders, 'Why should I help these buffoons? Why should I not enter politics myself?' He wins. The policemen who were chasing him are now deputed as his Personal Security Officers. Much of U.P. and Bihar today runs on the dictate of three *'babubalis'*—Mukhtar Ansari, the MLA from Ghazipur, Atiq Ahmed, the MP from Allahabad, and Shahabuddin, the MP from Siwan.

This is how Prakash Singh, who has been Director-General of Police of both U.P. and Assam, who has been Director-General of the Border Security Force, and who has made special study of Left-wing violence, describes the sway of Ansari:

> At least eight districts in eastern U.P. and four contiguous districts of Bihar are today completely under the grip of the mafia. The rule of law exists only on paper. District magistrates and superintendents of police kowtow before the mafia dons and take orders from them on critical matters. In Ghazipur district, most of the station house officers owe their position to Mukhtar Ansari, the local don. The S.P. and D.M. merely concur with his recommendations. Ansari, in fact, decides who is to get the contracts for major projects in U.P.'s eastern districts. His recommendations for an arms license have to be honoured. When he travels, he does so in style. A cavalcade of six to seven Qualis cars moves with a posse of about 12 policemen provided to him by the State Government and another of about 20–30 armed hoodlums. No S.H.O. dares check him for any violation of law. A case was registered against him in the context of the recent riots in Mau, but the state police pathetically said that it was not easy to arrest him.

The plain truth is that the police was not sure if the leadership in Lucknow would take kindly to his arrest. Mercifully, after pressure was built up, the don obliged by surrendering before a court. However, his wings have not been clipped and his assets remain intact. Once he comes out, he will be at his evil best again.

Shahabuddin's position in Bihar is comparable. There are no less than 30 cases against him, ranging from murder and kidnapping to keeping unaccounted foreign currencies...[1]

The police do not execute warrants against this Shahabuddin for months. He gives interviews to pressmen. He appears on TV. He lolls about in his well-known homes including the ones in Delhi. He, or, worse, his nominee writing the paper in Shahabuddin's name, sits for a *law* exam, no less! And he is a Member of Parliament, to boot. But the police do not serve the warrants on him saying they cannot locate him!

The Vohra Committee had reported in 1993. Nothing happened as a result. The Constitution Review Commission recalled in 2002 what the Committee had said in 1993. Nothing happened as a result. Prakash Singh's article set out the facts once again in 2005. Nothing happened as a result. And so it should be no surprise that, writing in *The Indian Express* of 27 February, 2007, Alka S. Pande reported, 'The international kidnapping kingpin Babloo Srivastava—after his acquittal in a murder case last week—declared his candidature on Monday to contest the Assembly polls from Lucknow Central, which comes under the parliamentary constituency of former PM Atal Bihari Vajpayee.' She recalled that 'In the current 403-member Uttar Pradesh Vidhan Sabha, about 200 members have criminal charges against them. Some prominent names are—Mukhtar Ansari, Amarmani Tripathi, Raghuraj Pratap Singh "Raja Bhaiya", Hari Shankar Tiwari, Mohd. Ashraf and Akhilesh Kumar Singh. And all these members are either part of the Government or are extending support to Mulayam Singh Yadav. Each of these *bahubalis* was facing criminal charges while contesting the Assembly polls in 2002, but none was convicted.' And not just ordinary criminal charges: 'Ansari,' she wrote, 'was once found to have been involved in

---

[1] *The Hindustan Times*, 17 November 2005.

terrorist activities as well. However, the STF personnel Shailendra Singh, who had found evidence against him, was transferred. Similarly, Raja Bhaiya was held under POTA, but all witnesses turned hostile and he had to be set free.' 'The statistics of the U.P. Police,' she reported, 'reveal that since 1985, there has been a rise in the number of leaders with criminal background from 35 in 1985 to 208 in 2002.' Everyone was, of course, duly concerned! Parliament was weighing provisions of a Bill to prevent persons with criminal records from contesting elections. A Bench of the Allahabad High Court had issued notices on a PIL filed before it. 'Even the Mulayam Singh Yadav Government had acknowledged the criminalization of politics,' Alka noted, Indeed, the U.P. Assembly itself had devoted an entire debate to the criminalization of its ranks after one of its members had been gunned down—that was in December, 2005. The result? 'February 26, 2007: The international kidnapping kingpin Babloo Srivastava—after his acquittal in a murder case last week—declared his candidature on Monday to contest the Assembly polls from Lucknow Central...'[1]

Police cases. Proceedings in the High Court. Debates in the Assembly. Accounts in newspapers. Committees. Commissions. And no consequence.

These dons run their operations from jails, *via* visitors and cell phones. Can it be that the police cannot search and sequester those wretched phones? Can it be that we cannot develop and install jammers in jails? It is the nexus that the dons have with politicians and policemen which prevents these obvious things from getting done.

Haji Mastan is already a member of the Maharashtra Assembly. Abu Salem, accused in the Bombay blasts case, awaits his acquittal to become an honoured leader...

Of course, the phenomenon is not limited to individuals. An entire mafia of smugglers runs much of coastal India, the sugar barons have sway over much of Maharashtra, the building and land mafias over swathes of one metropolis after another... The Naxalites are sought after in Bihar, in Jharkhand, in Andhra... Soon, no political party will be able to win elections unless it comes to an understanding

---

[1] *The Indian Express*, 27 February, 2007.

with them in stretches of Chhatisgarh, Maharashtra... ULFA has been decisive in tilting the balance from one party to the other in Assam...

Some way to select legislators and ministers to steer a billion people!

The myth of deciding, that of participation in governance

In what sense do the masses decide in a democracy? Do they decide the programmes of political parties? Or those sudden scriptures—the 'Common Minimum Programme'—that are knocked together *after* elections to rationalize arrangements to grab office? Do the people choose candidates? Do they determine how the one they elect will conduct himself subsequently, or the position he will take on specific issues? Each of these things, in fact, is decided by a small coterie which controls the political party. This is all the more so in regard to the day-to-day working of the parties. What is to be done that day in the legislature, for instance, is decided by two or three individuals, often by looking at nothing more substantial than the headlines of that morning's newspapers. To the outsider, of course, the average legislator is representing the people—and he strains to project himself as the one who is representing the people—and commands 'sovereignty' as their fiduciary. In fact, he, the average legislator, that is every member except those two or three controllers, does not contribute anything substantial to the decision; indeed, most often he learns about what is to happen only after he enters the House.

It is said that the coterie is influenced by what it thinks people will prefer in regard to each issue or person, and, in this sense, the masses exercise influence. But even this sort of influence, if it exists at all, is strictly limited. First, the masses scarcely have an opinion on the myriad issues that have to be settled at every turn: what is the opinion of the masses on the forthcoming amendment of the Patents Act? On FDI in insurance? The fact is that an opinion will be *created* for them through agitations, *dharnas*, statements to the press, and then invoked by the manufacturers of that opinion to support the position they have decided to take. Second, many random factors come to determine the position that these manufacturers of the 'people's opinion' will take—that the amendment is being espoused by their opponent or ally; that the controller of some business house has got to their leader or his rival brother. Third, the coterie has little information about what people actually feel regarding a candidate or an issue. This is evident from the way it is surprised by election results.

That the parliamentary system ensures 'participation by the masses in governance' is another hardy myth. Sheer numbers make 'participation' impossible. The issues themselves are too complex, and the people are both too little informed and too little interested to provide any substantial input. Which is the issue among the ones which come up daily for decision in a central ministry that you would want the 'people' to decide and administer? In fact, the more attention that the coterie pays to the opinion of the people, the more it will be prone to shorten even further its horizon, to lunge even more for populist boondoggles. 'Price control for drugs that the masses need'—how many times our governments go in for that: they win plaudits twice over: for serving the interests of the people and for standing up to 'multinational drug companies'! The net result? Leaders thus keep down the production precisely of the drugs that the people most need!

In a word, we find that the assertions by which the present system is justified turn out to be myths. The condition in which our institutions are today is standing proof of that.

- ❏ The system does *not* ensure accountability.
- ❏ It is *not* representative.
- ❏ It does *not* involve 'the people' in governance.
- ❏ It does *not* yield stable or strong and certainly not effective governments.
- ❏ It does *not* bring groups and interests together.
- ❏ It does *not* lead to any search for a consensus.
- ❏ The 'solutions' that emerge out of it are neither the ones the country needs, nor are they more durable.
- ❏ It just does *not* place power in the hands of persons who have the competence, nor even the aptitude for governance and legislation.
- ❏ It does *not* induce the persons in whose hands it places power to adopt responsible policies.
- ❏ It does *not* preserve the blocks on which it is built, the political parties.

5

Just one among many possible systems

In brief, the consequences of the present electoral system and of the parliamentary system, of which it is the starting point, that are most destructive of governance are:

❑ Candidates get elected with a woeful minority of votes.
❑ Hence, the system gives the maximum inducement to leaders and candidates to address their appeal to narrower and narrower sections and; in particular, it fans casteism.
❑ This leads to, and has already led to splintering the electorate. From that to splintering the legislatures. Thence to splintering the Executive. The end result is that no one has enough power to get things done, everyone has enough power to block everything.
❑ Every candidate has to depend on huge amounts of money.
❑ He has to field muscle. Increasingly, entire parties have come to turn to violent groups for assistance.
❑ Persons strive to enter legislatures not because they have any particular competence for legislation or for assessing policies, or even any special interest in these. Among the reasons for which they do so are that entering the legislature is the stepping stone to becoming a minister; entering the legislature can help shield one from the law; doing so confers several benefits—salaries, allowances, fees for attending sessions and committee meetings, accommodation, free telephone services, free travel, subsidized food... all the way to lifelong pension. In addition, as recent disclosures have shown, there are co-curricular windfalls, from voting for or against a government: recall the JMM bribery case; to what may be skimmed from MPLADS; to what may be charged for asking questions...

❑ Instead of attending to his duties as a legislator, the successful candidate has to cater to the personal needs of his constituents. The constituents, in turn, look to the winner not as one whose job is to assess legislative and policy proposals from the point of view of the country but as one whose duty is to advance their personal and family interests.

❑ The system does not yield the sorts of persons that are required for the complex tasks of governance.

❑ It shortens the horizon of those who are in office when the problems that confront us, from national security to economic development, require that policies be sustained for decades.

❑ Many of these policies are bound to dislocate some sections in the short run: these sections are liable to be localised, well-organized and aggressive. The policies will certainly yield benefits, in fact without them the country will be endangered; but the benefits will be a while in coming, and the ones who will benefit from those policies are today diffuse.

Structures and conduct

'No Constitution is perfect and the Drafting Committee is itself suggesting certain amendments to improve the Draft Constitution'— Dr. Ambedkar was moving the motion that the Draft be taken into consideration by the Constituent Assembly. The Draft had been in the public domain for eight months. Sharp criticisms had been hurled at it. Ambedkar answered them at length—what were going to be the special features of the federation; why it was no bad thing that the Constitution had borrowed heavily from other Constitutions—in particular from the Government of India Act of 1935; why the criticism that it had nothing in it that reflected our ancient systems of governance was misplaced; the clauses on amendment; those on Fundamental Rights... He had addressed these criticisms at length, and was winding up. The Draft had also been discussed extensively in the Provincial Assemblies, he recalled. Apart from criticism of the financial provisions in the Madras Assembly and the objections raised in regard to one clause, none of the Assemblies had advanced any serious objection to the Draft. And this, he said, gave him 'courage to say that the Constitution as settled by the Drafting Committee is good enough to make in this a start with. I feel that it is workable, it is flexible and it is strong enough to hold the country together both in peace time and in war time. Indeed, if I may say so, if things go wrong under the new Constitution, the reason will not be that we had a bad Constitution. What we will have to say is, Man was vile'[1]

Now, it is entirely true that there is no substitute for character in that, there is no structure that the perverse cannot pervert. But structures affect conduct. When processes of courts are so dilatory, so full of loopholes that punishment seems unlikely, naturally the criminal is emboldened to go on with his trade.

Recall the fact we noted at the outset, one that stares us in the face every day. Over the last decade and a half, a wide spectrum of new leaders has burst forth in industry. Narayana Murthy and his Infosys, Azim Premji and Wipro, FC Kohli and Ramadorai and their TCS, Sunil Mittal and his Airtel... not one of them was even heard of just ten-fifteen years ago. If we recall the names of the 'Ten Largest Industrial Houses' of twenty years ago, and compare that list with the ten largest houses today, perhaps the only common name would be TATAs. And, under Ratan Tata, TATAs today are completely different from what they were even ten years ago.

How is it that such leaders are bursting forth in industry, but not in public life? The question can, in fact, be sharper. How is it that leaders are emerging in industry who are taking India to new heights, while in public life the ones that are overtaking others are the very ones who will take, and are taking governance down?

The answer lies in the changes that reforms have brought about in industry. Till the 1980s, to get ahead, the best bet for the industrialist was to know the minister or civil servant in the relevant ministry. Knowing them, manipulating them was the way to score over one's rivals; it was the way to use the State to keep others out. Because of reforms, now the way to outdo others is to know the customer, the technologies; it is to reinvent one's operations on the shop-floor. Moreover, excelling has now become the condition of survival. An auto-parts maker in Pune cannot hold his own against rivals,

---

[1]*Constituent Assembly Debates, Official Report*, 4 November, 1948, Lok Sabha Secretariat, New Delhi, Volume VII, pp.31-44, at 44.

foreign as much as domestic; he cannot even survive unless he excels.

In a word, it is because the filtering mechanism and the criteria for locating the best have been changed that we are now getting so many new leaders in industry, and of such a different type. In politics, the reverse has happened; the selection procedure has become worse and worse—caste instead of performance, for instance.

And then there is the point about selectors. No UPSC, no DGTD could have spotted and nurtured the industrial leaders who are accelerating growth today. The scores and scores of factors that make up the 'market' are, as Professor Hayek had said, the 'discovery procedure' that has spotted them, and pointed them in the direction of steps that they must take. In several political parties, selection today depends on persons who have come up through, to take one instance, caste or money or the access to criminals. For the next round, they naturally select persons who are of the same qualifications.

In a word, structure affects conduct. Hence, it is important to inquire: what changes in the system will minimize the possibility of these outcomes?

Why not a lottery?

Assume that we had elections but no candidates. Computers register the names of all who have voted. By a lot, it picks 540 winners for the Lok Sabha. The advantages are at once obvious:

❑ There is no need for anyone to appeal to, or cater to any caste, etc.
❑ There is no need for him or his party to deploy any money.
❑ There is no need to seek the help of, and after elections repay some Naxalite group, ULFA and the like.
❑ The hold of party-bosses is minimized.
❑ The 'winner' owes nothing to the 'electorate'. By catering to their particular interests, she or he does not increase in the slightest her chances of being elected the next time.

❑ As the proportion of criminals in the population is liable to be less than the proportion who are being encouraged by the present system to contest elections, I would presume that the number of history-sheeters in those 'elected' by the lottery will also be reduced.

The drawback is also evident. The legislature is not liable to get enough persons who will have the competence that modern governance requires. But that is not an argument against 'elections' by drawing lots. It is an argument for introducing additional features. For instance, for limiting the lottery to those who have the qualifications in terms of education, professional experience, etc. that are required for governance. Better still, it is an argument, yet another argument for cutting the link between the Legislature and the Executive.

At this early stage, only two factors need be noted. First, the consequences that are debilitating us today are an inevitable result of the present system but this is not the only possible system. The consequences can be mitigated by other arrangements. Second, we should keep in mind for the future the advantages that accrue from introducing a step involving randomness, from introducing a lottery at some stage in the process.

Consider an alternate lottery, not to select the final winner, but to select the constituency from which a candidate will stand. Parties remain. They send lists of their candidates to the Election Commission. To determine which candidate will contest from which particular constituency, the Commission draws lots. Some of the earlier advantages are lost. Controllers of parties have clout now, parties have to muster all the resources that are required today— money, muscle. But some advantages remain: for instance, the link between the particular candidate and the constituency, though not between the party and the constituency, is weakened. And there is a new gain which is not there in an out-and-out lottery: as a candidate may have to stand from anywhere, parties will be under greater inducement to include in their lists persons who will be more acceptable across the board in different parts of the country or state, to different sections of the electorate. That the candidate is from a particular caste, etc., will matter less for who knows if that caste will be the decisive one in the constituency to which this candidate gets assigned?

Consider a third alternative. The figures that we had encountered earlier of candidates winning with the support of just 15–20 per cent of the electorate suggest that the smaller the constituency, the greater the incentive to hone one's appeal to a narrow group. Supposing the whole of India is one constituency, as it would be if we were electing the head of the Executive directly as in a Presidential System. There is no caste that has such a wide presence throughout the country that, by setting himself up as the champion and saviour of that caste, a person can sweep the country. Or consider the other, easier way of enlarging the number of persons that the candidate must persuade: make voting compulsory. As the number of voters will now be almost twice as large as it is today, the appeal that the candidate addresses will also have to be more comprehensive than the sectional ones that turn the trick today.

Many systems

The system we have is just one of many possible systems. Moreover, many of the alternative systems can, in fact, be said to be more 'democratic' than the one we have in that they would ensure, for instance, that the legislature would conform more closely with the preferences of the voters than does the present first-past-the-post system.

Even the present system is not one, unalloyed granite-whole. Legislators are elected by the first-past-the-post rule, with each voter having a single, equal vote. But that is not how our President is elected, nor the Vice President. In these cases, each voter—the legislators—has, in effect, a vote proportional to the population he represents. And the voter does not cast just a simple, 'Yes' or 'No' vote. He indicates his order of preferences among candidates. That last feature, of indicating preferences, also figures in the way we elect members of, say, the Rajya Sabha: when the legislature of U.P. is electing members for the Rajya Sabha, for instance, to win, a candidate may need, say, 35 votes; the U.P. legislators will indicate their second and third preference also; so that, once a candidate has obtained the necessary 35 votes, the second preferences of the surplus votes are counted and distributed among the remaining candidates. This system minimizes the number of votes that may be 'wasted'. It also enables the voter to choose not just between parties but also between candidates of a given party. Furthermore, in the case of the Rajya Sabha, the size of the 'constituency', that is the individual state, varies from states in the Northeast that return just one member to a state like U.P. that returns 30 members.

In a variant of this system each voter does not just put a 'cross' against one candidate. He is asked to indicate his preferences among candidates—preference 1 for 'X', preference 2 for 'Y', preference 3 for 'Z', say. If one of the three gets more than 50 per cent of the first preferences, he is declared elected. Otherwise, the candidate who gets the least number of first preferences is eliminated, and his votes are distributed among the remaining two in accordance with the second preferences that the voters for the eliminated candidate have indicated... The process of eliminating and redistributing is continued till one of the candidates gets an absolute majority. An obvious modification is possible. It doesn't seem quite right to attach the same weight to the second preference of an elector as to his first preference. Thus, we may assign 3 points to the first preference that an elector indicates; 2 to the second preference; 1 to the third. Once the votes are cast, we total the points that each candidate has secured. The one who gets the maximum points wins—provided she gets past the threshold...

In our system we are divided among geographically delineated constituencies, and we vote for one among a set of competing candidates. In others, voters vote not for one candidate but for a list of candidates put up by a party. As many candidates from the list that has been put up by a party get elected to the legislature as correspond to the share of votes that the party has received. In Germany, half the members are now returned from geographically delineated constituencies and half through lists. The proportion was 60:40 when the new Constitution was drawn up after the Second War. Each voter casts two votes—one for the candidate he prefers as far as the geographical constituency is concerned; and one vote for the party he prefers. There can be a further variation: the proportion of candidates that a party gets to send from its list may be determined in such a way that the overall share of members that it has in the legislature is proportional to the proportion of votes that it has received or, to confound matters, proportional to the votes its 'constituency candidates' have received. The seats that the party has in the House eventually can thus be brought closer to its share in votes. This can be done by reassigning seats of parties that fail to cross the prescribed threshold; or by keeping a certain number of seats from the beginning for such distribution. The geographical and list constituencies can be made to rotate or each voter can be given two votes. He casts one vote for a candidate in the geographical constituency and one for the party list.

Cut-off rules also vary. In countries which have been more particular about not excluding small fractions of voters, the cut-off below which a party does not get to send a candidate is kept very low. In countries which have been keen not to have the proportional system trigger instability by splintering the legislature into many parties, the cut-off has been kept high. Countries have adopted different rules to distribute the votes of parties that are ruled out by the cut-off rule. There are further differences depending on whether the parties are required to secure at the least a certain proportion of votes in just one region of the country, or in a given number of different regions, or only in the country as a whole. There can be a mix of these rules; in Germany, a party does not get to send a representative to the Bundestag unless it gets either five per cent of the votes across the country or it secures at least three seats on a regional basis.

In Italy, a country that has been plagued by chronic instability of governments, there was at one stage an ingenious provision for according a 'majority premium'. The party or pre-announced coalition of parties that secured an absolute majority of votes would get three-quarters of the seats in the legislature; the number of seats that the remaining parties would get would be correspondingly reduced, the share of each in the remaining parties would be in proportion to its share in the votes cast.

One could have a system in which each voter is given two votes—a positive vote and a negative one. He may cast the former for the candidate he prefers, and the latter for the one he least wants to see elected. Such a system is said to induce moderation among parties and candidates.

In a word, the system we have, even when we confine ourselves to this single point about how voters return a candidate to the legislature, is just one among a variety of systems. Each has its merits. Each has different consequences for the cohesion of governments that result; for the power that party-bosses have over their candidates; for the relative power that regional components of the party have *vis a vis* the national bosses; for the extent to which the final outcome reflects the preferences of the voters...

The present system is but a means

Such examples can be multiplied. The points to note are five:

❑ A system such as the present parliamentary system is a means. It is a means devised by persons more or less like us in the expectation that it will enable the country to achieve certain ends.

❑ The present system is just one among several possible systems.

❑ Nor is it the only possible democratic system. The American, British, Swiss, French, Scandinavian systems are very different from the one we have. They are no less democratic.

❑ We have to see not what the system is on paper, nor even what the Framers thought it will be at the time they put it in operation, but what it has actually become in practice.

❑ Adopting a new system is no disrespect towards the Framers: adopting a new system is not even a comment on the system they devised; it is a comment on what *we have made of the system they devised.*

Accordingly, of each system we must enquire:

❑ Is it yielding the strong Executive that our country needs?

❑ In particular, is it yielding the strong Centre that our country needs?

❑ Is it placing power in the hands of the right kind of people—that is, of persons who have the competence and integrity to manage affairs of State; who will automatically place the public interest above their own, above that of their relatives, community, caste?

❑ Is it inducing, is it inspiring the best and the brightest to enter and remain in public life? Or is it inducing persons to join public life as the surest and quickest way to make money?

❑ Is it keeping them and governments in place long enough for them to pursue policies?

❏ Is it enabling them to contribute their best?
❏ Is it ensuring that they are accountable for what they do?
❏ Is it flexible and open enough to keep receiving, accepting, accommodating new individuals and groups—but based always on their competence, integrity, talent, devotion to the public weal?
❏ Most important, under it, is the working of different limbs improving or getting worse? That is, are the corrective-mechanisms functioning, or have they also come to be infected by the same debilities as the limbs that are to be reformed?
❏ Finally, what sorts of activities does it reward?
   ○ To 'take rather than make'?
   ○ To violate the law rather than adhere to it?
   ○ To respect the rights of another, or to trample over them?

For answers to these will determine what will become of the system a few years from now.

If the particular system we have adopted is not getting us towards these ends, it is our duty by the country to think through alternatives.

6.

The alternative

The two basic elements we need are: an effective—that is, a strong and competent—Executive, especially at the Centre, and a continuing sense of belonging among the population at large, a feeling that the system of governance is responsive. For achieving these twin objectives, we should, on the one hand, weaken the link between the Executive and the Legislature, and, on the other, strengthen local government.

To ensure the first of these objectives, two features in the Constitution should be recast to provide:

❑ The head of the Executive, the President, is directly elected.
❑ He is free to select as his ministers persons from within or outside the Legislature.

The term of the President should be five years. A person should be able to be President for a maximum of two terms.

The President must be elected by more than 50 per cent of the electorate. As many candidates as are qualified for the Presidency and want to contest may do so. In case one of them gets the votes of more than 50 per cent of the electorate, she or he becomes President. If no one does, the election is held again as in France, within a fortnight, and only the two who have scored the highest number of votes are allowed to stand in the second round.[1] (Were it not for the

---

[1] It is indeed sad to read what happened in this regard in the Constitution Review Commission. In the Note of Dissent that the main author of the Report, Subhash Kashyap, felt compelled to annexe, he pointed out that the Commission had decided to recommend Compulsory Voting and 50% plus one votes and that the Editorial Committee had then unanimously endorsed the draft incorporating the Commission's decision. But suddenly this was diluted and omitted. In his Note of Dissent, Kashyap felt compelled to reproduce what had been agreed upon on both these points. Here is what he stated: ...

fact that many of our voters may find it difficult to indicate preferences, one way to 'economise' is to have not a second round but to make provision for it, so to say, in the first round itself. Instead of the second ballot, voters can be asked to indicate a 1st, 2nd, 3rd, etc., preference against the name of each candidate. If in the first round of counting, a candidate wins more than 50 per cent of the votes, she is declared elected. If not, the candidate polling the lowest number of first preferences is eliminated; the second preferences of the voters who voted for him are then assigned to the other candidates... tili one of them gets more than 50 per cent.)

It should not be possible to remove the President except by impeachment, and that on specified grounds. In other words, there should be no equivalent of the current 'vote of no confidence'.

The President may select anyone from outside or within the Legislature to be his minister. Any member of a Legislature who is chosen to be a minister, must resign his seat.

She or he may attend sessions of the Legislature, and participate in the debates. But she or he shall not vote on any measure on which the Legislature is voting.

'But how can we let outsiders participate in proceedings of the House? An outsider cannot even enter the lobby.' Such a reaction is yet another example of what management experts call IRI—the Instant Rejection Instinct, a reaction by which we exempt ourselves from thinking and doing anything. Ministers are today appointed from both Houses. Ministers who happen to be members of one House participate as fully in the proceedings of the other House as

---

..... In regard to Chapter 4 titled 'Electoral Process and Political Parties', I would like to reiterate the following unanimous decisions of the Drafting and Editorial Committee which were based on the decisions taken by the whole Commission earlier with one Member expressing some reservations in regard only to (a):

(a) The second approach which the Commission recommends for adoption, suggests that we should only have representatives who win on the basis of 50%+1 vote. If, in the first round, nobody gets over 50% then there should be a run-off contest the very next day or soon thereafter between the top two candidates so that one of them will win on the basis of over 50% of the votes polled. Several representations from organizations and individuals favoured this option to achieve the objective of better representation. The Chief Election Commissioner confirmed that the task of run-off elections ...

ministers who happen to be members of the latter. They answer questions, they participate in debates but they do not vote in the House of which they are not members. The most vivid example today is the Prime Minister. He is a member of the Rajya Sabha. In that sense, he is an 'outsider' to the Lok Sabha. Does he not participate fully in the proceedings of the Lok Sabha? But does he vote there?

The Judiciary

Just as the authority of Parliament *vis a vis* the Executive must be lessened, that of the Judiciary must be assiduously preserved. This will become evident as we recall what was said and argued by Mrs. Indira Gandhi and her subalterns as they pushed through the 42nd Amendment. For this reason, the methods of selecting judges, of transferring them, for verifying their conduct when the need arises, have all to be made more robust than they are—and several proposals have already been advanced for this purpose. But, as that discussion will also make evident, it is not enough to preserve provisions for judicial review. The judges have to act the freedom and independence that have been accorded to them by the

---

... can be managed. Actually, the run-off vote is like a re-poll in certain constituencies. There is no revision of electoral rolls, no fresh nominations, no fresh campaigning or the like. It is the same polling booth with the same administration and therefore there are no complications of heavy costs or fresh security arrangements. There are substantial advantages of following the policy of 50%+1 vote. On the one hand, it resolves the problem of representation. On the other, it also makes it in the self-interest of various political parties to widen their appeal to the electorate. It can help push political rhetoric in a direction that the mobilizing language might take on comparatively 'universal' tones as opposed to 'sectoral' tones of the present day. With the need to be more broad based in their appeal, issues that have to do with good governance rather than with cleavages and narrow identities might start to surface in the political vocabulary. With EVMs we can easily plan on a two-day election all over the country. The second day may be for run-offs. This means that at the end of the day, through the use of computer technology, the constituency will know whether someone has won by getting over 50% or that a run-off is necessary. If it is the latter, the announcement would mention the names of the two candidates. The final results can be announced with all others. If implemented properly, this suggestion has the potential of forcing political parties and candidates to think of strategies to obtain over 50% votes in the first election itself. This will discourage the ...

provisions. The assault on them through alterations like the 39th and 42nd Amendments was defeated. But ever so often, the judges themselves have leaned over to assist the Executive in its excesses. That is the point to which we return later in the book.

Elections and voting

So as to further minimize sectional influences, voting should be compulsory.

Both the Electronic Voting Machine and the compulsory Multi-purpose National Identity Card should have biometric identification marks.

Even these small steps will help. But the worst perversion has been the stuffing of electoral lists with the names of Bangladeshi infiltrators. These infiltrators are now estimated to number almost two crore. Successive Governors, intelligence agencies, every group and expert who has deliberated on national security—one and all of them have said that these infiltrators have changed the demographic composition of some of the most vulnerable and sensitive parts of the country. One Governor and former head of the Intelligence Bureau has publicly expressed his apprehension that, the way things are proceeding, there is a real prospect that a third Islamic Republic will

---

... non-serious candidates and fringe players from jumping in the fray and it will encourage making of pre-election agreements between parties and this should lead to moderation and stability. Also, while on the first occasion, there may be many run offs, with each successive election the number may be reduced to only a few.

The proposal evoked favourable response from the people. Also, it found overwhelming support in the Commission and the general feeling was that this one proposal had the greatest potential of service to the cause of national integration and ridding Indian politics of the scourge of casteism and communalism.

(b) Some scholars and concerned citizens suggested that voting should be made a citizenship obligation. Voting is compulsory in many countries. Many eminent Indians including the distinguished former President and elder statesman, Shri R. Venkataraman strongly favoured making voting compulsory. He suggested that the responsibility of ensuring that all the voters exercise their franchise may be entrusted to Panchayats at the village level. 'The advantage of compulsory voting is that the voter realizes that he is not conferring a favour on the candidate but exercising his duty as a citizen.' *The Commission recommends that voting be made compulsory as a fundamental citizenship obligation under the law.*

be carved out of India—consisting of areas from Bihar, Orissa, West Bengal and Assam. Already, the infiltrators determine the outcome in almost 40 per cent of the constituencies in Assam and in about a fifth of the constituencies in West Bengal. Their impact is palpable even in a constituency as distant from Bangladesh and as close to the rulers as New Delhi.

In a stinging rebuke to the political class, the Supreme Court struck down the nefarious IMDT Act, the device by which successive Congress governments made it impossible to identify and deport the Bangladeshis. The Manmohan Singh Government did the predictable thing. It incorporated the most disabling provisions of the IMDT Act into the Foreigners Act! This change has also been decisively struck down by the Court as being not just unconstitutional but also a grave threat to national security.

No electoral reform is as vital as identifying and deporting these Bangladeshi infiltrators, and removing their names from our electoral rolls.

It is an open secret that, in spite of the introduction of Electronic Voting Machines, officials manning polling booths are still able to manipulate the result by making a show of 'helping' the illiterate voter, and pressing the 'right' button before he does so. The technology certainly exists to eliminate such manipulation: the voter should be allowed to enter the polling station only upon production and verification of his National ID Card, a card that identifies him with a biometric mark, say his fingerprint; and the machine should respond only upon that biometric mark, say his fingerprint, being again identified as he presses the button.

Nor will there be the slightest problem in installing cameras to record everything that happens on polling day inside the polling booth. The film record should be treated as evidence, and, accordingly, be secured along with the EVMs, the moment voting closes, and be accessible to any candidate who contests the result.

Third, all elections must be held simultaneously. At present, some election or the other is always round the corner. This becomes the standard and unanswerable argument for deferring decisions that need to be taken. A corollary of this is that, should a seat fall vacant during the term of the House, it shall remain vacant. No by-election shall be held. Either the one who was the runner up in the preceding election should be given the seat, or, if the concern is that the balance of power in the chamber must be preserved, the party to which the member belonged should be allowed to nominate the successor member.

Legislatures

For elections to legislatures, three modifications are necessary:

❑ The size of the constituency has to be increased substantially so as to lessen the sway of one section or caste;
❑ The link between the electorate and the winner has to be weakened; and
❑ Qualifications and disqualifications for candidates have to be tightened.

Apart from scheduling elections simultaneously, the first step which is necessary was suggested by Mr. L.P. Singh in *Electoral Reform*.[1] The rationale for a modified list-system is as follows. The present system of single-member constituencies leads to the sorts of problems we have encountered earlier: for instance, the expectation, on the one hand, of the voter that the MP must attend to his personal problems; and, on the other, the compulsion of the MP to put catering to voters and their controllers before all else. By contrast, if all of India were one constituency; parties declared lists of candidates; voters voted for parties and not for individual candidates; each party got to send members to Parliament in proportion to its share in votes cast; in such a system, the link between the voter and the MP would be substantially reduced, and one set of problems would be minimized. But India is a continent. A person may have done exceptional service in Kerala and yet be unknown in the Northeast.

A *via media* is what will meet our objectives. Adjacent constituencies, say ten, should be clubbed. Each party submits to the Election Commission a list of triple the number of constituencies that have been clubbed; in our example, each party is to submit a list of

---

[1] L.P. Singh, *Electoral Reform*, Uppal Publishing House, Delhi, 1986.

thirty candidates. Electors are to vote for a party, or cast a negative vote, 'None of the above.' Each party gets to send members to the legislature from those ten constituencies in proportion to the votes it has received, with one caveat. The particular candidate who is to be sent shall be selected by lot conducted by the Election Commission. Assume party X secures 30 per cent of the votes. Of the ten members to be sent from this clubbed constituency, it shall send three. For the ten seats, it has submitted a list of thirty candidates to the Election Commission. The Election Commission shall conduct a lottery and select three from this list of thirty. They shall be MPs.

If the 'None of the above' entry wins, the election in that clubbed constituency shall be held again, and no one who had been included in the lists submitted by the parties shall be allowed to stand again.

Second, as Mr. B.K. Nehru suggested in his *Rajaji Memorial Lecture*, legislators shall have absolutely no privileges or perquisites.[1] They shall get a salary, and nothing else. They shall not be given any post whatsoever by the Executive, no membership of any board, or chairmanship of any corporation, etc. This way, only those who are actually interested in legislation and in policies will seek to enter legislatures. The current fraud of exempting office after office by defining it as not being an 'Office of Profit' will be ended. It is, of course, more than a fraud, it is an instrument for subverting the law that was passed. Parliament passed a law specifying that Councils of Ministers shall be below a certain proportion of the strength of the Assembly. Some states just made the persons who could not be accommodated as ministers, chairmen of government corporations with Cabinet rank!

Third, both positive qualifications and negative disqualifications must be made stricter.

As for qualifications, candidates for the lower House must be at least graduates. As for the Upper House, we need today not a Chamber of States but a Chamber of Talent. Therefore, in addition to being at least a graduate, a candidate must have distinguished himself in a profession including business and agriculture.

---

[1] B.K. Nehru, 'A proposal for Constitutional Reform,' in *Thoughts on Our Present Discontents*, Allied, Delhi, 1986, pp.73–85.

Disqualifications as they have been prescribed have become a farce: a list that lets criminals get into legislatures is actually worse than a farce—it is an accessory to a crime against the country. One principal source of problems is subsection 3 of section 8 of the Representation of the People Act, 1951. The first sub-section lists a number of crimes and provides that if a person is convicted for any of them, he shall be disqualified for six years from the date of his conviction, and, if he is imprisoned, for a further period of six years after his release. (There was a telltale incongruity between these subsections to which the Constitution Review Commission drew attention. Under subsection 1, the person was to remain disqualified for six years. The person convicted of rape would be punished with imprisonment for ten years. So, in the last four years of his imprisonment, while being debarred from voting, he could stand for election!) The deterrent as well as actual effect have been totally undermined by the self-serving text of sub-section 4. This subsection provides that, 'Notwithstanding anything [in the earlier sub-sections] a disqualification shall not, in the case of a person who on the date of conviction is a member of Parliament or the legislature of a state, take effect *until three months have elapsed from that date or, if within that period an appeal or application for revision is brought in respect of the conviction or the sentence,* until that appeal or application is disposed of by the court.'

Which fool will fail to file an appeal in three months? And, what will his incentive be, once he has filed an appeal? To go on getting the hearings adjourned, and elongated, and derailed till his term comes to its natural end!

Hence, the first change that is required is that, from the moment charges are framed by a court against a person—whether he is a sitting member or not—he should cease to be a member and be disqualified from contesting an election till he has been cleared of the charges. For the one who has been falsely implicated, the incentive would then be the opposite: he will strive to ensure as expeditious a disposal of his case as possible.

'But our opponents routinely implicate us in false cases,' politicians say. First, the disqualification commences once charges have been framed *by a court of law,* not from the moment the police or some investigating agency has filed them. Second, this apprehension can be allayed by requiring that the charges be framed at the level of a sitting judge of the High Court. Third, that such persons are inducted to man the courts as will serve the interest of the rulers of the moment, especially courts before which these cases are to come up, will only mean that, knowing that the next person could use the courts against them also, politicians will have an inducement to put more robust persons into courts.

The second change that is required is to make more comprehensive the list of offences, charges for committing which entail disqualification. In addition to the current definition—offences punishable with imprisonment for a maximum period of five years or more, and heinous crimes like murder, rape, smuggling, etc.—a former Chief Justice of the Calcutta High Court, D.S. Tewatia, writes, a person should be disqualified 'whose name had figured in *Basta* 'B' of the police or who had been chargesheeted by the court or convicted of an offence involving moral turpitude or who had been declared an absconder, a bankrupt or who has been facing eviction proceeding from government or public property or one who owes money to the government, local body, public undertaking and banks until by the prescribed date he leaves the encroached property and pays up the dues subject to his right as determined by the courts.'

Equally important for ensuring adherence to such provisions is a suggestion that was advanced by the Constitution Review Commission—that is, a political party that nominates a person with criminal antecedents to be its candidate, must be derecognized forthwith.

Such changes should be accompanied by the requirement that cases involving persons in public life—ministers, legislators, judges, civil servants—shall be tried on a day-to-day basis, by instituting special courts if necessary. And only one appeal should be permissible: an appeal to the Supreme Court.

Proceedings of legislatures

A host of changes are necessary, and these days you don't have to sit through a session of Parliament or a state legislature to realize how necessary they are. Just glancing at the proceedings relayed on television will provide all the evidence you need. A few illustrations will indicate the sorts of changes we need.

The first, of course, is the strict enforcement of rules, a point which transcends legislatures and one to which we will have occasion to return. Violation of the rules must, irrespective of the provocation that has led the member to violate the rule, invite, immediately and automatically, the maximum penalty that has been provided. Laxity in enforcing one rule cannot but clear the way for relaxing the adjacent rule. Accepting one sort of circumstance as an attenuating one cannot but become the justification for according the same latitude to the next provocation. Members naturally share the primary responsibility for what has become of our legislatures, but as much blame rests with presiding officers. Sometimes, out of the apprehension that the attempt to enforce rules might make the members even more intransigent; all too often, to remain in the good books of all sections of the House, presiding officers play along. Ever so often, the impatience that viewers see on TV is well-rehearsed. Prior discussion—and it is ever so convivial—has already settled the 'issue' on which members of this group or that will troop into the well of the House—a 'well' that really should be rechristened for what it is, 'the cremation ground of democracy'. That prior discussion has already settled the duration for which the shouting has to go on before the House is adjourned, as indeed it has already settled whether the House will then be adjourned for half an hour, till lunch, or for the whole day...

Second, if disorder has reached a pitch that the session just cannot be conducted, the House must not be adjourned for the day. If it must be adjourned, the adjournment must be for fifteen minutes at a time and the sequence of convening and adjourning and commencing again, must go on for the entire day. What kind of a school is it in which students can give themselves a holiday by contriving a ruckus for a few minutes?

Third, among the rules that must be strictly enforced is the rule about the necessity for a quorum. The rule requires only that one-tenth of the members be present. So few are present on ever so many occasions that twin conventions have in effect developed. Once the House has commenced its business, the presiding officer shall not ascertain whether enough members are present to constitute a quorum unless his attention is drawn to this by a member, and no member shall draw his attention to the matter. In fact, the rule must be enforced strictly and automatically. The moment the number falls below one-tenth, proceedings must automatically and invariably be stopped—till the deficiency is made up.

Fourth, 'innovations' like the 'Zero Hour' in which a member is allowed to raise any issue of urgent public importance must be done away with. In the years that I have been attending Parliament, I have not seen a single issue which could not have waited till the evening, that is, till the scheduled business of the day had been completed. The House has often been adjourned on the insistence that, far from waiting till the evening, the issue cannot wait for even a few minutes. And when the insistence has prevailed, has the issue come any nearer a resolution as a result of that discussion? The insistence has become not a device to solve a problem. It has become an instrument for asserting one's dominance. Such innovations must be scotched. Correspondingly, government must not be allowed to block discussion of an issue. Members who feel that the issue just must be discussed that day, must be allowed to have it discussed at the close of business for the day and it must be mandatory for every member to sit through that extra time in the late evening.

Fifth, the good that might have been secured from televising the proceedings has been set at naught by allowing only the official channel to televise them. What viewers see, therefore, is not what is happening in the House, but in effect a sanitized version of it. Even the simple device of keeping the camera focused on just the member who is speaking blacks out from the viewer how empty the chamber is. Proceedings should be opened to private channels as much as they are to the official channel. One thing should be mandatory: at all times that the House is in session, a blurb on the screen must indicate how many of the total number of members are present in the House!

Sixth, freedom of speech must be restored to members in one respect, and be curtailed in another. Today, if a member disobeys a whip of the Party to which he belongs, he falls afoul of Schedule X of the Constitution. If, for instance, he speaks or votes against another enlargement of reservations when his party has decided that it just can't oppose the proposal for fear of losing votes, he is taken to be guilty of defection, and is, therefore, liable to be expelled from the legislature. This has well-nigh killed free speech in our legislatures.

The provision in the Xth Schedule should be amended accordingly. Members ought to be obliged to obey whips only when the question is whether the government should continue in office or not, and party managers must not be permitted to issue whips on any other occasion.

That is one respect in which freedom of speech should be enlarged. But in another respect it should be cut back. By what is known as the Feroze Gandhi amendment, members are not liable to be proceeded against in any court of law for anything they say in the legislature. Over the years, persons with a very restricted sense of responsibility and a very expansive sense of their rights have become legislators. The protection is routinely abused with all sorts of allegations being hurled against persons who are not members of the House, with all sorts of untruths being asserted about events and issues. Indeed, *precisely because they are members of such an august body*, members should be held to even higher standards than are prescribed in, for instance, the ordinary law of defamation.

Accountability

The two changes we noted earlier—that the trial shall be held every day, and that only one appeal shall be permissible—will by themselves go far in ensuring accountability. But a few additional changes are necessary.

We should select a few laws the violation of which has particularly vicious consequences for the country—those relating to elections, national security, corruption, usurpation of public assets, misuse of one's office. Violation of any of these laws by a person in public life must be visited by punishment that is exemplary, and that increases in severity the higher the office a person holds. When a *patwari* accepts a bribe, the ill-effects are visited on the village, and perhaps on a few neighbouring villages; when a minister takes a bribe, the ill-effects are visited far and wide over the country through the license that it provides to others to do as he has done. Hence, the punishment for accepting the bribe must be several multiples higher in the case of the minister than it is in that of the *patwari*.

Second, the punishment must have two ingredients. The person convicted must undergo imprisonment—for fining such persons is of no consequence; and he must be permanently disbarred from public life.

Third, the standard of proof that is required in the case of these persons in regard to these laws must be less stringent than is required by the Indian Evidence Act. What a travesty of justice, what a crime against the country it is that a minister who is found with several crores of rupees of cash stacked in his bedroom escapes conviction altogether.

Fourth, as Mr. N. Vittal, the former Chief Vigilance Commissioner, pointed out, the *Benami* Transactions (Prohibition) Act must be made operational. The fate of this Act bears testimony to the subterranean power of those who would escape the law. The Act was passed in 1988. Section 5 of the Act mandates that all properties held *benami* must be acquired. And that this shall be done without any compensation. These properties, the Act specifies, are to be seized 'in such manner and following such procedures as may be prescribed.' Section 8 puts the duty of framing these rules and procedures on the Central government. Successive Central governments have not got around to framing the rules for *nineteen years!*

While strongly supporting the suggestion that this Act be made operational, the Constitution Review Commission made additional recommendations which need to be acted upon.

The Commission endorsed what the Supreme Court had urged in that notorious instance of misuse of authority and corruption, *Delhi Development Authority v. Skipper Construction Co. (P) Ltd*, namely that '...a law providing for forfeiture of properties acquired by holders of public offices (including the offices/posts in the public sector corporations) by indulging in corrupt and illegal acts and deals, is a crying necessity in the present stage of our society.' The Commission urged that a law for forfeiting such property be passed on the lines suggested by the Supreme Court. Lest such a recommendation lead to another infructuous authority being created, the Commission rightly pointed out that there is already a Tribunal to determine the property that is to be seized under other statutes, in particular under the Smugglers and Foreign Exchange Manipulators (Forfeiture of Property) Act, (SAFEMA) 1976. That very Tribunal can be asked to determine cases of confiscation arising out of the

Benami Transactions (Prohibition) Act, 1988 and the Prevention of Corruption Act, 1988 and other legislations which empower confiscation of illegally acquired assets.

The relevance of a related recommendation of the Commission is brought home to us every other day, by the fact that the numerous cases against politicians and civil servants for possession of disproportionate assets remain stuck. While recommending that the Prevention of Corruption Act, 1988 be amended to provide for confiscation of the property of a public servant who is found to be in possession of property disproportionate to his known sources of income, the Commission made two further proposals in this regard. First, that in this instance, the law should shift the burden of proof to the public servant who is accused. 'The presumption should be that the disproportionate assets found in possession of the convicted public servant were acquired by him by corrupt or illegal means,' the Commission observed. Second, it urged that in such cases 'A proof of preponderance of probability shall be sufficient for confiscation of the property. ...The law should lay down that the standard of proof in determining whether a person has been benefited from an offence and for determining the amount in which a confiscation order is to be made, is that which is applicable to civil cases, i.e. a mere preponderance of probability only. A useful analogy may be seen in Section 2(8) of the Drug Trafficking Act 1994 in United Kingdom.'

Our unrelieved and heartbreaking experience in regard to corruption cases also suggests two further requirements. We desperately need a central investigating agency that can investigate cases anywhere and everywhere in the country. What a travesty it is that even in a case such as that of Telgi involving a crime that is said to have covered transactions of anywhere up to Rs. 50,000 crore, the Government of Karnataka, some of whose leading lights were the subjects of suspicion, could refuse CBI permission to investigate the matter, and thereby hold up the investigation. Equally, and for the same reason, we need an independent office of public prosecutors modelled after the one in Japan.

But, of course, institutions are only as independent as the persons manning them. Hence, even if such agencies are set up, everything will turn on how the persons to man them are selected; on who are selected; on the extent to which governments and legislators allow them to function independently; and on the extent to which they themselves exercise the independence that has been given to them by the relevant legislation.

Two judgements that need to be reversed

One feature that may help both sides—the agencies that are set up as well as the innocent whom some governments may seek to persecute by using these agencies—is to provide for heavy torts in case of misuse of the agencies. The law should provide that at least a part of the tort, and a part large enough to actually hurt the one who misuses the agencies, must be paid personally by the person who has misused the agencies. I mention this in particular because of the curious reversal by the Supreme Court of its own judgement in *Common Cause v. Union of India*.[1] The original judgement had held that public servants are *personally* responsible for wrongful acts. Accordingly, it had fined two erstwhile ministers Rs.50 lakhs and Rs.60 lakhs respectively.[2] Later the Court reversed its decision and held that the petitioner, Common Cause, had not itself suffered any injury because of the illegal acts of the ministers. Therefore, while it could ask for cancellation of allotments that the ministers had made of petrol pumps and accommodation, it could not ask that ministers be fined! This from a Court that had been making the most far-reaching orders in response to public interest petitions, many filed by this very organization!! This from the Court which had been priding itself on taking matters up *suo moto* and passing the most far-reaching orders! Furthermore, in this new judgement the Court held that, as government would have to pay on behalf of ministers, there was no point in asking the government to pay to the government! The Court

---

[1](1999) 6 SCC 667.

[2]*Common Cause v. Union of India*, (1996) 6 SCC 530. *The Common Cause* judgements, as well as the judgement on the JMM bribery case which is taken up later, are the subject of detailed comments in two important papers prepared by Justice B.P. Jeevan Reddy for the Commission to Review the Working of the Constitution. *C.f., Report of the National Commission to Review the Working of the Constitution*, New Delhi, 2002, Volume II, Consultation Papers on 'Immunity of Legislators,' and 'Probity in Governance.' In the same volume, see also the Consultation Paper, 'Liability of the State in Tort,' by P.M. Bakshi.

needs to get back to its original judgement, and the law needs to specify that, once it is established that a person in public life has done an illegal act and obtained gratification for it, he shall have to personally pay for it.

There is another judgement that is as injurious to accountability, and therefore deserves to be roundly reversed. This is the mysterious judgement of the Supreme Court in the JMM bribery case,[1] and the construction it put on Article 105(2) in this judgement. The Article is meant to safeguard the independence of legislators. It provides, *inter alia*, 'No member of Parliament shall be liable to any proceedings in any court in respect of anything said or any vote given by him in Parliament...' The judgement also illustrates the sorts of legalisms which enable wrongdoers to flourish in India.

Mr. Narasimha Rao's Government was faced with a vote of no-confidence. Amounts were paid to certain members of Parliament to vote in his favour. Each of the beneficiaries, save one, voted accordingly. One of them who had also accepted the amount did not vote at all.

A five-Judge Bench heard the case. The case was hotly contested. All the five held that members of Parliament are public servants.

On the question of taking a bribe to vote or speak in a particular way, two Judges held that Article 105(2) does not confer immunity for the crime of taking or giving a bribe. Two Judges held that the Article gives an inviolable immunity to the member of Parliament so that, if an MP takes a bribe to vote or speak in a particular way, and then does so, he cannot be prosecuted: because, they reasoned, in such an event, there is a clear nexus between the bribe and what he has done on the floor of the House. Correspondingly, if he takes the bribe, and does not vote or speak in accordance with the deal into which he had entered, he has no immunity because then the bribe has no nexus with what was done on the floor of the House! In such an event, he can be prosecuted. The fifth Judge agreed with the latter two on this construction.

There was another technicality, and this too worked to the advantage of the ones who had accepted bribes. Who is to sanction

---

[1] *P.V. Narasimha Rao v. State (CBI/SPE)*, (1998) 4 SCC 626.

prosecution? the defence demanded. No authority has been specified as yet. Two Judges saw little difficulty in this: the Chairman of the Rajya Sabha in the case of members of the upper House, or the Speaker in the case of members of the Lok Sabha could sanction the prosecution, they held. On the other hand, two Judges deduced that, as no authority had been specified, no prosecution could be launched. One Judge expressed no opinion.

There was a third curiosity. There is the well-known decision of the U.S. Supreme Court in *Brewster's* case. In that case, of nine Judges, six had held that taking a bribe for doing something in the legislature is an offence. Three had declared that they could not hold it to be an offence because, to do so, they would have to go into the motive why a legislator did what he did, and the U.S. Constitution prohibits them from doing so. In the JMM bribery case, two Judges relied on the majority in *Brewster's* decision: 'The shield does not extend beyond what is necessary to preserve integrity of the legislative process.' They also noted that the American Judges had correctly held that the U.S. Congress is ill-equipped to investigate, try and punish. And they showed one way out. To simultaneously safeguard the freedom of legislators as well as the integrity of the parliamentary processes, they stressed, the expression in Article 105(2), 'anything said or any vote given by him in Parliament,' should be construed as 'liability arising from anything said or vote given by him in Parliament.' The member would thus be protected from an action for defamation in regard to a speech, for instance; but when he takes a bribe, the liability that would befall him would arise independently of and would not depend on his making the speech or giving the vote.[1]

On the other hand, two Judges invoked the *minority* opinion in *Brewster*, that to go into the charge that he had accepted a bribe for voting or speaking in a particular way, the Court would have to inquire into the motive of a legislator, and this it is not entitled to do. The conduct in question is reprehensible, they held, the offenders must be punished, but only by the House itself.

The Constitution Review Commission—in particular, Justice B.P. Jeevan Reddy in his Consultation Paper—analysed the judgement,

---

[1]Ibid, at 674, para 47.

and concluded, 'A charter of freedom cannot be converted into a charter of corruption.' The Commission recommended that, therefore, the Article must be amended to clarify that the immunity contemplated shall not cover illegal acts, i.e., giving and taking bribes for voting or speaking in a particular manner in the House. It went on to suggest that a special committee of the House should be constituted to give or deny sanction for prosecution, and it went into the modalities of the composition and term of such a committee. Given the condition of our legislatures, this seems to me to be needless genuflection to the claim that 'the House is master of its proceedings'. A committee of the House will be a committee of overly considerate peers. And, given the progressive homogenization of the political class, it will not be as stern in its standards as the situation requires. Members of the committee are also liable to be influenced by their political affiliation and to act on the direction of political bosses, as they did in the impeachment proceedings of Justice V. Ramaswamy. The better way would be to clarify the Article itself, and add provisions to the Prevention of Corruption Act so that taking and giving bribes to legislators becomes a crime under it, as much as giving bribes to civil servants or ministers or judges is, and leave the final verdict about guilt to the Judiciary.

The list of such imperatives can be lengthened. The basic points are two:

❑ Members of the Executive must be accountable. There can be no disagreement about that at all. But the presumption that the current system makes them accountable, by making the Executive accountable to Parliament and state legislatures, is a complete myth. Hence, accountability should be ensured by other devices.

❑ No law, no institution, no Lok Ayukta, and for the same reason no Lok Pal will ensure accountability till independent persons are appointed to such institutions, and till those who are appointed decide to exercise the independence that has been conferred on them by the law.

Few events nail the truth of these imperatives as our recent history. And it is to this that we now turn.

The sovereignty-mongers

7

The 'alert and quick-acting' sovereign

Mrs. Indira Gandhi had been elected to the Lok Sabha by a large margin in 1971. Raj Narain, who had lost, filed a petition alleging that she had indulged in corrupt practices to secure her victory. The case had been going on since 1971. On 12 June 1975, Justice Jag Mohan Lal Sinha of the Allahabad High Court held Mrs. Gandhi to have been guilty of corrupt electoral practices on two counts—that she had used the services of officials of the state government and that the person who had been her election agent, her trusted aide Yashpal Kapur, had at the time been a serving government officer.

An appeal was filed in the Supreme Court. Justice V.R. Krishna Iyer was the Vacation Judge. On 24 June 1975, he gave a conditional stay. Mrs. Gandhi could continue as Prime Minister and member of Parliament. She could participate in the proceedings of the House but she would not be allowed to vote. The Judge was solicitous to a fault. The High Court judgement may be overturned eventually, he noted, but as long as that does not happen, it stands. 'After all, the High Court's finding, until upset, holds good, however weak it may ultimately prove.' The law may be draconian, the grounds on which she has been held guilty 'may be venial', but as long as the law stands as it does, and till the High Court judgement is overturned, he is bound by them, and the debris of old orders, he said: 'Sitting in time-honoured forensic surroundings I am constrained to judge the issues before me by the canons sanctified by the usage of this Court.' He was at pains to explain that his order did not amount to much: the House is not in session, hence, the stipulation that she cannot vote is of little consequence: 'the veto on the right to vote is currently academic.' His order, he emphasized, 'substantially preserves the position of the petitioner as Member of Parliament and does not adversely affect her legal status as Prime Minister.' He was more than mindful that the case had larger dimensions: 'The proceedings in the Halls of Justice must be informed, to some extent, by the great verity that the sweep of human history is guided by sociological forces beyond the ken of the noisy hour or the quirk of legal nicety. Life is larger than Law.' And judges must address themselves to this larger universe: 'After all, judicial power is dynamic, forward-looking and socially lucent and aware.' He made light of the precedents that had been cited as 'a few orders... from the debris of old records...' And declared, 'the power of the Court must rise to the occasion, if justice, in its larger connotation, is the goal—and it is.' And he gave the vital, practical advice: 'Draconian laws do not cease to be law in court *but must alert a wakeful and quick-acting Legislature.*'[1]

That was on 24 June, 1975.

The date for hearing Mrs. Gandhi's appeal was set as 11 August, 1975.

The 'alert' Government summoned Parliament to an emergent session. The session is meant for transacting urgent Government business, the ministers declared. The much-flaunted Rules of Procedure were all suspended. The question hour, about not waiving which members are most insistent, was suspended...

On 4 August 1975, members of the Lok Sabha suddenly received 'Election Laws (Amendment) Bill'. The memorandum accompanying it stated, 'In view of the short duration of the current session of Parliament and the need to get the Bill passed in the current session itself, it is not possible to comply with the requirement in the direction 19B of the Directions of the Speaker...' about giving notice, etc.

But no reason has been given as to why the mandatory requirement for giving notice for such legislation has been set aside, Mohan Dharia pointed out. 'Is it because the Supreme Court is going to consider the appeal of the Prime Minister on the 11th August that this Bill is being introduced?... Why this indecent haste?' The Minister for Parliamentary Affairs recalled that he had already stated earlier that the session was meant for disposing Government business, and that the session was going to be a short one 'because Ministers were busy with the implementation of the economic programme.'

---

[1] *Indira Nehru Gandhi v. Raj Narain*, (1975) 2 SCC 159.

But government business was government business. Presiding over the sovereign House, the Speaker gave leave to introduce the Bill...

'Sir, the Bill is a simple one,' began the Minister of Law and Justice, H.R. Gokhale, as he was to do again and again in the coming days. All it does is to amend the existing law to specify that the date from which a candidate shall be taken to be holding himself forth for the election shall be the date from which the Election Commission notified the election and not any earlier date. Words tailor-cut to have Mrs. Gandhi not to have been a candidate on the date at which Justice Sinha had taken her to have been one.

Second, the Bill provides that, when any government servant 'in the discharge of or purported discharge of his official duty, makes any arrangements or provides any facilities or does any other act or thing, for, to, or in any relation to, any candidate or his agent or any other person acting with the consent of the candidate or his election agent (whether by reason of the office held by the candidate or for any other reason) such arrangements, facilities or act or thing shall not be deemed to be assistance for the furtherance of the prospects of that candidate's election.' Words tailor-cut to nullify one ground in Justice Sinha's judgement.

Third, the date on which a government servant's appointment or resignation is notified in the Government Gazette shall be taken to be 'conclusive proof' of the date from which he was appointed or he resigned. That took care of the other ground...

But the Allahabad High Court had already held Mrs. Gandhi guilty. No problem, Parliament is sovereign. It was asked to legislate that these 'clarifications' shall apply with retrospective effect in regard to any election that has been held before the commencement of the Act,

(i) in respect of which any election petition may be presented after the commencement of this Act; or
(ii) in respect of which any election petition is pending in any High Court immediately before such commencement; or
(iii) in respect of which any election petition has been decided by any High Court before such commencement but no appeal has been preferred to the Supreme Court...

(iv) in respect of which appeal from any order of any High Court made in any election petition under section 98 or section 99 of the principal Act is pending before the Supreme Court immediately before such commencement.

Clear enough? And within three days, by another device, these changes—'clarifications', as the Law Minister insisted they were—were put beyond the reach of courts all together. They were shoveled into that Swiss vault, the IXth Schedule.

'Sir, the provisions of the Bill are simple,' Gokhale reiterated, 'self-explanatory and long overdue...' And there is to be another change. Under the existing law, the moment a member is held guilty of corrupt practices, disqualification follows automatically—recall, Justice Krishna Iyer's expressions of helplessness. Hence, from now on, even after a person has been pronounced guilty, the matter will go to the President. He shall decide whether the infraction is grave enough to merit disqualification. In deciding one way or another, he shall take the advice of the Election Commission... Of course, the Minister did not have to say that, as the amendment would apply retrospectively, even to cases that had been decided but in which appeals were pending, it would apply to Mrs. Gandhi's case! The fact was that as some further tightening must have become necessary since the Bill was knocked together, amendments had been introduced to the text that had been circulated.

'Sir, it is most unfortunate,' Mohan Dharia began as the Law Minister sat down, 'that when we speak of the rule of law in the country, the whole rule of law should be circumscribed to suit some individuals...' 'Without going into the merits or demerits of the Allahabad High Court judgement,' he continued, 'there is no doubt in my mind that the Bill in the amended form has been brought forward in the House by the Law Minister to circumvent those issues which have been held by the High Court in favour of the petitioner and against the Prime Minister. Similarly, all possible care is being taken to take away the powers of the Supreme Court in deciding this matter on merits.' While Government is saying that there is a 20-point programme, he declared, actually there is a 20+1 point programme, the additional point being to save the Prime Minister from the judgement of the Allahabad High Court.

That was too much. The Emergency was on. Thousands had already been hurled into prisons. Loyalty had to be shown. The Speaker interrupted him, and the point we have to notice is the ground he gave. 'Don't attribute motives to Parliament,' declaimed the very man who was giving all assistance to reduce it to slavishness, '*Parliament is a sovereign body.*'

I am as much of a defender of Parliament's sovereignty, Dharia protested, as the next man. 'It is the Executive which has launched the severest attack on Parliament and parliamentary institutions in the country.'

He was interrupted again and again. He did manage to tell the ever-so-sovereign House, 'I would like to beg of you that let this House not be converted into a place to suit the dictatorial pattern as has been introduced in the country.'

The interruptions and shouting increased. 'I am not here to be cowed down,' Dharia said, 'You can raise your voice.' More shouting. 'You cannot cow me down that way. So, my submission to the House is that this Bill is nothing but surrender of parliamentary democracy to the coming dictatorship and therefore I oppose this Bill vehemently.'

The Speaker called on the Communist leader, Indrajit Gupta to proceed. 'Mr. Speaker, Sir, whether any particular individual at a particular moment will derive any advantage or benefit from these amendments or not, does not affect, in any way, the actual merit of the amendments,' he began, focusing, dialectically, no doubt, on the principal contradiction, no doubt. And soon he was having a swipe, insinuating that Dharia was a defector from his party. The cry was soon taken up. 'He is a born defector,' shouted another progressive about Dharia.

Indrajit Gupta was Jesuitical: the amendments are not going to help only the Prime Minister. So, there is nothing wrong with them. They will be available to everyone else also.

And then the opposite argument: 'Everybody in the country knows why it is being brought now. What is wrong with that?' He immediately shifted the debate to a higher plane, as they say, to principle and ideology!

The High Court judgement has thrown up certain issues. They are being addressed in the Bill. And that is but right. There are those who say that the Executive, Legislature and Judiciary are three pillars of equal status. We do not accept this, Gupta said. '*The Parliament represents the sovereign will of the people. We have seen, time without number, in the past that matters which have been decided by this Parliament, which have been legislated by this Parliament, are completely overthrown by the will of some judge sitting in a court somewhere.* And because that is the Judiciary—I have got all respect for the Judiciary—it should not be put on a pedestal higher than the Parliament *which represents the sovereign will of the people.*'

The judgements are so often contradictory. In any case, the matters dealt with by these amendments 'are not such fundamental issues.' And the basic reason: 'This [the Bill] will apply to everybody hereafter. Whether it applies to Shrimati Indira Gandhi or not today, *I am not concerned with it*'—a well-practised evasion of the dialecticians. 'It will apply to everybody hereafter.'

Why give it retrospective effect, then?, Mohan Dharia asked.

'It applies to all cases which are pending,' Gupta said. 'There is not only Shrimati Indira Gandhi's case. There may be other cases also pending.'

Dharia: 'How many cases are there?'

Indrajit Gupta: 'I do not know.'

Dharia: 'Let them tell us how many cases are there.'

From '*Them*', only silence!

Indrajit Gupta proceeded to extol the provisions one by one. And soon turned to the ideological point, to the bourgeois notion, so to say. 'About taking away the Supreme Court's powers,' he said, 'Well, I am all for taking away the Supreme Court's powers in many things, and I think more things will come. I am not prepared to put the Supreme Court on a pedestal. *The Parliament is supreme. Otherwise say good bye to democracy...*'

But one has to maintain a show of independence. So, he was sorry, he said, that the several recommendations that had been given by the Joint Committee on electoral laws had not all been brought together...

Only one other speaker, another progressive, spoke.

That was enough of a national debate. Gokhale had been fortified by Indrajit Gupta. What Dharia had said was 'completely irrelevant and beside the point,' he began...

He swiftly tagged the amendments to sovereignty! To enact them so as to overturn the verdict of a Court will be to establish sovereignty of Parliament—that was his reasoning! '*This Parliament had assured its supremacy when its supremacy and sovereignty was questioned by the judicial decision,*' he said. '*It is not necessary to remind the House of the number of occasions on which this Parliament has acted to establish the sovereignty and supremacy which it always had and which I assert it will continue to have in future.*'

And then the fateful words which were to presage what the Government was already planning: '*I agree that we might have to have an overall look, may be, even at the Constitution itself, to see that no future situations arise where the final word of Parliament itself is challenged.*' And we shall soon see where this 'reasoning' about establishing the sovereignty of people and, therefore, of Parliament led.

The Bill was passed. No votes needed to be recorded—so overwhelmingly did the sovereign parliamentarians endorse their sovereign right to overturn a judicial verdict.

That was on 5 August 1975. But this was the Emergency. Trains were running fast, and on time. Parliament could not be slower. So, the very next day, 6 August, the Bill was taken up by the Rajya Sabha.

There was no Dharia here. 'The Bill is a simple one,' Gokhale intoned again. '...The provisions of the Bill are self-explanatory and are long overdue,' he repeated. Other than Gokhale, only two members spoke. Both wholeheartedly acclaimed the provisions. Of the 23 columns their speeches occupy in the official record, 21 are taken up by the resident dialectician, the Communist leader, Bhupesh Gupta. He proved to be even more liberated from bourgeois inhibitions than his Lok Sabha counterpart, Indrajit Gupta.

The matter has come in a political context, Bhupesh Gupta said. Otherwise the amendments 'would not have attracted so much attention or controversy.' 'I am quite conscious about the background against which this Bill has come,' he said. 'But I am not apologetic'— this was the refrain that was to embolden Gokhale even more. 'In the other House, an honourable member, Shri Mohan Dharia, said that it was only an attempt to cover a particular case and the case of the Prime Minister. Sir, I am not one of those who are apologetic about this.' 'Well, there comes a time in the life of a nation or, for that matter, in the life of Parliament and the polity of a country when experience throws up a new vision and when decisions have to be taken in the light of the challenges we face now.'

'Sir, many of the things which should have been done earlier are done at a crucial moment because we are forced to do so by the circumstances of the development of life itself,' he said, and asked, 'Therefore, what is wrong with that?'

'Is it a joke that the Prime Minister of a country was sought to be removed from office and debarred from contesting an election because of what a single judge said in one of the High Courts of the country and simply because he has held her guilty of corrupt practices under an Act which was passed 22 years ago? Are we to accept that position?'

The real question is who is sovereign? 'Are we to accept this position that a judge will decide as to when the Prime Minister should go or whether the Prime Minister should remain or not simply because her election case has been adjudicated upon by him and he has found some technical, legal and narrow violations of law? Are we ready to give such powers in the hands of a judge? It is not a question of Prime Minister alone. *It goes to the root of sovereignty of Parliament, legislative institutions...*'

'Sir, what is wrong there if somebody says that our minds are exercised when an issue has come centering round the case of the Prime Minister?,' he repeated. The institution of Prime Minister is 'something which is important and "pivotal"...'

Have you not seen how in the *Golak Nath* case, the Supreme Court judges have reversed their judgements 'creating a crisis in the law and the Constitution, and above all in the socio-economic life of the country, giving *carte blanche* to forces of reaction and making Subba Rao and others come out as the champions of liberty and democracy with Masanis and others on their side?' Notice how he refers to one of the most distinguished of the judges who have sat in the Supreme Court. Notice that Gupta and his comrades were among the major proponents of a 'committed judiciary'. Notice, the guilt-by-association...

'Judges are not angels,' he declared. 'They are subject to pulls and pressures of the society. They live in the society. They are not completely free from the influences of the society.' And then the unstated canard from which you may infer anything: 'I am not using other bad expressions about their families and surroundings.' Having repeated himself twice or thrice in this refrain, he catapulted from the general to the particular: 'Therefore, Sir, I cannot take the facile view that the Allahabad judgement has been one which is above board, beyond reproach, and does not warrant any suspicion and questioning, apart from the legal view that will be taken in the Supreme Court.' In fact, he had a hunch, he said, that the Supreme Court will strike down the judgement.

Notice the reasoning: judges are not angels; therefore, judges are subject to pulls and pressures; therefore, the Allahabad judgement cannot be said to be above suspicion; therefore, it is suspect.

Notice too, the comrade's 'hunch'—that the Supreme Court will throw out the judgement, and notice what he says next.

Having cast judges in doubt, and through that the particular judgement in doubt, he was off to the favourite device of comrades, the conspiracy theory.

The Opposition has 'raised a hue and cry as if the Allahabad judgement is the biblical utterance which must be implemented here and now or heavens would come down crashing on us.' 'But I can tell you that the Allahabad judgement has political overtone...' 'Sir, I tell you, even before the judgement was given by the Allahabad High Court, those quarters which are shouting against our country today, crying hoarse, they had already come to know the conclusion what the judgement would be like...' The BBC made a broadcast... 'It was the BBC judgement. Allahabad has followed the BBC judgement.' The seed having been thrown for others to pick up, he said immediately, 'Now there may be or may not be a nexus between the two. But we are politicians, we are not judges'. That, presumably, entitles persons like him to manufacture conspiracy theories. 'We must try and find out the connection between the BBC broadcast and the pronouncement by Justice Jag Mohan Lal Sinha.'

A member much known for his pro-Soviet affiliations, butt in to widen the conspiracy. The news also appeared in the *International Herald Tribune*, he said.

Bhupesh Gupta was by now in full flight, the stock words came naturally: 'What the BBC said in the language of imperialism and hostility, animosity and malice for our country, the Allahabad judgement said in the profundity of its judicial language...' The judgement is 'a weapon for the rightist forces and for their offensive.'

If the fact that the BBC could anticipate what the Allahabad High Court would conclude is proof that it and the Court were in conspiracy, is the fact that the Supreme Court subsequently did what the comrade's 'hunch' had said it would do prove that the two—the comrade and the Court—were in conspiracy?

But Bhupesh Gupta was not one to be detained by doubts. He was off to sovereignty. Who is to decide who is to be Prime Minister? A mere judgement of one judge? *'Sir, this is substituting the judgement of a court, which is again* sub judice, *as it is now, for the will of the people reflected through the sovereign Parliament of this country.'*

From that he flew to the RSS, the Anand Margis... 'Crisis sometimes brings out the best in human beings,' he said, 'crisis sometimes compels society to think of measures which had been deferred in the past but to brook no more delay in so far as the required change is concerned. This is what we are going to do.'

'Therefore, let us not be apologetic,' Gupta emphasized. People say you are supporting the Prime Minister, he said. Yes, 'But we are supporting not an individual. We are supporting here certain basic things in political life and certainly we would not like the institution of the Prime Minister to be attacked, to be mauled, to be assailed in the manner in which the Anand Margis, the RSS and their rightist political patrons wanted to do. It is a question of the defence of democracy. It is not a question of defence of Indira Gandhi. Indira Gandhi can look after herself very well and this massive array of supporters are there...'

'But as a citizen of the country, as a democrat, as a champion of the working people of our country, as one who believes in going forward by smashing all the way the forces of reaction and counter-revolution,' Gupta maintained, 'I am certainly interested in how the Prime Minister's office and certain norms and digits [*sic.*] that surround it are defended and protected against the undue encroachments by the judiciary...' 'The issue today is not merely of one Indira Gandhi but the issue is that of the basic institution of Parliament and the Prime Minister occupies, as I said, a pivotal position in that set-up.'

A law that has been devised to save an individual thus becomes one that is necessary to save an institution. A law that Parliament is passing because it is totally servile becomes one, passing which is necessary to establish the sovereignty of Parliament!

Having established the principle, so to say, Gupta extended it to matters beyond mere election law. 'I wish more changes were made as far as the courts are concerned,' he began. 'Why should the court sit in judgement on everything?' Here is the Constitution which has made property a Fundamental Right... And then this matter of who is to be disqualified from Parliament. This is not something that should be left to one judge to decide, not to some court to decide: 'It is not a matter of law. It is a matter of how our institutions are functioning, the parliamentary institutions. It is a matter that goes to the root of democracy. Why should a judge decide as to who should remain or should not remain a Member of Parliament, as to who should remain the Prime Minister or should not remain the Prime Minister? It is for the people to decide through their representatives in the legislative houses...'

Sovereignty, the question is who is sovereign: 'Sir, the jurisdiction of the court is absolutely uncalled for in a situation of this kind. The Prime Minister's case has underlined the fallacy of the law existing, and we are amending the law to remove that fallacy. Does the judge decide, on grounds of only technical offence, whether the country can have a Prime Minister, irrespective of whether the country wants it, irrespective of whether the Parliament wants it, or not? Does he remain the sole arbiter? That is the position. That has gone.'

But that is just one step. Sovereignty demands more. 'In many other matters, the jurisdiction of the court should be taken away,' Gupta declared, anticipating, like the BBC, what was about to unfold! 'Sir, in matters of social and economic policies, in matters which concern the destiny of a nation, *the nation has to take charge of it, and on behalf of the nation, the Parliament has to take charge. We cannot leave it to the vagaries, prejudices, biases, the learning and knowledge of these judges, or for that matter, the collective body of judges. That we cannot do. That should be within our domain. And this is in line with the concept of sovereignty of Parliament and of democracy as well.'*

Nor is it just the case that we are to pass laws and the courts are to interpret them. 'If it [a law passed by Parliament] is ambiguous, it is our job to set things right'—as was being done! 'It is our job to give plain meaning and ambiguity there should be left to Parliament and not to the court to interpret in this manner. Therefore, Sir, there should be a second look in this matter as to the interpreting power of the High Courts and the Supreme Court. We must know where the courts should interpret. We must also lay down where we do not want interpretation by the court, where things will be left to ourselves to be interpreted by us in sovereign Parliament and Assemblies...'

Back to the conspiracy: arguments of the Opposition are drawn 'from the argument being voiced every day by the Western press, Western television, Western Radio—America, West Germany, Britain and France particularly... the forces of subversion, reaction, communalism and those who are ready to gang up with the Anand Margis and the RSS in order to achieve their diabolical political ends... the conspiracy of the internal forces of reaction and the external forces of imperialism and neo-colonialism...'

Gokhale, the Law Minister, was soon on his feet. 'Mr. Chairman, I am very grateful to my honourable friend, Mr. Bhupesh Gupta... for having made a speech which was very scintillating and logical, not merely in eloquence but also in content...' He agreed with everything that his esteemed friend had said... And then the vital phrases that presaged what was already being planned: *'I have personally felt, and I am quite sure that most of us would feel, that we must have a second look at the whole framework of the Constitution itself and this process has to start as early as it can...'* As for the existing electoral law, the President, Vice President, Prime Minister, Speaker, etc., occupy high offices: 'To my mind it appears that it is a ridiculous machinery under which they are subjected to judicial scrutiny while they are elected by a vast majority of the people and electoral colleges...'

The Bill was passed—there was no need to record how many voted for it.

That was on 6 August 1975.

Another sovereign act

Not sure that even that made-to-measure change in the election law would be sufficient, and with the hearing of Mrs. Gandhi's appeal set for 11 August, the very next day, on 7 August, Government rushed the 39th Amendment to the Lok Sabha. This sweeping Amendment was passed within two hours. The very next day, it was rushed to, and passed by that other limb of sovereignty, the Rajya Sabha. The next day was Saturday. No problem. State legislatures were summoned for emergency sessions. They endorsed the amendment! On 10 August 1975, the President gave his assent. So, literally a day before the hearing was to begin, not just the law on the basis of which the Supreme Court was to judge the appeal was changed, the Constitution itself was changed ruling the Supreme Court to be completely out of court!

The minutiae of the Election Law apart, the real question is, 'How can the Office of the Prime Minister be exposed to the vagaries of judges?,' the loyalists reasoned. What if they find some way to uphold the Allahabad verdict in spite of these changes in the Act? Why not amend the Constitution itself, and put the election of the Prime Minister beyond the scrutiny of courts all together?

So, two and a half hours before the Lok Sabha was to meet on 7 August, 1975, members suddenly received the Constitution (Fortieth Amendment) Bill.

The Speaker read out the formula text, 'Motion moved. "That leave be granted to introduce a Bill further to amend the Constitution of India."' Mohan Dharia, one of the Young Turks of those days, got up, 'Sir, so far as the sovereignty of the Parliament is concerned, it is unchallengeable. But regarding the special merits of the Bill, I would like to point out that the Bill was received by me at 8.15 A.M. this morning...' The rule is that Bills for amending the Constitution should be received at least two days before they are to be taken up. I realize that rules have been suspended for this session, Dharia said, but at least for amendments to the Constitution, the rule should not be suspended... The Minister for Law has said that this is being done because of urgent need, but he has not stated what that urgent need is... 'My information,' Dharia said, spilling the beans, 'is that the Bill is to be passed today. It is to be passed tomorrow by the Rajya Sabha. State Assemblies are being convened to get it ratified by more than 50 per cent of the state Assemblies. I am also told... that on 10th an Ordinance creating this machinery—the statutory body or authority—will be promulgated and no sooner it happens than the hearing fixed for 11th August in the Supreme Court will automatically lapse.'

The Law Minister; H.R. Gokhale, was brevity itself: 'I have nothing to say because the point was with regard to the notice. You,

Sir, in your wisdom and in your discretionary power waived the rule, for which I am very grateful.'

The sovereign House, accordingly, took up the Bill. The Law Minister just summarized the provisions. Even thirty years afterwards, the audacity they embodied chills one's spine.

The designations of the President, Vice President and Speaker were thrown in but the target was only the case against Mrs. Gandhi. In the name of the people and principle, the 39th Amendment provided:

❑ The election of a person who at the time of the election or thereafter is appointed Prime Minister shall not be called in question 'except before such authority... or body and in such manner as may be provided for by or under any law made by Parliament and any such law may provide for all other matters relating to doubts and disputes in relation to such election including the grounds on which such election may be questioned.'

❑ 'The validity of any such law... and the decision of any authority or body under such law shall not be called in question in any court.'

❑ 'Where any person is appointed as Prime Minister... while an election petition... in respect of his election to either House of Parliament or, as the case may be, to the House of the People is pending, such election petition shall abate upon such person being appointed as Prime Minister...'

❑ The shameless and conclusive clause (4): 'No law made by Parliament before the commencement of the Constitution (Thirty-ninth Amendment) Act, 1975, in so far as it relates to election petitions and matters connected therewith, shall apply or shall be deemed ever to have applied to or in relation to the election of any such person ... and such election shall not be deemed to be void or ever to have become void on any ground on which such election could be declared void or has, before such commencement, been declared to be void under any such law and notwithstanding any order made by any court, before such commencement, declaring such election to be void, such election shall continue to be valid in all respects and any such order and any finding on which such order is based shall be and shall be deemed always to have been void and of no effect.'

❑ 'Any appeal or cross appeal against any such order of any court as is referred to in clause (4) [the preceding sub-para] pending immediately before the commencement of the Constitution (Thirty-ninth Amendment) Act, 1975, before the Supreme Court shall be disposed of in conformity with the provisions of clause (4).'

Opportunity was also being taken, the Law Minister said, to place a few laws in the IXth Schedule—that was his euphemism for shovelling, in just one heave, thirty-eight laws beyond the reach of courts. Among these were the changes that had been enacted in the election laws; among these was the notorious MISA, the Maintenance of Internal Security Act under which the Opposition had been herded into jails across the country.

The Bill has been introduced in a great hurry, the first speaker said. He advanced two reasons. First, the Bill sought to place the election of the Prime Minister, etc. beyond the reach of courts. But the case which is to be heard by the Supreme Court does not have to do with Mrs. Indira Gandhi's election as Prime Minister. It has to do with her election as an ordinary member of Parliament from Rae Bareilly. Being elected Prime Minister is a subsequent event. Elected members of the majority party elect their leader, he is invited to become Prime Minister. This stage does not figure in the case. This Bill, by putting only the election to Prime Ministership beyond the reach of courts may confound the problem. Second, the entire Constitution needs a thorough review. Bringing amendments like this, piecemeal, one by one, creates the wrong impression, he said. 'So, this bit by bit amendment when one case is pending in a High Court or the Supreme Court or one judgement has been delivered by any court, does not look very healthy or good. At least this creates a bad taste in our political, social and economic life. Even those who want that such changes should be made feel hesitant in defending it in the background in which it is introduced...' This should have been done as part of an overall scheme to overhaul the Constitution. It should have been done earlier—especially because 'a basic threat has been posed in the last one and a half years to our democratic order, to the very fundamental structure of democracy...' backed by 'the moneyed-class, landlords and foreign imperialists...'

Is he opposing the Bill in the guise of supporting it, or is he supporting it while maintaining the veneer of independence? It wasn't clear. The Speaker asked him to wind up. He is the only member who is listed to speak, and you have not allotted any fixed time for this discussion, some members protested. Why are you not letting him speak?... But the member soon sat down of his own volition.

The chorus began. The Prime Minister holds a vital/pivotal/key position in our structure... A member's name was called to speak. He did not respond. A while later his name was called again. 'Sir, I am quite astonished,' he said, getting up this time. 'I have not given my name at all. I have not given notice of any amendment also...'

Things were obviously being done in a hurry. A mistake has been made, the Speaker said. The slip that the member had sent earlier for some other purpose had got mixed up with papers regarding this discussion...

The chorus of the sovereign members resumed. Even in the House of Commons, the election of the Speaker is not opposed. If we elevate the post of our Speaker to the same level, there would be nothing wrong. 'But some hallucination is there to some of us, when we speak of the Prime Minister,' the member charged. 'We say she is the Prime Minister of the nation; she reflects the nation and she speaks for this Parliament and for the ruling party. Because of the hallucination, certain colour is given and you read it with a coloured glass. If you accept that the institution of the Prime Minister is something above, or something safe or serious, then there is nothing wrong in including the Prime Minister along with the President, Vice President and the Speaker...'

'If you view it from a serious angle,' he went on, 'we know the things that are existing in this country; let us not pay lip service, let us really realize it, and I think, it is high time that serious consideration is given to this Bill under the given time.' 'The time is very important,' he said, with more candour than some would have wanted to go on record. 'We know pretty well that certain things are going to take place after 11th or 12th,' alluding to the hearing that was coming up in the Supreme Court; 'that is there...' Three days ago, we amended the Representation of People Act, he acknowledged. 'There itself it is clear' that the Allahabad judgement can no longer stand. 'But I know, Sir, there are certain bad elements; they can challenge even that, and they can create confusion in this country. They will not stand, but they can create confusion...' Hence, this Bill...

It has been drawn up in a hurry. The authority that is to be instituted under it has not been spelled out... 'But I tell you that we all agree here and say that *Parliament is the supreme authority and we are the law making authority. Nobody can question it,*' he declared, affirming the doctrine of sovereignty.

'But the Parliament is represented by whom?,' he asked, elucidating the lemma of that doctrine of sovereignty. *'By the Prime Minister who holds the majority, who speaks for the majority and for the nation.'*

Hence, the manifest conclusion: 'So, we take the institution of the Prime Minister, not Mrs. Indira Gandhi as she says. It is the institution of the Prime Minister that we take from that pedestal and put it there.'

But erecting this fortress around this institution could only be one clause in fulfilling the doctrine of sovereignty. The member, therefore, moved to state, 'The other day we also discussed and classified the Executive, the Legislature and the Judiciary. *Now the question is which is superior? A time has come for us to judge, because after 27 years, we are unable to move forward for the simple reason that there are so many impediments in the way. These impediments must be removed once and for all. That is why we have this Emergency; that is why we are welcoming this Emergency...'*

What clear light the doctrine of sovereignty provides! And where it leads!

So, the Constitution 'needs a lot of amendments,' he said. 'But that cannot be done in a day.'

And there *is* something, the unspoken one, that needs to be done in a day! 'These are the things which are very essential at the moment and be brought forward immediately...' 'All of us know about the judgement of the Allahabad High Court,' he continued. 'I do not want to go into the merits of this judgement,' he said. So, he turned to its motives!! 'But everybody is of the opinion that it is a political judgement; it is not a judgement that is based on law. The other day when we amended the Representation of the People Act, we tried to remedy certain things so that in future such calamities may not arise...'

'So, I support this piece of amendment,' he concluded, 'not from the angle of any sentiment, not from the angle of just supporting it, not from the angle of criticizing it, but because it is the need of the time. We have to feel the pulse of the nation and I know disruptive forces are still active. As they are still active, it is essential to do so and we have to give up the argument that there is no time and we should have been given two more days.'

And what is this about not giving members two days? 'I know in a number of legislations even two months time had been given but none of us cared to study them and then come here,' the member said with the candour he had been displaying. 'They are viewing this legislation from the coloured glass. In the past we have not cared even to look at the title of the Bills, not to talk of going through the papers. But today we come and say that time to go through it is not enough. I will simply say that we should get along otherwise time will overcome us and we will be nowhere.'

It was Mohan Dharia's turn. He could go only so far and no further in the face of the sovereignty-franchisees. He agreed that the Constitution needed to be recast. And for this, there was no need for any Constituent Assembly. When Parliament sits to consider an amendment to the Constitution, it does so as a Constituent Assembly, he said. In fact, the original Constituent Assembly had been elected only on limited franchise and indirectly. Therefore, 'I do feel and believe that this House is more sovereign than that Constituent Assembly,' he declared. 'I do feel that as a Parliament we are a completely sovereign body and there is no need for a new Constituent Assembly,' he reiterated. And so he wanted the Government to 'bring forward package programme of having structural amendments to the Constitution.' His objection was that this amendment was being brought forward because a decision had gone against 'a particular individual,' that is why he was not supporting it, Dharia said. For the comprehensive amendments that were needed, he urged that the Government consider initiating a 'national dialogue'. The speech was seen as a brave one given the circumstances.

Indrajit Gupta, the CPI leader, gave, as you would expect, a dialectical speech. The Bill had just come to them. They had not had time to assess its merits and implications. Could it not be challenged on the ground that it was setting up a common authority to decide on challenges to elections of the President, Vice President, Speaker and Prime Minister—for they were different types of offices: the first three were above and beyond parties, but the Prime Minister was Prime Minister by virtue of being the leader of the majority party.

His main grouse was that the Bill had been sprung on the House. We are supporting you in the Emergency. But you have not consulted us at all in regard to this Bill. To ensure 'meaningful cooperation', you should not take parties like ours for granted... Take this as a 'friendly warning'.

With that, he swiftly shifted to safer ground—the ham-handed way in which censorship was being applied to proceedings of Parliament. 'Now, in the beginning, at least by the great mercy of the censor, the names were being printed that so and so spoke. In the second stage, the names were cut out. In the third stage the fact that the debate has taken place at all was also cut out...' So much for the Parliament-that-is-sovereign.

And then to even safer ground, to the common ground so to say. The 'sort of vituperative stuff' that is being printed in the *London Economist, Time* and *Newsweek.* And, of course, he knew who was behind this ham-handedness: 'I demand that the whole censorship should be properly screened and scrutinized to see who are the agents of the Jan Sangh sitting there doing all these things,' he declaimed.

The Communists are supporting the Emergency, he reminded the House. That is why we agreed to the suspension of rules for this Session. But we do not want Parliament to be emasculated in this way for all time to come... Then the operational line, 'Of course we are not going to oppose this Bill.' Then the plea-cum-'friendly warning': 'But I think in the interests of the country, it is necessary for all democratic forces to cooperate with each other and stand united. If you want that cooperation, which we are quite willing to give in regard to all measures against the rightists and reactionaries, then please treat us, like the ADMK and other groups, as independent parties, with their own independent identities, their own policies and their own view of looking at things and not as your subsidiary agents. If you take that attitude, it will become very difficult to cooperate. I hope in future, this will be done in a more meaningful manner.'

Who would have any difficulty in treating the other as an independent entity when that entity is ever-willing to endorse every measure against those whom both in chorus dub 'rightists and reactionaries'?

In any event, the operational phrase for this Bill was the one that had just slipped by: 'Of course we are not going to oppose this Bill.'

The next speaker was another stalwart of secularism—from the Muslim League. Had the Prime Minister not acted, 'the right reactionaries, the militant communal elements and extreme leftists would have taken our country to anarchy,' he declared... He too wanted changes in the Constitution. 'We have actually been demanding that there should be a ban on these right reactionary elements like RSS and armed militant communal forces. This has been done now...' The only caution that must be taken is that, while amending the Constitution, the 'fundamental rights of the minorities' must not be affected.

As all the members, save Dharia with his caveat, had supported the Bill, the Law Minister was brevity and graciousness personified. He only pointed to the results of the law as it stood. Here we have these high dignitaries like the Prime Minister. And their election can be challenged in courts. 'A situation where all these dignitaries, when elected by the support of a very vast majority of the people, are subject to judicial determination as to the validity of their election is a very ridiculous position. It is ridiculous that the Prime Minister, for example, who has not only been herself elected in her constituency by a vast majority of the people but who has been recognized throughout the length and breadth of the country and even outside as the undisputed leader of the nation—not only as head of the Government but as the undisputed leader of the nation—should be subjected to a process in which judicial scrutiny takes place and it becomes all the more ridiculous when it takes place on flimsy and even ridiculous grounds...'

Notice the linear ascent:

❑ The people are sovereign.
❑ Therefore, the Parliament is sovereign.
❑ Therefore, parliamentarians are sovereign.
❑ Therefore, the majority of parliamentarians is sovereign.
❑ Therefore, the leader/controller of that majority, the Prime Minister, is sovereign.
❑ Therefore, subjecting him/her to judicial scrutiny is ridiculous.
❑ For the same reason, anyone who opposes her or him is an impediment in the march of the sovereign people.

❑ So that the people may continue to march forward, that impediment must be removed out of harm's way.

What sort of an authority would be constituted under this Amendment, the Law Minister recalled that he had been asked. He could not indicate anything specific, he replied, except that it will *not* be court-like. The 'absolutely untenable' situation that has arisen because of 'judicial interpretations'—from what date is the Prime Minister to be taken to have held herself out for an election; to what extent can the assistance of a government servant be taken before it becomes a corrupt practice... Such things have been clarified by the amendments that have been made in the Representation of the People Act. That applies to all members. This Amendment has been brought about for and is limited to these high dignitaries...

And then the declaration. We cannot allow the country to continue to be 'imprisoned' by the Constitution. The Constitution was framed in very different circumstances, British imperialism... Hence 'I would very much like—I said this yesterday in the Rajya Sabha—and I want to repeat it here that the time has now come when we have to have a fresh look at the whole fundamental structure of the Constitution itself...'

Time to vote. Dharia left the House. The Amendment Bill was passed: Ayes: 335; Noes: Nil...[1]

The very next day, the Bill was put to the other limb of sovereignty, the Rajya Sabha.

As sovereign, as obsequious

The Law Minister needed to do no more than go through the motions—to repeat what had been asserted in the statement of Objects and Reasons. The discussion opened with the in-House expert on dialectics, the CPI's stalwart, Bhupesh Gupta. We got the Bill just today from the Lok Sabha, he began. We have not had time to discuss it among ourselves. Naturally, we should be given time to examine it, to look up the Constitution and 'see whether things have been properly formulated in the Bill even when we are prepared to

---

[1]For the foregoing, 'Constitution (Fortieth Amendment) Bill,' *Parliamentary Debates, Lok Sabha, Official Report,* Lok Sabha Secretariat, 7 August, 1975, 6–115.

support it.' 'But there was no time. Is it nice? I said it before. There is a sense of urgency on the part of those who are sponsoring the measure. I do not mean anything ill. Nor do I want to cast any reflection on the sincerity and the urgent desire of those who want to get it passed as quickly as possible. I do share their anxiety. All the same... Under the Rules, we should have two days. But at least give us four–five hours. Give us reasonable time to read and assimilate...' A devotee's plaint.

And the reason he was making this suggestion, the leader explained, was because they were on the same side, and because of their common regard for Parliament and institutions. How touching his solicitude for Parliament and other institutions sounds even thirty years later:

> I say this because I would not like a situation when we would be unwittingly, with all good intentions, be denying the Parliament its right in any manner. Of course, we know there are people whose policy and plan are to pull down the institutions of democracy in our country and you have to deal with them. Those who want to bring down the institutions of democracy defile and defame them; but they shower affection on them so long as it suits them. They denounce them the moment it does not suit them.

A textbook description of the tactics prescribed for Communists in Lenin's *Collected Works!*

'Sir, we do not belong to that category of people.' And then the dialectic:

> Institutions must be changed, if necessary, and they cannot be a stagnant pool. They must be given some purpose and direction and they must be renovated from time to time to bring them in line with the changing situation, to meet the challenge of our times. I entirely agree with that and hence I also agree that it is necessary to have a second look even at our own Constitution.

He was all for the Amendment. He marshalled what passes as wit for it. It is necessary that persons occupying these high offices be kept 'from being hijacked by somebody at the judicial gun-point.' 'Hijackings are of various types,' he elaborated. 'Now, hijacking can take place in many ways. Here, Sir, one can take a gun—you do not need a revolver or a pistol—the High Court judgement is your gun, point it and hijack the Prime Minister and take him or her away. Sir,

I think we are protecting him or her against this hijacking business at the judicial gun-point or gun-point of a judgement, if you call it. Well, nobody of such high eminence or such high position... should be hijacked like that. So, we are stopping this hijacking business by this Bill. We shall deal with them in the House...'

In the case of the Prime Minister, where is there the need to go to a court of law at all? She or he has been made Prime Minister because she has the confidence of the majority of the Lok Sabha. So, the Lok Sabha should settle the matter. It should decide whether it still has confidence in the person. And this does not imply any discrimination in favour of the Prime Minister, the dialectician explained, by an argument that was to become an embarrassment the very next day:

Sir, it does not mean that the Prime Minister is not equal before the eyes of law. Suppose, Prime Minister drives a car and violates the traffic rule. She is as much liable as I am. Suppose Prime Minister commits a crime. He or she is as much liable as I am. The Prime Minister cannot claim immunity from criminal and judicial proceedings when he or she has committed a crime. Therefore, law stands there. Law is not discriminatory between the Prime Minister and others...

And what is so special about immunizing such high dignitaries from 'this hijacking business'? After all, each of us has some privileges because of the position we hold; as member of Parliament I enjoy immunity from being sued for defamation on account of anything I may say here, the member explained. The very case and judgement which had given rise to the present situation constitute the argument for the changes, he explained. An officer's help was said to have been taken. The Court was told that he had resigned. But, said the opponents, the resignation had not been gazetted. 'Whether his resignation should have been gazetted or something happened earlier became such a mighty, terrible, devastating thing that the Prime Minister's office crumbles and the Prime Minister is brought down. Crisis is created and some people start calling it a total revolution but we call it a total counter-evolution. Naturally, Sir, you have to amend the law, you have to do that, there is no other way.' And look at the harassment: 'The case went on for months and months, where everything was dug up. Many other things which had nothing to do with the election case, which had nothing to do with how an election could have been won, were brought in. Sir, this is not good even for an ordinary member of Parliament, leave alone the Prime Minister. So, I can quite understand that kind of thing.'

And this does not have to do with Shrimati Indira Gandhi. ...Tomorrow another Prime Minister may be there but our projection of parliamentary institution is that the Prime Minister's office occupies a very crucial place. It has an international image, and it is not good for a country to allow its Prime Minister to be subjected to all these things, it is not good particularly for a country like ours so long as we proceed on the progressive road...

And it is this proceeding on the progressive road which was the heart of the matter. This is why there was all this obstruction and denunciation, the member declared, moving to the principal contradiction. 'So, Sir, those are the things. The Americans dislike what is happening in the country. The West Germans dislike it. The imperialist class, the British imperialists dislike it. They are denouncing it. They are running a campaign—some of them—in support of Jayaprakash Narayan. They are denouncing it.'

'What conclusion do I draw from it?,' the anti-imperialist asked, and answered:

I draw the conclusion that perhaps we have struck a blow against them. Sir, I take this action against the rightist forces as a blow struck against the strategy of American neo-colonialism... the blow that has been struck against the right reaction in our country to the Anand Marg, RSS and others is a blow which has struck at the very basis of the American strategy of destabilization, the strategy of these elements within the country to bring about a rightist takeover of the country so that neo-colonialism can have an upper hand. Therefore, Sir, we are happy from that angle also. It is not because the action has been of international significance. It is because all the progressive sections of the world, not to speak of the socialist countries, the people of the socialist countries, have been fully supporting these actions. Sir, these measures have been brought in line with them.

And there must be no flinching:

We are amidst a fight. We may not be fighting as some people are fighting in the streets of Lisbon or the Northern Portugal. May be the hordes of reaction and reactionaries are not out in the streets with guns in their hands. That will be a fatal day for us. But the fact remains that ideologically we are in the midst of a fight. But we do not have to be forced constitutionally, politically, legally or economically but we have to conduct the fight from a position from where we can strike them most effectively and beat them down into total surrender. Let us involve the brave soldiers, fighters and generals of total revolution into a situation of total surrender. That is what we should like. Hence, this measure justified itself even from the moral and political angle, leave alone the constitutional angle because they are counting on it; they are counting on certain facts, certain other opportunities open to them. So, Sir, I think it is quite all right that we have it now.

That feat of single-handedly lifting the discourse to the moral plane, as we shall see, evoked special gratitude from the Law Minister! .

The next member, he was from Tamil Nadu, was brief. This Amendment is like the others. Most have been 'necessitated consequent on the judicial interpretation or phraseology of the Constitution, not being in consonance with the spirit of the Constitution,' he said. The institution of the Prime Minister has 'a pivotal position in the Indian constitutional structure.' And what has happened?

That dignified position has been vilified by frustrated politicians day in and day out. The sinister move by right reactionaries is nothing but to malign the reputation of the Prime Minister, Mrs. Indira Gandhi. The habitual Indira-haters can do anything. But the country is now well aware, Sir, that Indira Gandhi is the only leader with national following. She is the only visible, political leader commanding respect of all sections of the people of India. Is this authority and is this dignity to be at the caprice and whims of political frustration? I think that the 39th Amendment has prevented this catastrophe.

I can't understand why such an Amendment escaped the attention of the Law Ministry so long, the member from Uttar Pradesh exclaimed. And what happened as a consequence? 'Some time back someone from a street-corner filed a petition against the Prime Minister. And what happened? The judgement on two small issues or points, came in her way. And the word used was "corruption". My friends, who can question or say something against the integrity, honesty of the Prime Minister of this big nation, who on earth can say something against the Prime Minister, as was said at times by some irresponsible people? The Prime Minister won by a majority of 80,000 or 90,000 votes.'

A member corrected him, 'More than one lakh.'...

The Law Minister rose. He had thought of not giving a reply at all, he said, as he had already covered most of the points during the discussion on amending the Representation of the People Act. 'But I take this opportunity to fully endorse what my friend and colleague, Mr. Bhupesh Gupta, said, that the present amendment is not only constitutionally and legally justifiable but it is also morally justifiable.' And that was something that needed to be understood clearly:

> I would like to emphasize that it is morally justifiable because underlying the amendment is the basic concept that the persons holding these four high offices *who have been elected by a vast majority of the people and who represent the people at large and are occupying these positions by virtue of the electoral mandate, cannot be displaced by any authority which is an outside authority like the judicial authority, may be the Supreme Court or the High Court or for that matter, any other authority. It is an accepted principle that the will of the people is the last word and no judicial interpretation given by anyone howsoever high can override the verdict of the people.* That is why I say that it has the strongest foundation not only on legal or constitutional ground but also on moral ground...

Time for the vote: Ayes: 161; Noes: Nil...[1]
The people vindicated!

Sovereignty redoubled

Putting a gloss on their support for the Emergency and the spate of changes that were being enacted, Bhupesh Gupta of the CPI had said on the 8th that the protection which was being crafted for the Prime Minister so that her election could not be challenged did not amount to her being placed above others in the eyes of law. She would still be liable for any crime—recall his reference to violating traffic rules!—that she or he may commit. That was the argument on the 8th.

By the next day, 9 August 1975, that is just two days before the Supreme Court was to hear her appeal, the fight against imperialist/communal/reactionary forces advanced further!

Why shield the Prime Minister only from challenges in regard to her election? After all, she is the highest representative of the people, she embodies the aspirations of the country, the dignity and honour of the country, the sovereignty of Parliament. She should be shielded from *all* proceedings. Period.

---

[1] 'The Constitution (Fortieth Amendment) Bill,' *Parliamentary Debates, Rajya Sabha, Official Report*, 8 August, 1975, 9-64.

And that is exactly what the Rajya Sabha, exercising its sovereign power no doubt, did in The Constitution (Forty-first Amendment) Bill. The Bill was introduced by the then Law Minister, H.R. Gokhale, on 9 August 1975. Every member who spoke exerted to outdo others in expressing his whole-hearted and enthusiastic support for the Bill. One after the other, members said that they were astonished that such a Bill had not been brought earlier.

It is 'a brief Bill,' Gokhale told the House, 'and a very simple Bill.' Just a few changes are being suggested in Article 361 of the Constitution.

The Article shall now provide,

No criminal proceedings whatsoever, against or concerning a person who is or has been the President or the Prime Minister or the Governor of a State, shall lie in any court, in respect of any act done by him, whether before he entered upon his office or during his term of office as President or Prime Minister or Governor of a State, as the case may be, and no process whatsoever including process for arrest or imprisonment shall issue from any court against such person in respect of any such act.

Furthermore,

No civil proceeding against the President, or the Prime Minister, or the Governor of a State, shall be instituted or continued during his term of office in any court in respect of any act done or purporting to be done by him in his personal capacity, whether before or after he entered upon his office as President, or Prime Minister, or as Governor of a State...

How brief! How simple!

And what acclaim.

It is anomalous that protection, though to a lesser extent, has been available thus far to the President and Governors, it has not been available to the Prime Minister, Gokhale told the House, even though the latter 'holds a most pivotal position'. Hence, the Bill.

There has been a 'grave omission' in the Constitution, the first member who spoke said. 'It is true that the incumbent to the office of the Prime Minister is the leader of a particular political party and continues to belong to that party,' he conceded, only to add, 'But the moment he or she occupies that high position, she becomes the leader of the people. The Prime Minister has the responsibility of securing the welfare and well-being of the people as a whole, irrespective of the party affiliations of the people.' Of course, the member couldn't be detained by the thought whether by the same words those who became chief ministers of states or indeed ministers should not also have been included in the Bill! He was in full flight. 'Therefore,' he continued, 'this high position of the Prime Minister deserves all our respect and it is the bounden duty of each and every citizen to hold the incumbent in respect and honour. But, unfortunately, this sense of understanding was not witnessed in the recent past and such an attitude of denigrating the office of the Prime Minister has to be restrained. Therefore, I welcome this amendment.'

But amendments of this kind are not enough, he said. He was, therefore, very glad that the Law Minister had stated that the whole Constitution needs to be looked at again.

We are in an Emergency, the next speaker explained, 'which is very necessary in certain periods of a nation's history.' 'We will have to make quick strides.' But 'there are people in this country whose mind is conditioned and even fossilized to that extent who say that the Constitution is sacred and should not be touched.' But the Constitution is 'man-made'. In making it, because of the circumstances prevailing at that time, the Framers gave 'preponderance to the idea of freedom,' he said. But that freedom 'has been misused and abused to such an extent that freedom has degenerated into license and democracy has degenerated into mobocracy.'

When situations change, the Constitution has to be changed. Do we not have the example of God Himself? 'Sir, changes are necessary. It is said: Old order changes yielding place to new; and God fulfils Himself in many ways lest a good custom should corrupt the world. When God Himself changes, Parliament should change. No system is absolute. No Constitution is absolute. No virtue can be absolute in life. All things are relative. The Constitution is relative. The system of Government is relative. The parliamentary democratic system is also relative to the particular needs of the situation. Therefore, where the Constitution needs changes, we have got to change it, and that does not mean that the change we make should be permanent. Tomorrow another situation may arise, when we have to change it. That is the law of life. If we go against the law of life, as the reactionaries are doing in this country under the pretext that the

Constitution is sacred as if the Constitution has been given by God Himself directly to this country. *This attitude is reactionary, anti-progressive and anti-people.'*

The Prime Minister occupies 'a very key position', the next speaker declared, the Prime Minister is 'actually the pivot of the whole structure now.' 'In fact, in this federal polity, it is the personality of the Prime Minister and it is the image of the Prime Minister that is the unifying force.' And 'now what is required for our country is mostly the strengthening of the bonds of unity in this country...' 'Therefore, we shall not allow anything to be done to denigrate that image.'

But what has been happening in the last few years? These anti-Congress parties got together to destroy democracy from below by defeating the Congress. As, after seeing the performance of these parties, the people came back to the Congress, and these persons saw that 'anti-Congressism was not paying dividends,' 'they wanted to destroy it from the top, from the apex of the pyramid.' 'From anti-Congressism to anti-Indira Gandhi, that was the transformation that took place from 1971... They were only attacking personalities, denigrating the image of the leadership and only trying blackmail...' Hence, the Bill...

The speaker was not finished. He trained his guns at the root of the immediate problem—the Judiciary! The Judiciary 'wanted to play the role of the Executive,' he said. 'Sir, let the Judiciary realize where the demarcation line is between the judicial functions and executive functions.' Let the judges rise above 'their mania for precedents.' The Judiciary should not work as a brake, he declared. 'Let it not work as a brake, as a permanent brake. We are determined about it,' he said. 'Secondly, Sir, *the question is as to who is to rule the country.'*

'*Parliament,'* interjected another representative of the people, another spokesman for sovereignty.

'I think we have decided it once already,' our speaker continued. 'Probably our Judiciary needs to be told about it time and again. I think we would be failing in our duty if we do not make them realize this. *It is the people's institution, the representative institution, the Parliament, which has the last word and this must be made known to them...'*

'*Der aayaad, darust aamad*,' the next speaker declared. When we grow up, we cannot keep wearing clothes that were made when we were five. We cannot wear in the winter clothes that were made for the summer. We cannot wear in Ladakh and Kashmir the clothes we had stitched for the plains. We are in the twentieth century. Change is a hundred times faster than it used to be. We cannot go on eating food that was devised by our forefathers thousands of years earlier when we are in a world that is going to the moon. When the airplane has come into being, we cannot go on travelling by the bullock cart.

The position of the Prime Minister is far more vital than that of Governors and the like, he said. In the personality of the Prime Minister, the entire *shakti* of the country is embodied. He speaks for the country, for the nation. When he takes a step, it is on behalf of the country. He shows the way to the country. He takes the nation forward. It is this person who keeps the country secure, who strengthens the unity of the country. 'When such a person gets ensnared in trifling matters because of trifling persons, it is not just his status that is lowered, the status of the country is dragged down...' But bringing such individual amendments is not enough, he echoed. We must review the Constitution as a whole. In fact, when we bring individual amendments one by one, questions are raised about our motives, and it is inferred that we are bringing about these changes because of some thing in the present situation... Therefore, the entire Constitution must be reviewed, and for this a committee should be set up...

Speakers were soaring higher and higher, both in proclaiming sovereignty of the people, as well as in demonstrating loyalty to the highest symbol of those people, the embodiment of sovereignty, Mrs. Indira Gandhi. The next speaker outdid them, doubly so. Pointing out repeatedly that he was just a layman, telling Parliament that he did not even know English, he exercised the rights of a layman and let fly. The Constitution was drafted by the Framers in completely different circumstances, he said. 'They never envisaged a time when such persons would man the opposition parties who, taking shelter behind the Constitution, would do such deeds in this country as would injure the people...' Under these laws and this Constitution, recognition has been given to such parties, these regional parties. They first tried to capture power by preventing with their *lathis* the poor from voting. When that did not work, they conspired to get the courts to pass strictures against rulers so that the rulers would vacate the chairs for them. 'The Framers of our Constitution had no clue that the opposition parties would come to consist of such rotters that, unable to constitute parties, they would begin talk of partyless democracy,' alluding to JP's thesis in that regard.

'They could not even have imagined that the Judiciary would become so cheap that it would join hands with foreign agents and work,' he declared. Here is Indira Gandhi whose grandfather worked in Uttar Pradesh, whose grandmother worked in Uttar Pradesh, whose father nursed Uttar Pradesh, whose revered husband nursed Rae-Bareilly, in *that* constituency Indira Gandhi has won because of the help of Yashpal Kapur?[1] 'Did the Framers of the Constitution even contemplate that this country could get such lowly and such diabolic judges?,' he demanded. That deserves to be repeated in the original: '*Kya constitutional framers ko yeh pataa thaa ki aise ghatiya aur kamine judge bhi is desh mein ho sakte hain?*'

So, while we should of course pass this Bill, two other things should be done—he, as the sovereign representative of the sovereign people, told the sovereign Parliament. First, the Constitution should be amended to ban regional parties. Second, 'We should not let any such person become a judge. In fact, I say that such judges, whose mental capacity doesn't work sufficiently for them to know as to who is more important, Indira Gandhi or Yashpal Kapur, that such judges should be punished.'

The layman wasn't finished. 'In fact, I am of the opinion that this judge could be an agent of the CIA or he is mad. Either his place is in America or in the lunatic asylum in Agra.'

'There is a lunatic asylum in Bareilly also,' another sovereign representative of the people chimed in.

'Yes, as Bareilly too has a lunatic asylum, that too is a fit place...'

And who is to say that the member does not have the right and authority to say all this? After all, he is the common man speaking. A man who revels in not knowing English. A true representative of the people. A spark of their divinity-that-is-sovereignty.

---

[1] Her long-time aide who had figured in Justice Sinha's indictment.

When the Constitution was framed, the next speaker began, it was necessary to protect offices of honour. Today it is necessary to protect offices of work. Sir, the Constitution is the symbol of a nation's life. Life flows. That water alone remains clean which continues to flow... At that time, because of Gandhiji's assassination, RSS had vanished; because of the Partition, Muslim communalism had vanished... How could the Framers have contemplated that this knot of poison—'*yeh zehar ki gaanth*'—would form again after 25 years? Yes, the princes of that period have gone. But with their jewels and hidden millions, they are conspiring to throw society into danger. And they are joined by the new money-bags, the capitalists. In such circumstances, we must think of a complete overhaul of the Constitution.

Today the Prime Minister of India is not just the Prime Minister of the country, he proclaimed. She has become the symbol, the embodiment of Indianness, of India's unity, of India's progress. In these circumstances, should some case commence against her in some criminal court, the prestige of the country itself will be destroyed. This amendment should have been brought earlier...

It was time to speak not just on behalf of the people in general, that the earlier speakers had already done. It was time to speak in the name of the poor.

We socialists have rejoined the Congress as what we used to demand—abolish privy purses, nationalize banks, nationalize import-export trade—has all been enacted and implemented by the Congress, the socialist declared, explaining his homecoming. So, it is not the Congress of those days. Sir, I would, through you, urge the Law Minister to ensure that the franchise of these capitalists—of whoever has five or ten lakhs or more—is taken away. 'In this land of the poor, these *crorepatis* should have no franchise, these moneybags who with their crores are out to poison society...'

Notice how well the ingredients fuse into one another: the people, the poor, their representative, the layman, the progressive... And, fused together, where they lead.

The Prime Minister is the cornerstone of our Constitution, the next speaker began, around whom the mill of our democracy rotates. If the Prime Minister is not protected, if the Prime Minister remains exposed to such attacks, the person cannot discharge the responsibilities of his office. This has nothing to do with any individual, he declared, it is a matter of principle... We must rethink the Constitution, especially provisions relating to property... We must change it so that our goal is attained, so that our viewpoint prevails...

Sir, there is one other matter, the speaker said, warming up to the theme of the people, in particular the poor and deprived, and their true representatives. Sir, there has been talk of judges of High Courts and the Supreme Court. I think that no one can get out of the circumstances into which he has been born, in which he is nurtured, in which he lives. This is the reason that these courts are filled primarily with persons from the well-off sections of society. They just cannot represent the poor, the oppressed, the hungry people. They just cannot comprehend their sentiments. They have been brought up in such an atmosphere that they just do not have the capacity to understand what the poor are saying. Therefore, I urge the Law Minister, appoint such persons as judges whose sentiments are linked to those of the poor, who can represent them, who will always keep them in mind... The obstructions they have been causing in *zamindari* abolition, in tenancy legislation... So, keep such persons in High Courts and the Supreme Court who are in tune with the sentiments of the poor. And who have the same ideology as we in the ruling party do. Then alone will they decide in accordance with our thinking...

Every member having spoken for him, in his reply to the 'debate', the Law Minister was as brief and simple as he said the Bill was.

The Bill was passed the same day, at the same sitting. Ayes: 154. Noes: Nil.[1]

That was on 9 August 1975. The Parliament, what with its powers as sovereign, had changed the election law, declaring as 'legal' what had hitherto been illegal. It had amended the Constitution so that the election of Mrs. Indira Gandhi now fell outside the reach of the Supreme Court. Now one-half of that sovereign had put all her acts—past, present, future—beyond criminal and civil law.

---

[1]For the foregoing, 'Constitution (Forty-first Amendment) Bill, 1975,' *Parliamentary Debates, Rajya Sabha, Official Report*, Rajya Sabha Secretariat, 9 August 1975, 1 to 58.

The sovereign had prepared Mrs. Gandhi well for the Supreme Court!

As the months went by, the last twist of the knife began to seem unnecessary. Could it even give the wrong impression? Enemies were saying that the election law had been amended because Mrs. Gandhi had been found guilty of corrupt practices. Would they now say that she had criminal acts to hide and that is why this last Bill had been passed?

In any case, where is the need? A lakh are in jail. The country is quiet. The trains are running on time...

8

Sovereignty in full spate

But the people must march ahead. Socio-economic revolution has to be ushered in. Courts are the obstacle. Fundamental Rights are the obstacle... The Constitution itself needs to be overhauled. And as the sovereign, Parliament can do what it wants with it.

A paper appeared, 'A Fresh Look at Our Constitution—Some Suggestions'. Its proposals would emasculate the Judiciary completely. The captive Congress passed a Resolution advocating that for 'the misery of the poor and vulnerable sections' to be alleviated, it was imperative that 'our Constitution be thoroughly re-examined.' The infamous Swaran Singh Committee was set up, and produced the proposals it thought were required of it. As was her custom, Mrs. Gandhi also had a parallel group drafting even more draconian changes. Soon, the Forty-second Amendment was before the sovereign Parliament.

Three aspects of this Amendment are important for the matter we are considering:

The relationship between the citizen and the State was overturned. Article 31C was generalized, so to say: no law which so much as contains a declaration—a mere declaration—that it is for giving effect to the Directive Principles or even one of them shall be called into question in any court on the ground that it violates Fundamental Rights, in particular Article 14[1] and Article 19.[2] Second, through a new Article 31D, it was laid down that no law which provides for preventing or prohibiting 'anti-national activities' or formation of 'anti-national associations' shall be deemed to be void on the ground that it is inconsistent with Articles 14, 19 or 31.[3] Third, Article 26 was replaced so that

---

[1] The right to equality.
[2] The rights to freedom of speech, to assemble, to form associations or unions, to reside and settle anywhere in the country, to practise any profession, occupation, trade or business.
[3] The right to property.

henceforth Courts would be able to issue writs, etc, to Government only where the injury or injustice was 'of a substantial nature'. The Judiciary was crippled. Henceforth, there shall be no limit at all to the power of Parliament to amend the Constitution. A new clause was added to Article 368 laying down, 'No amendment of this Constitution (including the provisions of Part III),[1] made or purporting to have been made under this Article... shall be called in question in any court except upon the ground that it has not been made in accordance with the procedure laid down in this Article.' Even that last bit— that the Amendment could be challenged on ground of impermissible procedure—was dropped during discussion in the Lok Sabha so that no Amendment could from now on be questioned in any court on any ground at all, full stop. Second, building on the command performance of the Swaran Singh Committee's proposals, a new Article 144A was inserted providing that the constitutional validity of a law shall be considered by Benches of at least seven judges; and that no law shall be declared unconstitutional unless a majority of not less than two-thirds of judges constituting the Bench hold it to be so.[2] The dykes around Mrs. Indira Gandhi's election were thickened. Recall how expeditiously the sovereign Parliament had approved amendments to election laws on 5 August 1975, to declare as legal the practices on account of which Mrs. Indira Gandhi had been held to be guilty of corrupt electoral practices. By these changes, the power to decide whether a member, having been found guilty of corrupt electoral practices, had incurred disqualification and if so for how long was taken away from the courts and vested with the President. While commending the change, H.R. Gokhale had twice said that this power would be exercised by the President on the advice of the Election Commission, 'and the Election Commission's advice is binding on the President.'[3] Articles 103 and 192 were now replaced: if a question arises whether a member of Parliament or of a state legislature respectively has become subject to disqualification, and if so for how long, the question will be decided by the President, and the President's decision shall be final. Before giving his decision, the President shall, merely 'consult' the Election Commission; there was nothing about the advice of the latter being binding. Simultaneously, Article 74 was changed to ensure that the President shall adhere to the advice of the Council of Ministers headed by the Prime Minister in all matters. Hence, the Prime Minister would in effect have power over every member of Parliament as well as every member of every state legislature whose election came to be disputed. There was another tell-tale

---

[1]That is, the part guaranteeing Fundamental Rights.

[2]The new Article 228A made similar provisions for High Courts that would assess constitutionality of state laws—Benches of not less than five judges ... to hold a law to be unconstitutional more than two-thirds of the Bench must hold it so...

[3]*Lok Sabha Debates*, 5 August, 1975, 5.

change: during the hearings of her election case, it had been claimed on Mrs. Gandhi's behalf that the work that officers had done was nothing exceptional, that it was standard practice and was laid down in the 'Rules and instructions for the protection of the Prime Minister when on tour or travel'. Raj Narain asked that this manual be produced; Mrs. Gandhi's side resisted. The 42nd Amendment inserted a new clause into Article 166: '(4) No court or other authority shall be entitled to require the production of any rules made under clause (3) for the more convenient transaction of the business of the Government of the State.'

Of course, the Constitution was changed in a host of other ways: the Preamble was changed to give a 'secular' and 'socialist' veneer to what was being done; two new Parts and nine new Articles were grafted; 50 Articles were amended, many out of recognition. The net effect of this exercise of sovereignty is well described by Granville Austin in his meticulous and thorough study:

The shift in the balance of power within the new Constitution made it all but unrecognizable. The Supreme Court had been divested of much of its original jurisdiction. The high courts had been hobbled. Parliament had unfettered power to preserve or destroy the Constitution. Parliament now sat in judgement over the elections of its own members and those of the President and Vice-President. The President had to assent to Parliament's enactments as presented by the council of ministers... Neither the central nor state governments were restrained from acting in their respective legislatures by quorum requirements for the amendment abolished these. A single government supporter in an otherwise empty house could pass a bill. Parliament's and the legislatures' terms had been extended to six years from five. Finally, the council of ministers had extraordinary powers given by the amendment's final clause. This provided that if there were any difficulties in giving effect to the Constitution as amended, 'the President may, by order', for up to two years, adapt or modify the provision to remove the difficulty...[1]

And how was all this justified? The people are sovereign; hence, Parliament is sovereign; hence, the Prime Minister, whom they have elected to head the government, has to saved from mere judges; the judges are an obstruction to our helping the poor and vulnerable sections...

---

[1]Granville Austin, *Working a Democratic Constitution, The Indian Experience*, Oxford, New Delhi, 2001, pp. 373–74.

The 42nd Amendment was 'debated'—hailed and acclaimed, would be more appropriate—for eight days in the Lok Sabha, and six days in the Rajya Sabha. One significant change was made as a result of these 'debates'. As we have noticed above, even that toehold, that an amendment to the Constitution may be taken to court on the ground that the procedure prescribed for constitutional amendments has not been followed, was erased.

But the 'debates' are valuable in that they show where those propositions—the people are sovereign; therefore, Parliament is sovereign... —lead.

October 25, 1976: Lok Sabha

H.R. Gokhale rose to introduce the Amendment: 'The objective is to bring about a socio-economic revolution in the country after the achievement of this freedom,' he declared. Some provisions of the Constitution have proved to be obstacles in the march of our socio-economic revolution... The obstacles lie even more in 'judicial history', he said: 'it shows that at every stage when something was done with a view to give effect to the objectives, hurdles were thrown up...'—privy purses, bank nationalization... And, ever so often, the Judiciary executed somersaults, ever so often it became very difficult to understand what the law really was... The Amendment is being brought to remove these obstacles.

He soon warmed up to the main target—the judgements in which the Supreme Court had held that, while Parliament could amend the Constitution, it could not injure its Basic Structure or features. 'We do not know what are the basic features,' Gokhale told the Lok Sabha. 'I think *we should not lose any time in once for all stating categorically and unambiguously, that there is no question of anything like basic features*, about which they themselves do not know what they are. But so far as what Parliament regards as basic for the purpose of making changes is concerned, *there can be no impediment in the way of Parliament to amend any provision of the Constitution.*' Therefore, he said, socio-economic objectives apart, 'the most important feature of this Constitution Amendment Bill is that *we are reasserting with all emphasis that the Parliament is supreme and there are no limitations on Parliament in respect of the amendment of the Constitution.* We have made proposals to give effect to this assertion of *Parliament's supremacy and its sovereignty* and that to my mind is one of the most important features of the present Constitution Amendment Bill. In one of the clauses we have said that after this amendment becomes effective, *no court, howsoever high or low, will be entitled to go into the question of the validity of a Constitution Amendment, i.e. its constitutionality or otherwise.'*

'Howsoever a court may be composed, of eminent, learned and distinguished judges and so on, it may be,' he told the fiduciaries of sovereignty, 'the fact remains that it is the people sitting here, in this House and in the other House, who are responsible to the people, who are answerable to the people, not they who determine whether a certain amendment should be made or not, and whether an amendment is constitutional or not...'

He held forth on the first instrument for ensuring this sovereignty: henceforth, no law Parliament passes for giving effect to even a single Directive Principle, no law which Parliament so much as says is for giving effect to even one Directive Principle, shall be called in question on the ground that it violates Fundamental Rights.

He dilated on the clauses by which the original jurisdiction of the Supreme Court was being hacked, and the one by which its power to adjudicate constitutional amendments was being taken away, and then, in keeping with the Goebbelsian temper of the Emergency, declared that those who were saying that the independence of the Judiciary was being trampled upon were totally wrong: 'How? Because no provision in the present amendment has affected the status, the position, the dignity, the independence of the Judiciary. The mere fact that by a provision you re-allocate or distribute matters in which jurisdiction or powers will be exercised certainly does not take away the independence of the Judiciary or its dignity or status.'

The dialectician took over. Indrajit Gupta of the CPI said that his Party had 'no quarrel whatsoever' with the objective of socio-economic revolution that Gokhale had mentioned, and the provisions drafted for furthering it. 'In fact, our Party has been pressing for a long time that the Constitution requires to be amended, to be radically amended, precisely in order to facilitate the advance that we all want towards a better and more equitable society, towards the achievement of socio-economic reforms in the interest of the vast majority of the people, and towards the removal of obstacles and hurdles which experience has proved, stand in the way of bringing about such reforms.' His mild objection, as he was to state later, was that some of the proposals did not bear on this objective— for instance, the proposal to do away with the requirement of a quorum in sessions of legislatures. 'In our opinion the Constitution reflects to a large extent a sort of a compromise between the interest of the affluent or exploiting classes, the privileged classes in our society which naturally do not want to give up those privileges and the interests which actually are of the vast majority of people in this country—the toiling people, the wage earners, the poorer sections who want the Constitution to be amended more and more in such a direction that their rights and their interests would find proper and effective guarantees in the pages of the Constitution.' The Amendment was a step towards rectifying the compromise.

Gupta's specific endorsement was of greater import: his colleagues and he share the opinion, he said, that '*the right of this Parliament to amend the Constitution is supreme and unchallengeable.*' 'I am glad that Government has decided to go ahead with the consideration of this Bill which asserts, as the Minister has said just now, *the supremacy of Parliament.*'

Gupta was naturally gratified about the ideal of socialism being incorporated in the Preamble, and the provisions that would further this: 'The attractive power of the idea of socialist order or society and correspondingly the extent to which, I think, the capitalist system is getting discredited throughout the world, all these things combined together make the people of our country aspire to a socialist order which should be spelt out in due course as to what it means and what it should mean...' The Amendment reflects 'the correct aspirations of most of the people of our country,' but, of course, more would need to be done than introducing the word in the Preamble.

One of cheerleaders of the Emergency and such changes, Priyaranjan Dasmunsi, now Minister for Parliamentary Affairs, soon followed. From the 'core of my heart, I welcome this Bill and congratulate the Law Minister for having brought forward this measure to fulfill some of the aspirations and dreams of our great leaders of the national struggle, specially our great leader Pandit Jawaharlal Nehru,' he began. 'This Bill exclusively deals with provisions relating to socio-economic changes in our country,' he said with another Goebbelsian flourish. 'The Bill before the House expresses the views and aspirations of the people of the country,' he maintained. '...The Constitution is the document of the people of the country and as such, it is a national document,' he said, not just a legal document. 'In that context, we have to examine as to *who can express the will of the people, the aspirations of the people, better than the elected representatives of the people.* This Parliament is not only competent but also has the responsibility and the duty to fulfill the promise which they gave to the people during the elections with regard to socio-economic changes, to the extent they can.'

'The comments which were offered by the Opposition in this regard, as I have already said, are old ones and if I am not wrong, they are largely anti-national.' The Amendment rectifies the greatest blunder: 'I think, the greatest blunder that we have made in this country since adopting this Constitution in 1950 is not to make clear to the people, what is anti-national, what is anti-country and what is anti-people. If we had done this earlier, many crises could have been avoided.' In keeping with the times, he urged the Government to be alert to the hostility and conspiracies of 'super powers' and 'nuclear powers' and 'imperialist forces' and 'foreign agents'...

As a progressive, Dasmunsi knew why the Judiciary had been coming in the way, and how it had to be dealt with. 'I do not mind if the role of the Judiciary is amended,' he proclaimed. 'I am all for the *supremacy of the Parliament.* If you feel that Judiciary claims more power than the Parliament, then there is a class struggle. It is clear that Judiciary has taken a path which is not to the liking of Parliament and, therefore, Parliament had to jump upon in this class struggle. While Parliament tries to adopt a policy for the people, whatever jargon you may use "socialism" etc., the Supreme Court comes for struggle. It means a class struggle. It means that a group of vested interests wants to oppose us. Until and unless we do have the capacity to change the class character and concept of judicial wisdom of the country in regard to the central law and the state laws, this will continue.' 'The Government has shown the courage and the wisdom to bring in such a bold and courageous measure and those who brought this measure should be considered as the greatest patriots of the country, for all time to come.'

The day had gone well. With the Opposition in jail, the Amendment was being endorsed by member after member from 'the core of the heart'. The highlight of the next day, 26 October, was the long discourse of none other than the head of the infamous Committee which had paved the way for many of the provisions, Swaran Singh.

Much of his speech was devoted to establishing who was responsible for pushing the Government to make these amendments. The respective functions of the three organs of the State had been well-defined, he said. '...*Unfortunately the courts transgressed the limits prescribed for them.* They did not have the authority to examine the constitutional validity of acts amending the Constitution, and *they arrogated to themselves the jurisdiction and the authority to go into the constitutional validity of constitutional amendments.* It is that imbalance which had been created, that excess of jurisdiction that became evident at various stages that we are now trying to rectify and trying to restore the original division as was contemplated by the Framers of the Constitution. So if there was any disturbance of that line of demarcation which defined the functions, which laid down the contours within which the three wings were to function, *the transgression, if anything, took place on the side of the courts.* They started examining and they thought they could go into this question. In the initial stages—I must be fair—they came to the conclusion that Parliament has got the authority to amend the Fundamental Rights also, and it appeared that things were stabilizing. Later on, they went back upon the original thing and they said that Fundamental Rights cannot even be touched. What is most disquieting is that they thought of this concept of "basic structure".'

All the Government was doing was to help the judges: 'They took up an attitude and now we are trying to help them to get out of that attitude. This is what it comes to.'

The words 'basic structure' do not occur in the Constitution, he said. 'So what the courts were doing when they brought in this concept of basic structure was that in a sense they were taking upon themselves the right to amend the Constitution and they brought in these words "basic structure"... the Judges themselves imported this concept of basic structure into the Constitution, for which there was no justification.' 'I say in all seriousness that these are symptomatic of assumption of jurisdiction. It is a crude sort of invasion, if I may say so, into the domain of Parliament by using expressions for which there is no warrant whatsoever in our Constitution. All that we are doing is to tell them: leave us to amend the Constitution; leave us to add new words to the Constitution; you confine your activity only to interpret what is in the Constitution and do not bring in other concepts which are ethereal. In a sense we are trying to help them by defining their domain so that they may not be in unchartered seas and do not lead the country to some imponderables.'

And underlying all this is the principle on which all are agreed: '*So far as the supremacy of Parliament is concerned, I think it is axiomatic; it is the will of the people in all spheres which will prevail; there is no doubt about it. Parliament is the only authority which can amend the Constitution and we are saying that if they amend it, it is in the exercise of that authority which is the right of the people which is exercised by their chosen representatives and that is final. This therefore is the concept of the non-challengeability of the constitutional amendments.*'

'Let courts for a change learn to understand that certain fundamental things cannot be altered by a razor-sharp majority,' he said endorsing the two-thirds of the Bench rule, which, of course, the Amendment had taken from the report of his Committee.

And then the warning: 'The Constitution undergoing an orderly change, is the greatest protection of the country and protection of the rights of the people. Who can stop the vast socio-economic changes to help the poorer sections taking concrete shape? They must come. *If the Constitution stands in the way, or anybody stands in the way that person would be wiped out, that institution would be wiped out, but the things must change.* So, if we facilitate the change and make the change orderly and constitutional, it is in the best interests of the society and we should not at all be apologetic about changing the Constitution.'

With even the mild Sardar Swaran Singh having delivered himself in such terms, others were freed from all inhibition. C.M. Stephen, another person who passed for an authority on law and the Constitution these days, declaimed, 'The nation felt that it was held up and the march was stolen from it.' The feeling of Parliament that the restriction imposed by the Court was 'a stone hanging on its neck...' It was removed by our amending the Constitution. But the Court put even heavier restrictions... Here we were, representatives of the people, by the 25th Amendment, 'We said that we are sovereign, we are supreme and in Article 31C we said that if we enact any law and if the Parliament or the Legislature declare that it is in pursuance of the Directive Principles, then it shall not be set aside on the ground that it is not in pursuance of the Directive Principles...' But the Supreme Court again, in *Kesavananda Bharati*...

But times have changed: 'We framed this Constitution when the property right was considered sacred; we framed this Constitution when socialism was an anathema; we framed this Constitution when the princely rights were considered sacrosanct; we framed this Constitution when the path was not clear. Today, the path is clear, the vision is clear, the goal is clear, the leadership is clear and we know where we want to go. We want to be armed under the Constitution where we will not be put under trammels and under fetters. A Constitution is necessary which will reflect the aspirations of the people and will give us freedom to operate in a particular manner...' 'Now, the funny thing is that the law is binding on every court, not on the Supreme Court,' he continued. 'They are free. What a wonderful thing. We may get a ruling in our favour tomorrow. What is the guarantee that day after tomorrow some other blooming Bench will not sit and strike it down? Are we to function in this eternal, perennial, never-ending and continuing threat of a super chamber sitting in judgement on us?'

The ground had been prepared for Mrs. Indira Gandhi herself to speak. She did so first on 27 October. She was contemptuous of the decision of the Opposition—leaders of which she had thrown in jails across the country—not to participate in the debate. 'To non-cooperate with Parliament is to non-cooperate with the people. My advice to the un-reconciled Opposition parties would be to give up their negative opposition and return to the path of reason and responsibility. Of course, this negative opposition is not born out of the Emergency, as some hon. Members opposite have hinted. It started long before Emergency; and, in fact, it was one of the causes for the Emergency...'

'We have gone ahead with our programmes in spite of tremendous odds and unforeseen difficulties, external as well as internal,' Mrs. Gandhi declared. 'It was the abuse of democracy by some of the Opposition, the obstruction in the way of our legitimate functioning which necessitated further consideration and action...'

She is the one who had led the call for a 'committed judiciary'. She is the one who had superseded judges in the Supreme Court to place her handpicked judge in the Chief Justice's chair. She is the one who had transferred judges who had given judgements that inconvenienced the Government in *habeas corpus* cases. Her party is the one that was to give political positions to the head of the Election Commission as well as the Supreme Court. But Goebbels is Goebbels: 'Justice Subba Rao's trying for Presidentship was a blatant indication, not only of the political bias of some of the Judiciary, but of their intention to be involved in and to interfere in politics. The question was not of a particular individual, it was symptomatic of the basic struggle, the spearhead of the entire movement against everything that the Congress Party as a representative of the freedom struggle, had advocated and struggled for, the programmes and ideas on which not just one but all our elections were fought and won...'

She improved on Swaran Singh. 'Various theories, as to what constitutes the core of our Constitution, have been put forward. Some say Fundamental Rights, others, the Directive Principles Chapter. Yet others think it is judicial review. *A doctrine of constitutional supremacy has been propounded. The true supremacy is that of the people.* While the Constitution is a very important document, it is but an instrument to serve the people. The Constitution exists for the people. People should certainly respect it, but they cannot be sacrificed for it...'

The election laws had been overturned, for the people. The election of the Prime Minister had been placed beyond the reach of the courts, for the people. For anything and everything that the Prime Minister did, howsoever grave a crime, howsoever gigantic an extortion she or he extracted, she had been put beyond the pale of law, for the people. The jurisdiction of the Supreme Court had been hacked away, for the people. The requirement of quorum in the Houses was being jettisoned, for the people...

There is the law of life: 'There can be stability and responsibility and law only if the Legislature, the Executive and the Judiciary respond to the changing needs and aspirations of our people... This is what the present Bill does: it is responsive to the aspirations of the people and reflects the realities of the present time and the future...'

And then that basic curse which the judges had let loose: ' *We have always maintained that Parliament has an unfettered, unqualified and unabridgeable right to amend the Constitution.* We do not accept the dogma of the basic structure. Sardar Swaran Singh remarked that some Judges have imported the phrase "basic structure". I would not say they have imported it since it does not exist in any other Constitution, *they have invented it...*' Not just the bar of the people, the bar of history: 'The Constitution has to face a bigger than the judicial scrutiny and that is the scrutiny of history. It has to be capable of meeting the challenges of historical forces. There is something greater than all of us and that is the nation and its future. That is the importance of this Bill.'

The next day, 28 October, Gokhale rose to elaborate the points and sharpen the attack on the Judiciary, and to commend that the Bill be taken up for consideration. With *Golak Nath*, with *Kesavananda*, the Judiciary 'made an *intrusion into the field of the Legislature and its supremacy...*' Accordingly, *'we regarded it our duty, our primary duty, to do everything that we can within our power to establish and to assert that supremacy of Parliament...'*

And there was Panditji to invoke. 'I intend to quote again something which has been quoted many a time,' Gokhale said. 'These are words of such prophetic significance that they will bear a little repetition—because, at this time, when we are talking of changes, we should be reminded over and over again of what Jawaharlal Nehru said in the Constituent Assembly. He said:

> 'So far as we are concerned, we who are connected with the Congress shall give effect to that pledge naturally, completely, 100 per cent and no legal subtlety and no change is going to come in our way: that is quite clear. We will honour our pledges within the limits and no judge and no Supreme Court can make itself a third Chamber and no Supreme Court and no Judiciary can stand in judgement over the sovereign will of Parliament representing the will of the entire country. It is obvious that no court, no system of Judiciary can function in the nature of a third House, as a kind of a House of Correction. So it is important that, within this limitation, the Judiciary should function.'

'This warning was given to the Judiciary not now when, as some people are inclined to say, we are really trying to say things about the Judiciary and trying, as it were, to denigrate or lower its importance,' Gokhale told his fellow sovereigns, 'but these words were said even when the Constitution was being framed and was being discussed. Yet, *unfortunately for us and more unfortunately for the Judiciary, this prophetic warning fell on deaf ears and we have had, from time to time, situations where an atmosphere of confrontation was sought to be created by these very judges who were to see that confrontation does not occur.'*

Who is responsible for the confrontation? The judges! For whom is the confrontation unfortunate? For the judges! 'So, it was our duty to see that they did not encroach upon the field which did not legitimately belong to them.'

And in the discharge of this duty we must go to the farthest extent: '*Our anxiety now is naturally to see that we don't allow this kind of thing to happen again and in the present amendments which we are considering we should not leave any stone unturned, we should not leave anything undone, which is necessary to be done to see that, in future, such a thing does not happen again.* And that is why, in Article 368... we have unequivocally stated that the Supreme Court will have no jurisdiction whatsoever to entertain, and much less to decide, any question relating to the validity of a constitutional Amendment. *If, even after this warning is given again, not by mere spoken words but by incorporation of an express provision in the Constitution of this country, things like this recur, which I hope will not, I think, it is a bad day for the Judiciary of this country.* It is this which, I hope, they will understand even now, so late, and will so direct their attention to other matters which can be regarded as belonging to their legitimate field and not to any other.' This from the Minister of Law and Justice!

And it was really out of his concern and compassion for the judges! 'Yesterday, Sardar Sahib has very properly pointed out that we are not doing anything to infringe on their powers,' Gokhale said, '*but we are really trying to save them from the temptation of intruding into powers which do not belong to them. It is not really that we want to save ourselves, the people, from them, but it is really to enable the judges to save themselves from this temptation—to save them from themselves.*' 'Ourselves, the people,' to save Judges from themselves!

The changes that are being affected 'are, in that right spirit of telling the courts where they stand and where Parliament stands.'

Had the top-sovereign not explained it all? 'It is in that context that the Prime Minister has said yesterday—of course, she did not use these words—that the Supreme Court is not that supreme, that *there is something else which is more supreme, there is a forum which is more supreme, than that Court itself, and that is the forum where the representatives of the people sit, this Parliament.*'

'With regard to the supremacy of Parliament...,' he said, 'it is the desire and the effort of everyone of us here to see... not to leave any stone unturned, not to leave anything undone, which is necessary, so that the real position comes back again, and we are trying to restore that position back and nothing more.'

And again that total lie, with the artful qualification: 'We know... the power of the court, the jurisdiction of the court, is not taken away *in matters which really, truly, belong* to the sphere of a judicial decision... So what I am trying to point out is that on all basic and important matters and *in matters which can legitimately be said to belong to their area,* on all those matters, the Judiciary is yet entitled to adjudicate as against an Executive action or against judicial or quasi-judicial action...'

The lobbies were cleared. 'The question is: "That the Bill further to amend the Constitution of India be taken into consideration."' Division. Ayes: 346. Noes: 2.

The cheerleaders got their chance again during the clause-by-clause consideration of the Amendment. The concept of 'socialism' is being incorporated into the Preamble, Priyaranjan Dasmunsi declaimed. Hence, 'socialism is no more a slogan of the Congress Party or the Communists; it is no more a monopolistic, theoretical conception of a group or individual, it is the desire and demand of the whole nation, from Kashmir to Cape Comorin.' Hence, 'If anybody propagates something against the concept of socialism, if anybody preaches anything against the concept of socialism, if anybody organizes something to motivate the people against the concept of socialism, *then that activity should be treated as an anti-national activity.*' He explained what he had in mind: 'At present in the country the larger mass media, the newspapers, etc. are controlled by the monopoly houses. The Chambers of Commerce in South, East, North and West are dominating the trade and commerce of this country. The Rotary Club and the Lions Club have a tremendous influence over the mass intelligentsia of the country. Whatever may be their character, whether right or left that is not important. But what is important is this. Suppose tomorrow the *Indian Express* or the *Hindustan Times* management, after this Constitution Amendment is adopted, tries to publish a series of articles to justify to the people of this country why socialism should not be accepted in this country, *then that should be considered as an anti-national activity* because the nation as a whole is already committed to the concept of socialism...' Munsi is the Minister for Information and Broadcasting today! Conspiracies all round: Right-reactionary forces... Naxalites... Radio-Peking... Voice of America... Gandhi Peace Foundation... India Harmony Society... In West Germany, the Indian National Club... The International Krishna Consciousness Society of Calcutta... The Prajapita Brahmkumari Ishwarya Vishwavidyalaya... In the 1969 report of the CIA it has been mentioned that these are the subsidiaries of CIA...

And all this because Parliament is supreme: 'I congratulate the Leader of the House and the leader of the country, our leader Shrimati Indira Gandhi *for once again proving to the world that parliamentary democracy and Parliament as such in the country is supreme and it is Parliament which is representing the will of the people.* It is due to her courageous leadership from 1969 up to this day that the politics of the entire nation got a new strength and confidence and I feel that by amending the Constitution through this Bill, it is not Government alone which will get a new strength, but, it is the whole country which will get a new strength and confidence to make further fresh break-through in the socio-economic transformation...' There is no need for a Constituent Assembly: 'The concept of Constituent Assembly in such great issues as the constitutional amendments is not only against the wishes of the people, but also, *it is against the interest of parliamentary democracy and the concept that Parliament is supreme. Our leader Shrimati Indira Gandhi has shown by her courage that this Parliament is not only supreme but that it is the custodian of the will of the people and there shall not be any alternative to it... At present, under the leadership of Mrs. Gandhi, the people's will, through this Parliament, is supreme in the country and nothing whatsoever can come as an obstacle in our way.'*

And so, 'for God's sake, for heaven's sake, do not revive this idea of a Constituent Assembly. *Let us revive the idea of the people's spirit, the idea that Parliament is supreme, nothing can come in the way of Parliament, that Parliament represents the people's will, that Parliament is the main custodian of the nation and the Constitution.'*

Gokhale was on his feet again: '...when this House will pass the Bill, that will be our finest hour...,' he began. And the most important thing is that the supremacy of Parliament is being put beyond doubt. Far from him to denigrate the judges, far from him to say that they lack in patriotism. 'All that I was trying to do was to emphasize that judges have to be in tune with the movement of the times and with the felt necessities of the times. *If that does not happen, it is not that the people can be held back. If that does not happen, it is the Judiciary which comes into disrepute. It is to prevent that thing from happening that I emphasized... that we wanted to tell the judges, understand what the people demand, keep in tune with what the people want.* While nobody ever disputed the right of the judges to interpret the Constitution or the other laws *within the sphere which is allotted to them,* what we undoubtedly disputed and will dispute is the fact that in that process of interpretation, they will not succumb to the temptation of importing their own political philosophy for good or for bad...'

'Therefore, I would like to remove the doubt raised by some of my friends and most of them from the opposite side, when they tell me that I had been attacking the judges, opposing the judges and denigrating them and I seize this opportunity to make it clear that denigrating them was the farthest thing from my mind,' Gokhale said. He was in fact doing his duty: 'I would have been failing in my duty if I had not said what I had said because I was only communicating to them, what the whole country felt and what the entire Parliament representing the people of this country felt in the last several years...'

Sovereignty reinforced

The proposals were now in the Rajya Sabha. The other day this Bill was passed with great acclamation by the Lok Sabha, Gokhale told the House, and he was sure, he said, 'this House also will accept this Bill with the same joy and acclamation.'

He explained the major advance: 'This Parliament now is putting beyond any doubt that *Parliament is the supreme authority to amend any provision of the Constitution or all provisions of the Constitution.*' Under the Bill as it was originally introduced and moved in the Lok Sabha, there was a provision which allowed an Amendment to be taken to court if the prescribed procedure for amending it had not been followed. But now all doubts have been removed; those words have been removed all together from the amended Article 368... 'Not only that,' Gokhale told the sovereigns who were soon to pass the Bill with joy and acclamation. '...A new clause has been added saying that on no ground whatsoever Parliament's right to make an amendment can be the subject-matter of any issue before a court of law... Now the Article as has come before this House makes it abundantly clear that the courts have no jurisdiction whatsoever to deal with any challenge to a constitutional amendment...'

The courts are the ones that had forced the hand of Government, he said. They had been handing down judgements on the basis of the 'political philosophy of the judges who decided the case,' matters were decided on 'political consideration'. As a result 'many unusual, unknown things were done apart from saying that Part III [the part of the Constitution that deals with Fundamental Rights] is unamendable.' We used to say that the basic structure notion had been imported, Gokhale said, adding, and giving credit where it was due, 'but the Prime Minister rightly pointed out in the other House that it has not been imported but it has been invented; it has come from the thinking of the judges who thought that they should reserve to themselves some power which really they did not possess and which they, in their heart of hearts knew that it really belonged to only one authority in India, *the highest authority, namely, the Parliament.*'

Gokhale expanded on how the hand of Government had been forced: 'Now, all these cases of judicial determinations left us with no alternative but to place before Parliament, in unequivocal terms, a proposal where not the Supreme Court or any other court in India but *Parliament alone can have the authority and has the necessary supremacy which, as we all know, always existed.* But we had to reassert because of the situation created by judicial determinations. Therefore, what we are doing now by accepting this proposal in the constitutional amendment is really, once again, to assert, without any shadow of doubt, that the courts will have no function in the matter of determining the validity of a constitutional amendment which function is only of Parliament and of no one else.'

Next, socio-economic revolution... Hence, Directive Principles to supersede Fundamental Rights... The mere declaration by Parliament that a law is intended to further the Directive Principles or even one of them, the mere declaration to this effect, shall put it beyond the scrutiny of any and every court... And this for good reason: 'Experience unfortunately has shown in the last 10 or 12 years that *in every case, in every important matter where things were considered as very vital from the point of view of the people at large and the country, the Judiciary transgressed its limits* and entered into a field which really did not belong to it.' Some critics are saying that we are taking away the jurisdiction of the courts: 'This is a motivated criticism with a view to create a feeling of suspicion in the minds of the judges. The people who criticize are those who have a vested interest in the present functioning of the courts...'

The provisions have been discussed far and wide. 'Has the Emergency in any way come in the way of holding the discussion?,' Gokhale demanded.

Some Hon. Members: Yes.

Shri H. R. Gokhale: No.

Shri Omprakash Tyagi (Uttar Pradesh): All the seminars were banned.

Shri H. R. Gokhale: Nothing was banned.

Shri Omprakash Tyagi: Here in Delhi.

Shri H. R. Gokhale: Listen to me. The real thing is that under the guise of holding discussion on the constitutional amendments, some meetings were sought to be used for other purposes. But I can say with confidence that every meeting *which really wanted to discuss constitutional amendments,* was allowed not only recently but even after the question was raised for the first time in the country that the Constitution was going to be amended.'

The House returned to joy and acclamation...

What the Amendment is doing, in fact, is to strengthen and advance the Rule of Law, the Minister of Law and Justice explained. His exposition is worthy of being taught in Law Schools: 'When a situation comes in the country where any further progress can be achieved only by this,' he said, 'one thing was clear in our minds that whatever we do in this country we do it on the basis that there is the rule of law. If there is the rule of law, we will do things if the law enables us to do them. But if the law comes in the way of doing them, it becomes the paramount duty of Parliament to see that the law conforms to the wishes and aspirations of the people. It is for the purpose that even the fundamental law is being amended to see that no one at any time can say that something extra-constitutional was done, that something illegal was done.' The critics can say and do what they want, 'But the fact remains that in the country as a whole, among all sections of the people, the proposals for amendments have been extremely well received and there is a general consensus. In fact, people have been complaining that this is something which should have been done ten years back, why did you not do it at that time? So much is the feeling that what is being done is so necessary. "Better late than never," some of them have said.'

The road that the courts had to follow was now amply clear, there was no need to say much more: 'All that I would say is that I hope that even after these amendments are made, the people who are charged with the responsibility of judicial determination will see what the feelings of the people are, that they will bear in mind where the people want us to go and why the hurdles which come in the way of doing those things have to be removed. If this is done and if people do not import their political philosophies in their judicial determination, then I believe no court will function in the way in which it has behaved for the last ten or fifteen years.'

The theme was taken up by the other great authority on matters constitutional—the ever-law-abiding, A.R. Antulay. The amendments are being made 'to remove hurdles in the path of progress, in the path of the poor,' he said. 'According to me, to be very honest and frank, they are not frightening. In fact, they are much less than what India needs today.' He wanted to ask the Law Minister, *'Why should there be the power for the Supreme Court to interpret the Constitution? Why should they have the power of judicial review even of ordinary legislation?'* They are accountable to no one. 'The very root, the very base of their authority by way of interpretation and by way of judicial review will have to be taken

away one day or the other in the interests of the people of this great
country,' declared this great Barrister. 'And judicial review of law is
no inseparable part of a democratic Constitution. France, a full
blooded democracy, does not have it...' And for good reason: 'The
three wings to the State are the Executive, the Judiciary and the
Legislature. The Executive is removable by the people and the
Legislature is removable by the people. But has anybody given any
thought to the question as to how the third wing of the State, that is,
the Judiciary, is removable by the people? Even if the whole people
of India think so, can they remove one judge?'

An Hon. Member: You want that also?

Shri A. R. Antulay: Yes, I want that, I want the Judiciary to be
responsive to the urges of the people.

Another champion of sovereignty, Harsh Deo Malviya, equally
progressive, equally committed to socialism, declared, 'Basic
structure is a figment of imagination.' It has been clearly stated by our
Prime Minister that this is something which is concocted.
It does not exist. It is nowhere there in the Constitution. It has been
brought in only to protect private property and to protect the vested
interests. According to me and according to us in this House, if there
is anything basic in this country, it is the people of the country. What
are basic are the rights of the people. *Nobody, no power, no
Judiciary, however highly placed they might be and in whatever high
a chair they might be sitting, will have the right to interfere with the
basic will of the people which is expressed through Parliament and
this is fundamental.'*

The President of the Congress, D.K. Barooah, who had
proclaimed, 'Indira is India. India is Indira', gave one of the longest
speeches. Mrs. Indira Gandhi was soon to single it out: 'It was
comprehensive,' she told the Rajya Sabha. 'He dealt with brilliance
and humour, with all aspects of the question. This was expected for
he has been most intensely involved with the drawing up of these
amendments. Himself widely read, he has added to our education
and introduced us to the thoughts and words of eminent writers and
thinkers, men of politics and men of law. I might add that he has just
loaned me a book from which there will be some quotations in my
speech...' Can you imagine the palpitations that triggered?!

'Sir, I would like to submit that the Emergency which is a child of
the Constitution has brought about all these things,' he declared. 'It

has tried to bring food to the people, clothes to the people, houses to the people and many opportunities of development. Therefore, it is necessary that the gains are consolidated and not frittered away. So, Sir, I suppose that the Emergency was necessary and I suppose it still continues to be necessary...'

He wanted the House to appreciate what, he said, is 'the biggest point of all of them', 'the question of the Supreme Court *vis-à-vis* this Parliament.' 'Sir, our Constitution... has one characteristic, one basic characteristic, and that is *the sovereignty of the people expressed through Parliament. That is the only basic quality of the Constitution, that is, it has founded the sovereignty of Parliament and nobody else's sovereignty in this country...*' The Judiciary can claim autonomy, he said. It cannot claim sovereignty—as if that is what the courts had been doing. And then the veiled warning: 'Therefore, Sir, any effort of extension of judicial authority would be fatal for the Constitution and *certainly fatal for the Supreme Court itself.*'

He did not need to say anything about the basic structure, he said. 'Nobody knows what it is... It is not even a chaotic idea. It is only a term which they have used which has no meaning...' We can't even bury it or cremate it: how can you bury or cremate what is not there?... Learning, humour, as Mrs. Gandhi was soon to say. 'Therefore, we leave it at that and march along with the amendments in order that we implement what Pandit Jawaharlal Nehru wanted to do when he moved the Objectives Resolution for the founding of the Constitution...'

8 November: The highlight of the day is the speech of Mrs. Indira Gandhi. She is relaxed, full of the same learning and humour, loaned quotations and all. The Opposition members are keeping away, not because the country is imprisoned but because 'they sensed the massive support which the Bill received in the Lok Sabha.' 'Sir, there is a rumour,' she says washing the stains off her hand, 'I do not know what to call it—being spread that we are against judges or against the Supreme Court. The Congress President went out of his way to express our view with clarity. But I also would like to assure this House and the world outside that no such feelings exist in our minds and a wrong meaning has been read into what has been said by some of my colleagues...' But facts are facts: 'Most judges do not jump into the political arena. But one did...' Forces inside and outside working against the country... An organization has been set up abroad,

'Indians for Democracy'. 'An American in America' has written to her about such persons and organizations, and she takes the House into confidence about what this American has written: 'All these Indians who have taken up residence abroad, who have no compunctions about deserting India for what they consider greener pastures, are now criticizing the efforts of your country to go ahead.' Some Americans are not 'the foreign hand', clearly!

The matter is straightforward: the people, the march of the country, continuation of the Struggle for Independence, sovereignty of people and Parliament, removing the cobwebs which have been spun by some recent attempts of the Judiciary...

> The objective of this Bill is the rejuvenation of the nation and the Constitution. *We are bringing into a sharper focus the intention of our founding fathers. We are re-establishing harmony between the Legislature, the Executive and the Judiciary as originally provided in the Constitution. We are removing the cobwebs created by some recent attempts of the Judiciary to encroach into political and legislative spheres. We are re-asserting the sovereignty of the people and pointing out that everything else, including the Constitution, is for the people. We are trying to end once for all some needless controversies which stood in the way of quicker progress. We are clarifying again beyond any doubt the sovereign constituent power of Parliament when it is amending the Constitution.*
>
> There is nothing radical or new in the amendments. Whatever appears as new is a clearer expression of the urges which moved the nation before and after Independence and which guided the founding fathers. But, as I said, *we are for the sovereignty of Parliament*. But the sovereignty of Parliament is itself dependent on the people of India. Parliament is a creature of the Indian people. Therefore, what we are really trying to do is to strengthen the Indian people, to enable their voices to be heard and to enable the quicker solution of their problems.

The flag having been unfurled, many rose to hail it...

9 November: The House is soon to act with joy and acclamation. Gokhale again. What is this about Fundamental Rights being imprisoned? Did the member—it was the great lawyer, C.K. Daphtary, who had pointed that out—not notice that we have freed the Directive Principles from imprisonment?... This business about judicial review: 'If we talk of judicial review, traditional jurists in this country and outside have come to the conclusion that *if there is any undemocratic feature in the Constitution, it is the feature of judicial review*. It is undemocratic because what is democratically done and decided by the elected representatives is set at naught by people who are not so elected and who, in that sense, do not represent the people...'

The 42nd Amendment is passed with joy and acclamation...

Notice the steps:

❑ The people are sovereign.
❑ Therefore, Parliament is sovereign.
❑ Therefore, parliamentarians are sovereign.
❑ Therefore, the majority of parliamentarians is sovereign.
❑ Therefore, the one who controls the majority is sovereign.
❑ Therefore, anyone, any institution, any law or Constitution that comes in the way of the sovereign is thwarting the will of the people; he is working to perpetuate the exploitation of the poor.
❑ Therefore, he must be 'wiped out'.

Another point is just as vital. The propositions are hurled, institutions are debased by servitors, by bullies, by louts. Who remembers Gokhale the jurist, Swaran Singh the rationalizer, Barooah the scholar, C.M. Stephen the law-giver, who remembers the cheerleaders of those days? But their shouts and screams, their vituperation, their lies, prevailed. The injury was inflicted...

To this day

That sequence of propositions, indeed the very words are heard today, each time the courts establish that what politicians are doing violates the law and the Constitution. Recall what the very politicians who have plunged the country into vicious casteism let loose recently after the Supreme Court nailed the misuse to which Schedule IX has been put. 'The Court should not transgress the limits that have been laid down... Parliament is supreme...' The DMK Chief Minister, M. Karunanidhi, immediately saw in the judgement, reason to have the Constitution reviewed...

As I close this chapter further news comes from Tamil Nadu. 'DMK tells judiciary: Don't exceed limits,' reports *The Asian Age*. One Arcot N. Veerasamy—who the paper points out is a senior minister in the Tamil Nadu Government, who is close to the Chief Minister, Karunanidhi, who is the Treasurer of the DMK—this worthy declares at a public meeting in the presence of the Chief Minister, 'Some judges are behaving as though they have jumped from heaven. Everyone has a limit and must function within that. There is no legal sanction to criticize an elected Chief Minister or unnecessarily fault his Government. My only worry is that courts should not end up as *kattapanchayats* [kangaroo courts]. If the courts continue to function in this manner, people will lose confidence in them.' 'Some courts in Tamil Nadu are functioning in a manner as if they command more authority than a democratically elected Chief Minister,' Veerasamy continues. 'I do not consider High Court judges superior to the Chief Minister. Who has given the authority to the High Court to usurp the powers of the Chief Minister? Has the High Court been given more responsibility than the Chief Minister?...'

And what is Karunanidhi's reaction? 'There has been a raging debate in recent times,' *The Asian Age* reports him as saying, 'as to who will bell the cat, and now Veerasamy has accomplished that. At least now, after this bell's ringing, let there be honesty and justice here.'[1]

And now another avalanche—the moment the Supreme Court has stayed the operation of Arjun Singh's *diktat* about reservations... The people, the poor, Parliament, sovereignty...

---

[1] *The Asian Age*, 5 February, 2007.

9

Some important lessons

'Nobody knows what it is...,' the President of the Congress, D.K. Barooah, had proclaimed of the Basic Structure. He needn't say anything about it, he said, as 'It is not even a chaotic idea. It is only a term which they have used which has no meaning...' We can't even bury it or cremate it, he had said: how can you bury or cremate what is not there at all?[1]

It has been imported by the judges, Sardar Swaran Singh told the Lok Sabha. It is an invention, Mrs. Gandhi declared. The cheerleaders took up the refrain: No one knows what it means, they said, the judges themselves do not know what it means...

---

[1]As is well known, the Supreme Court initially held that there was no restriction on the amending power of Parliament. True, the Supreme Court noted, Article 13(2) prescribes that 'the State shall not make any law which takes away or abridges the rights conferred by this Part [that is, Part III dealing with Fundamental Rights] and any law made in contravention of this clause shall, to the extent of the contravention, be void.' But, it held, the expression 'law' in this clause does not cover the constituent power—that is, the power to amend the Constitution. [*Sankari Prasad v. Union of India*, AIR 1951 SC 458.] This view was reiterated, and, in a sense, enlarged, to state explicitly that an Amendment to the Constitution could even take away Fundamental Rights, and yet not fall afoul of Article 13(2). [*Sajjan Singh v. State of Rajasthan*, AIR 1965 SC 845.] That was in 1965. In 1967, the Supreme Court decided that 'law' in Article 13(2) did, in fact, include amendments to the Constitution, and that, therefore, no amendment could take away or abridge Fundamental Rights guaranteed to us in Part III. [*I.C. Golak Nath v. State of Punjab*, AIR 1967 SC 1643.] The extent of the amending power continued to be a matter of contention. As politicians made more and more extravagant promises; as they were able to fulfil fewer and fewer of them, they began blaming the Judiciary for standing in their way. Leftist rhetoric was at its apogee, and with it, the hurling of blame on others. The matter came to a head in what became one of the pivotal cases in our constitutional history —*Kesavananda Bharati v. State of Kerala*. [(1973) 4 SCC 225.] The judgements in this case have become the cornerstone of the Basic Structure edifice, and, therefore, the discussion in the text centres round these judgements.

If such a vague concept is enunciated, namely, that Parliament can amend the Constitution but not emasculate some ethereal thing called its 'Basic Structure', Parliament will not know what the contours are within which it can legislate, the Government argued then, and has argued ever so often since. 'It was strenuously urged on behalf of the Union and the States,' the Judges recorded in *Kesavananda Bharati*, 'that if we come to the conclusion that there are implied or inherent limitations on the amending power of Parliament under Article 368, it would be well nigh impossible for Parliament to decide beforehand as to what amendments it could make and what amendments it is forbidden to make.' 'According to the Counsel for the Union and the States,' the Court noted, 'the conceptions of basic elements and fundamental features are illusive conceptions and their determination may differ from judge to judge and therefore we would be making the task of Parliament impossible if we uphold the contention that there are implied or inherent limitations on the amending power under Article 368.'[1]

But the scheme of the Constitution is plain, the Judges showed at length. The Preamble sets out the kind of polity and society we are to build. The provisions that follow are devices by which that objective is to be obtained. The distinctive mark of our polity is to be that we are to secure socio-economic change while preserving the dignity and freedom of the individual and the democratic structure that the Constitution has set up.[2]

Is the concept too vague to be a guideline to legislatures? What about each of the objectives that are set out in the Preamble? the Judges inquired. Can the same charge not be hurled at them? Does that mean that they are of no consequence? Or that they also throw our legislatures into confusion? Recall the Preamble:

WE, THE PEOPLE OF INDIA, having solemnly resolved to constitute India into a SOVEREIGN SOCIALIST SECULAR DEMOCRATIC REPUBLIC and to secure to all its citizens:

---

[1] *Kesavananda Bharati v. State of Kerala*, (1973) 4 SCC 225, at 485.

[2] See, for instance, *Kesavananda Bharati v. State of Kerala*, 1973 (4) SCC 225, at 365, paras 283, 287; 427, para 533; 435 para 546; 454, para 581; 640, para 1161. Reiterated often: for instance, *Minerva Mills v. Union of India*, (1980) 3 SCC 625, at 673 para 83; 645, para 27; 654 57, paras 56, 57, 62, 63.

JUSTICE, social, economic and political;
LIBERTY of thought, expression, belief, faith and worship;
EQUALITY of status and of opportunity;
and to promote among them all
FRATERNITY assuring the dignity of the individual and the unity and integrity of the Nation...

Socialist? Secular? Justice, social, economic and political? Liberty of thought, expression, belief and worship? Equality of status and opportunity? Fraternity? Dignity of the individual? Which of these is so specific as to not require further deliberation? Have not controversies attended the meaning that should be read into each of them? Are treatises, and law books and judgements not full of the different shades of meaning that can be read into each of these concepts and objectives? And the devices that can and cannot be deployed to attain them? Are they, therefore, to be erased? Or is it that, because these concepts are not the '4' that results from '2+2', they do not exist? 'It is not correct to say that what is difficult to decide does not exist at all,' the Supreme Court had pointed out.

Natural rights? In what sense are they more specific? In what sense are their contours more concrete?

What about the power that has been given to the State to put *'reasonable* restrictions' on Fundamental Rights enumerated in Article 19? Is what is 'reasonable' in a particular circumstance in regard to a particular right self-evident? Is the uncertainty lessened or compounded when the Constitution lays down further in the same Article that such reasonable restrictions as may be imposed must be, *inter alia*, in the interests of *'morality'* or *'public order'*? That they must be *'in the interests of the general public'*?

Do the legislatures know the precise limits to which they can delegate their power to legislate? Have the courts not had to strike down many a law on the ground that its provisions exceeded permissible limits of delegation? Does that mean that there are no limits to what the legislatures may delegate to bodies lower down, or that the limits need not be kept in mind? 'The position as regards the ascertainment of the basic elements or fundamental features of the Constitution can by no means be more difficult than the difficulty of the legislatures to determine beforehand the constitutionality of legislations made under various other heads,' the Supreme Court pointed out. And it zeroed in on to the real intent of such contrived apprehensions: 'Arguments based on the difficulties likely to be faced by the legislatures are of very little importance and *they are essentially arguments against judicial review.*'[1]

If Parliament's power is 'unlimited'

Judges pointed to the consequences that flow from assuming that Parliament has unlimited power to amend the Constitution. Indeed, they were led to spell these out in detail by a claim that the then Attorney General himself advanced before them on behalf of governments, both Central and state. 'According to the learned Attorney-General,' Justices J.M. Shelat and A.N. Grover noted, 'the declaration in the Preamble to our Constitution about the resolve of the people of India to constitute it into a sovereign democratic republic[2] *is only a declaration of an intention which was made in 1947 and it is open to the amending body now, under Article 368, to change the sovereign democratic republic into some other kind of polity.*' 'This by itself shows the consequence of accepting the construction sought to be put on the material words in that Article for finding out the ambit and width of the power conferred by it,' the Judges said, and, hence, that 'The Court cannot ignore the consequences to which a particular construction can lead while ascertaining the limits of the provisions granting the power.'[3]

The Court recalled that during the deliberations of the Constituent Assembly itself, Mr. H.V. Kamath had proposed an amendment which would in effect have reposed unlimited powers in Parliament to amend the Constitution. The amendment had been specifically rejected.[4] And for good reasons.

If the claim is accepted that there is no limit to the power to amend the Constitution, the Chief Justice, Justice S.M. Sikri noted, 'Article 368 can itself be amended to make the Constitution completely flexible or extremely rigid and unamendable. If this is so, a political

---

[1] *Kesavananda Bharati v. State of Kerala,* (1973) 4 SCC 225, at 485.
[2] That other word, equally vague, 'Socialist', was to be added during the Emergency and was still in the future.
[3] *Kesavananda Bharati v. State of Kerala,* (1973) 4 SCC 225, at 427.
[4] *Ibid,* at 415, para 499.

Notions

10

Lessons from liberals, for liberals

Through its judgement in *Kesavananda Bharati*, the Supreme Court constructed a dyke to shield the country and the citizen from the political class. By its dogged refusal, during the Emergency as well as later, to reopen the question of the Basic Structure, in the face of enormous pressures, the Court has safeguarded it. But the dyke has just about survived. The enthusiasms of individual judges for the causes that caught their fancy, the trusting natures of the simple and good among them, not to say, the fact that some outside the Judiciary reached high office precisely because they were eager to please those in authority—these and other factors have often brought the dyke perilously close to being breached.

As I have had occasion earlier to illustrate the legal legerdemain by which our jurisprudence has often played into the hands of the political class,[1] just a few examples will suffice to show that there *are* traits that we have to guard against.

The first source of danger

The first of these is the somewhat fitful adherence to the Basic Structure doctrine by the judges themselves. The most blatant instance, of course, occurred within just two years of the Court enunciating the doctrine—that is, during the Emergency. Freedom, Fundamental Rights, and all things good and noble having been declared to be inalienable elements of our Constitution, the Supreme Court had little difficulty in justifying the suppression of all these by the Executive. Yes, they are elements of the Basic Structure, the Court declared. But so are the Emergency provisions. Hence, when

---

[1] *Courts and their Judgements, Premises, prerequisites, consequences,* Rupa, Delhi, 2001; *Falling Over Backwards, An essay against reservations and against judicial populism,* ASA and Rupa, Delhi, 2006.

these provisions say that citizens shall not have the right to approach the courts for the enforcement of their freedoms and rights during an Emergency, that too is something that flows from the Basic Structure. Here is how one Judge put the matter in *ADM, Jabalpur:*

> ... We were asked to at least interpret the emergency provisions and the Act in such a way as to preserve what was represented to be the 'rule of law' as a part of the basic structure of the Constitution.
>
> It seems to me that the theory of a 'basic structure' of the Constitution cannot be used to build into the Constitution an imaginary part which may be in conflict with constitutional provisions. The Constitution cannot have a base cut away from the superstructure. Indeed, ... it seems to me that the emergency provisions could themselves be regarded as part of the basic structure of the Constitution. At any rate, they are meant to safeguard the basis of all orderly Government according to law.[1]

Another Judge was even more circumspect in applying the doctrine. The notion of the Basic Structure is to be a touchstone for amendments to the Constitution, not for ordinary laws, and this incarceration of people is not even an ordinary law, it is Executive action pure and simple. Where does the Basic Structure come in? That in ordinary times, the Executive must obey laws passed by the Legislature cannot be extended to times of Emergency. The Emergency provision also is a part of the Basic Structure. And, in any case, the provision enabling the Executive to impose an Emergency, does not provide that the Executive is free to disobey laws made by the Legislature. All it says is that citizens shall not have the right to approach the courts for relief in case the Executive—or the Legislature, for that matter—goes against the provisions of law or Constitution during an Emergency...[2]

But what about the Rule of Law? Haven't you declared repeatedly that it is a basic feature of the Constitution? Is the Government free to throw that also to the winds? The Court was unmoved:

> A facet of the same argument was presented on behalf of the respondents with even greater force. It was urged that Article 359(1) may remove fetters imposed by Part III [the part of the Constitution setting out Fundamental Rights] but it cannot ever remove the fetters arising from the principle of rule

---

[1] *ADM, Jabalpur v. Shivakant Shukla*, (1976) 2 SCC 521 at 640, paras 312-13.
[2] *Ibid*, at 657, paras 365-66.

of law or from the principle of the limited power of the Executive under a
system of checks and balances based on separation of powers...

That the rule of law must prevail in normal times is the rule of law under the
Indian Constitution. But it is necessary to clear a misconception. Even though
the compulsion to obey the law is compulsion of normal times, Article 358
takes in those cases only in which the Executive purports to act under the
authority of a law. It does not envisage that Executive can act without the
apparent authority of law. In other words, *Article 358 enables the Legislature
to make laws in violation of Article 19 and the Executive to act under these
laws, despite the fact that the laws constitute an infringement of the
fundamental rights conferred by Article 19...*

The 'rule of law' argument like the 'basic feature' argument is intractable.
Emergency provisions contained in Part 18 of the Constitution which are
designed to protect the security of the State are as important as any other
provision of the Constitution. If the true construction and effect of Article
359(1) is as I have stated it to be, it is impossible to hold that such a
construction violates the rule of law. The rule of law, during an emergency, is
as one finds it in the provisions contained in Chapter 18 of the Constitution.
There cannot be a brooding and omnipotent rule of law drowning in its
effervescence the emergency provisions of the Constitution.[1]

Grave constitutional consequences follow upon the proclamation of
Emergency, the Judge declares. Legislatures can make laws curbing
Fundamental Rights. The right to move courts for the enforcement of
any right can be suspended. The power of the Executive to give
directions to the states gets enlarged out of recognition. Parliament
gets power to make laws on matters included in the state list. In a
word, 'The democratic structure of the Constitution stands severely
eroded in such a situation.' Hence, declares the Judge,

If consequences so fundamentally subversive of the basic federal structure of
the Constitution can ensue during emergencies, *it is not as revolting as may
appear at first sight* that even if the Executive does not obey the mandate of
the Legislature, the citizen is powerless to move any court for the protection
of his fundamental rights, if these rights are mentioned in the Presidential
Order.[2]

Because something is 'not as revolting', it passes muster!

---

[1] *ADM, Jabalpur* v. *Shivakant Shukla*, (1976) 2 SCC 521, at 658-61, paras 368-75.
[2] *Ibid*, at 658, para 367.

The moment the people trounced the Emergency and threw out its perpetrators, that very doctrine of Basic Structure began working the other way—rather, that very approach of making light of it when doing so seems convenient, began working the other way! And, ever so often, it began doing so at the hands of the very same judges. 'Federalism', for instance, has often been listed as being a basic feature of the Constitution. And such is the respect for a crippling law that the Central Bureau of Investigation is not able to investigate the most violent of crimes, the most blatant acts of corruption without the permission of the state government. Were it to so much as lift a finger to do so, the courts would be certain to immobilize it. But when the Congress governments were dismissed in several states after the rout of Mrs. Indira Gandhi, the Supreme Court found good grounds to approve their dismissal—'federalism' did not come in the way. Democracy is a basic feature, the Court held; the essence of democracy is that people shall choose their legislatures; as events show that these legislatures have lost the confidence of the people, it cannot but be right that the Assemblies have been dissolved—thus went the reasoning. In a typical passage the Court declared,

> One purpose of our Constitution and laws is certainly to give electors a periodic opportunity of choosing their State's legislature and, thereby, of determining the character of their State's government also. It is the object of every democratic constitution to give such opportunities. Hence, *a policy devised to serve that end could not be contrary to the basic structure or scheme of the Constitution.* The question whether they should have that opportunity now or later may be a question of political expediency or executive policy. Can it be a question of legal right also unless there is a prohibition against the dissolution of a legislative assembly before a certain period has expired? If there had been a constitutional prohibition, so that the proposed action of the Union Government could have contravened that constitutional interdict, we would have been obliged to interfere, but, can we do so when there is no constitutional provision which gives the legislature of a State the right to continue undissolved despite certain supervening circumstances which *may, according to one view,* make its dissolution necessary?[1]

Similarly, while even elementary investigations into a Telgi-like scam would be barred by courts unless the state government, some of the controllers of which seem to figure in it, accorded permission;

---

[1] *State of Rajasthan v. Union of India,* (1977) 3 SCC 592 at 614, para 32.

while even to investigate heinous killings as in Nithari, the CBI would have to wait upon a state government to invite it to examine the crime; while the pursuit even of Naxalites and terrorists across state boundaries is hampered by the notion that federalism is a basic feature of the Constitution, when, the Emergency having been overthrown by the people, the Central Government set up a Commission of Inquiry to go into the allegations against the then Chief Minister of Karnataka, Devraj Urs, the Court made light of the federalism-is-basic-feature argument. Declaring that 'it is clear that whenever the doctrine of the basic structure has been expounded or applied it is only as a doctrine of interpretation of the Constitution as it actually exists and not of *a Constitution which could exist only subjectively in the minds of different individuals as mere theories about what the Constitution is,*' the Court held,

> the *so-called federalism* as a fetter on legislative power must find expression in some express provision to be recognised by Courts. It may be mentioned here that a majority of judges who decided the *Kesavananda Bharati* case have not treated 'federalism' as part of the basic structure of the Constitution. And, none of them has discussed the extent of the 'federal' part of this structure. It is not enough to point to Article 1 of the Constitution to emphasize that our Republic is a 'union' of States. That, no doubt is true. But, the word 'union' was used in the context of the peculiar character of our federal Republic revealed by its express provisions. We have still to find, from other express provisions, what this 'union' means or what is the extent or nature of 'federalism' implied by it. The Constitution itself does not use the word 'federation' at all.[1]

This dexterity—of detecting alternating principles— reminds us that, to have the Basic Structure wall shield us, we must shield it from the ingenuity of lawyers and judges!

Further sources of danger

The second danger to guard against is that on occasion judges have found the Basic Structure doctrine to be a good instrument for pushing their favourite hobby horses. The Preamble declares our aim is socialism, the Judge reasons. Socialism aims at economic and social egalitarianism. And these require a planned economy—'It would be necessary for both the efficient working of socialist enterprises and the prevention of unplanned and anarchical expansion of private

---

[1] *State of Karnataka v. Union of India*, (1977) 4 SCC 608 at 681, paras 128-29.

enterprises...' And therefore the nationalization of coal mines. And all this flows from the various streams that have contributed to our heritage, 'Buddhism, Jainism, Vedantic and Bhakti Hinduism, Sikhism, Islam, Christianity.'[1] Ever so often, like so many others, judges too have been carried away by their commitment, so to say, to these lofty goals, and made light of the banks within which the Constitution, and in particular the doctrine of Basic Structure, binds us to operate.

The third source of danger stems from the fact that, even among the judges who have had to reconcile themselves to the notion that the Constitution has a Basic Structure, two streams have continued to flow separately. One set of judges has held that such Basic Structure as is there must be related to specific provisions of the Constitution, that there is no structure 'floating, like a cloud in the skies, above the surface of the Constitution and outside it or one that lies buried beneath the surface for which we have to dig in order to discover it.'[2] The other set has held that there *is* indeed a Structure that arches over the specific provisions, that there *are* elements that link the separate provisions and parts of the Constitution, that give coherence to the Constitution as a whole.[3] An Executive, or indeed a Legislature

---

[1] *Samatha v. State of Andhra Pradesh*, (1997) 8 SCC 191, at 248, 262, 264, paras 79, 102, 103, 106.

[2] *State of Karnataka v. Union of India*, (1977) 4 SCC 608 at 677, para 120.

[3] As in the following: 'Therefore, it is important to note that the recognition of a basic structure in the context of amendment provides an insight that *there are, beyond the words of particular provisions, systemic principles underlying and connecting the provisions of the Constitution. These principles give coherence to the Constitution and make it an organic whole. These principles are part of constitutional law even if they are not expressly stated in the form of rules.* An instance is the principle of reasonableness which connects Articles 14, 19 and 21. Some of these principles may be so important and fundamental, as to qualify as 'essential features' or part of the 'basic structure' of the Constitution, that is to say, they are not open to amendment. However, it is only by linking provisions to such overarching principles that one would be able to distinguish essential from less essential features of the Constitution. The point which is important to be noted is that principles of federalism, secularism, reasonableness and socialism, etc. *are beyond the words of a particular provision.* They are systemic and structural principles underlying and connecting various provisions of the Constitution. They give coherence to the Constitution. They make the Constitution an organic whole. They are part of constitutional law even if they are not expressly stated in the form of rules.' *M. Nagaraj v. Union of India*, (2006) 8 SCC 212, at 243, paras 23-24.

that wanted to ride roughshod over the confines of Basic Structure would have little difficulty in deploying the former set of pronouncements to whittle down the Basic Structure to a toothless conception.

The fourth danger is even greater—for there has been a continuous stream of judges, all of them happen to have been hailed as progressives, who have scoffed at the very notion that the Constitution has a Basic Structure which cannot be violated. Justices A.N. Ray, K.K. Mathew, Chinnappa Reddy, and several of their acolytes have spent much wit to belittle the formulations of the Court in *Kesavananda, Minerva Mills*, and similar cases. The striking words and colourful imagery they have used—'vague', 'amorphous', 'indefinable', 'an exercise in imponderables'—can always be drummed up by those who will trample away the doctrine. On occasion, even those who after the Emergency had been overthrown spoke up conspicuously for liberty, and became famous for reading more and more facets of liberty into Articles of the Constitution, have thought fit to make elaborate statements in their judgements which can be grist to predators.

Several instances can be recalled. We can begin with *Kesavananda Bharati* itself. Justice Y.V. Chandrachud chose to preface his judgement with observations that were to be soon hurled back at him. He had wanted to avoid writing a separate judgement, he began. But, alas, the choice 'seems no longer open'. 'We sat in full strength of 13 to hear the case,' he noted. He had hoped that he would be able to share the views of colleagues 'after a free and frank exchange of thoughts.' But they had been overtaken by 'adventitious circumstances,' he continued. Counsel had taken so much time that little time had been left for exchanging views. 'And the time factor threatened at one stage to assume proportions as grave as the issues arising in the case,' he wrote. The Chief Justice was to retire, hence in the end there had been no time for views to be exchanged or even for draft judgements to be circulated...[1] A most worrisome observation—for it showed that judicial conventions had somehow been cast aside—'only "adventitiously"?,' those interested in doing down the judgement would insinuate.

---

[1]*Kesavananda Bharati, op. cit.,* at 959-60, para 1997.

A few years passed. Justice Chandrachud had by now become the Chief Justice. He was the one presiding over the *Minerva Mills* case. Tensions—subliminal if not subterranean, of course—between him and Justice P.N. Bhagwati were the talk of the Bar, and beyond. When it came time to deliver the judgement, Justice Bhagwati flung the very same passage at Justice Chandrachud—and added much spice of his own. Arguments in the case had gone on for three weeks, Justice Bhagwati pointed out. They had commenced on October 22, 1979 and ended on November 16, 1979. He had hoped, he said, that 'after the completion of the arguments on questions of such momentous significance, there would be'—Justice Chandrachud's expression—'a "free and frank exchange of thoughts" in a judicial conference either before or after the draft judgment was circulated by My Lord the Chief Justice.' This would have enabled him either to share the views of his colleagues, the Judge said, or to persuade them to his views. 'But,' Justice Bhagwati said, 'I find myself in the same predicament in which the learned Chief Justice found himself in *Kesavananda Bharati v. State of Kerala,*' and he quoted the passage we have just encountered. As in *Kesavananda,* so in this case, 'so much time was taken up by counsel to explain their respective points of view that very little time was left to the judges "after the conclusion of the arguments, for exchange of draft judgments".' 'Here also, I am compelled by similar circumstances'—and here Justice Bhagwati added—'*though not adventitious,* to hand down a separate opinion...' 'Somehow or other,' the Judge wrote, adding a possible explanation only to slight it, 'perhaps owing to extraordinary pressure of work with which this Court is overburdened, no judicial conference or discussion was held nor was any draft judgment circulated which could form the basis of discussion, though, as pointed out above, the hearing of the arguments concluded as far back as November 16, 1979.'

Months had passed. There had been no news. 'It was only on May 7, 1980, just two days before the closing of the court for the summer vacation, that I was informed by the learned Chief Justice that he and the other three learned Judges, who had heard this case along with me, had decided to pass an order declaring the impugned constitutional amendments *ultra vires* and void on the ground that they violated the basic features of the Constitution and that the reasons for this Order would be given by them later.' 'I found it difficult to persuade myself to adopt this procedure, because there had been no judicial conference or discussion amongst the judges where there could be free and frank exchange of views nor was any draft judgment circulated and hence I did not have the benefit of knowing the reasons why the learned Chief Justice and the other three learned Judges were inclined to strike down the constitutional amendments.' Had there been a judicial conference or discussion or had a draft judgment setting out the reasons for striking down the constitutional amendments been circulated, the Judge said he could either have 'as a result of full and frank discussion or after considering the reasons given in the draft judgment,' either agreed with what 'My Lord the Chief Justice and the other three learned Judges' had concluded, or persuaded them to change their view and agree with his.

And he proceeded to cast doubts at the way the Court had been made to function—obviously by the Chef Justice. 'That is the essence of judicial collectivism,' Justice Bhagwati noted, nailing what in his view the Chief Justice and his colleagues had violated. 'It is, to my mind, essential that a judgment of a court should be the result of collective deliberation of the judges composing the court and it would, in my humble opinion, not be in consonance with collective decision-making, if one or more of the judges constituting the Bench proceed to say that they will express their individual opinion, ignoring their colleagues and without discussing the reasons with them and even without circulating their draft judgment so that the colleagues have no opportunity of participating in the collective decision-making process'—stating in effect that the Chief Justice and others on the Bench had ignored and slighted a colleague. And more: 'This would introduce a chaotic situation in the judicial process and it would be an unhealthy precedent which this Court as the highest Court in the land—as a model judicial institution which is expected to set the tone for the entire judiciary in the country—should not encourage'—a more direct charge of mismanagement, of setting a wrong precedent and a bad example could scarcely be made.

And matters were made worse by the fact that his colleagues had chosen to pronounce an order striking down constitutional amendments of all things,. and declaring that they would give the ·

reasons later. True there are exceptional circumstances when an order is given and the reasons are put out later. But those are very special circumstances, the Judge elaborated—where the case involves the liberty of the citizen or the execution of a death sentence or where the time taken in preparing a reasoned judgment might prejudicially affect the winning party. In such circumstances of urgency and irremediable injury is such a procedure adopted—that of departing 'from the legally sanctioned course'. But what was the position here? 'The court had in fact waited for about 5 months after the conclusion of the arguments and there was clearly no urgency which required that an order should be made though reasons were not ready... The delay of about 2 months in making the order was not going to injure the interests of any party... there would have been no prejudice to the interests of justice if the order had been made on the reopening of the court after the summer vacation supported by a reasoned judgment.' It is for these reasons that he had recorded that he would 'prefer to pass a final order in this case when I deliver my reasoned judgment.' But this 'unfortunately led to considerable misunderstanding of my position' and that is why he was now explaining 'my conduct', the Judge said.[1]

The Judge himself has shown that this judgement was not properly considered, the lackeys were soon to proclaim. Accordingly, it must be reviewed...

The same sequence was enacted in *Tulsiram Patel*. Here an important judgement that had held the ground for ten years was in question, as were important points of constitutional and administrative law. The majority had come to one view—it entailed overruling that judgement. Justice M.P. Thakkar was of a different opinion. He did not just state that. No meeting has been held, he said. There has been no 'give and take of ideas' 'with due respect for the holders of the opposite point of view in a true democratic spirit of tolerance'—that is, his colleagues were being undemocratic, that they were lacking in tolerance and respect for him. Such an exchange would not have injured the cause of justice, it may have enabled one side to persuade the other. Justice Madon—he is the one who had written the majority judgement—'also appears to suffer

---

[1] *Minerva Mills Ltd. V. Union of India*, (1980) 3 SCC 625 at 664, para 78.

heartache on the same score', Justice Thakkar let fly, and proceeded to pluck a sentence from the covering letter that Justice Madon had attached to his draft judgement. Far from a dialogue, the draft judgement of 237 pages had been sent to him just three hours before the deadline by which the final judgement just *had* to be delivered, Justice Thakkar disclosed—the Chief Justice was retiring that day, and, if the judgement was not delivered, the hours of 'judge-time' that had been invested would have gone waste... Hence, his dissent...[1]

Bent on mischief, even schoolboys would need no more...

In a word, we have a dyke. But it also needs to be safeguarded—not the least from judges committed to—how should one put it?—better working of courts, and 'progressive' agendas.

Progressives

For the commitment of progressive judges to their own agenda often becomes a handy instrument for the rulers. Determined to sanction a step that was taken to be progressive, we have a Judge, who in other cases is quite punctilious about precedents, proclaim, 'The power of judicial review to strike at excess or *mala fides* is always there for vigilant exercise untrammeled by the narrow precedents of Victorian vintage...' He is as impatient with the dyke as the sovereignty-mongers:

> The question of basic structure being breached cannot arise when we examine the *vires* of an ordinary legislation as distinguished from a constitutional amendment. *Kesavananda Bharati* cannot be *the last refuge of the proprietariat* when benign legislation takes away their 'excess' for societal weal. Nor, indeed, can every breach of equality spell disaster as a lethal violation of the basic structure. Peripheral inequality is inevitable when large-scale equalisation processes are put into action. If all the judges of the Supreme Court in solemn session sit and deliberate for half a year to produce a legislation for reducing glaring economic inequality, their genius will let them down if the essay is to avoid even peripheral inequalities. Every large cause claims some martyr, as sociologists well know. Therefore, what is a betrayal of the basic feature is not a mere violation of Article 14 but *a shocking, unconscionable or unscrupulous travesty* of the quintessence of equal justice. If a legislation does go that far it shakes the democratic foundation and

---

[1] *Union of India v. Tulsiram Patel*, (1985) 3 SCC 398, at 526, paras 178–79.

must suffer the death penalty. But to permit the *Bharati ghost* to haunt the corridors of the court brandishing fatal writs for every feature of inequality is judicial paralysation of parliamentary function. Nor can the constitutional fascination for the basic structure doctrine be made a *trojan horse* to penetrate the entire legislative camp fighting for a new social order and to overpower the battle for abolition of basic poverty by the 'basic structure' missile. Which is more basic? Eradication of die-hard, deadly and pervasive penury degrading all human rights or upholding of the *legal luxury of perfect symmetry and absolute equality* attractively presented to preserve the *status quo ante?* To use the Constitution to defeat the Constitution cannot find favour with the judiciary!...[1]

How very serviceable such pronouncements are to those who would blow up the dyke! The judgement in *Kesavananda Bharati* becomes a 'ghost'. Concern that it be adhered to becomes a 'Trojan horse'. The one relying on it comes to be acting on behalf of the 'proprietariat'. The one whose rights are being trampled becomes a 'martyr' to the 'large cause'. The infraction falls short of being the 'shocking, unconscionable or unscrupulous travesty' that alone shall concern the committed Judge. The ones who show up the injustices that are being heaped turn out to be indulging in 'the legal luxury of perfect symmety and absolute equality' to 'preserve the *status quo ante*'...

The same sort of assistance has been provided by the fine distinctions that have been crafted along the way—between ordinary law and constitutional amendments, between legislative power and constituent power. Ordinary laws are not to be struck down on the ground that they violate the Basic Structure of the Constitution, the Supreme Court has ruled in many a case. Only constitutional amendments are to be tested on this touchstone. What about the prohibition in Article 13(2) that 'The State shall not make any law which takes away or abridges the rights conferred by this Part [that is, Part III which lists Fundamental Rights] and any law made in contravention of this clause shall, to the extent of such inconsistency, be void'? The Court crafts a helpful distinction! 'Although "law" must

---

[1]Justice V.R. Krishna Iyer in *Bhim Singhji v. Union of India*, (1981) 1 SCC 166, at 185-86, paras 18–20. For several examples of this kind, see *Falling Over Backwards, An essay against reservations and judicial populism*, ASA, New Delhi, 2006.

ordinarily include constitutional law,' the Supreme Court declares, 'there is a clear distinction between ordinary law, which is made in exercise of legislative power, and constitutional law, which is made in exercise of constituent power...' As Mr. Seervai was to point out later, in the hands of creative and progressive parliamentarians such a distinction would come to mean that, when they could not amend the Constitution in the way they wanted as the proposed change would patently injure the Basic Structure, they could just pass an ordinary law, put it in the IXth Schedule, and thus achieve their goal of amputating what was inconvenient in the Basic Structure.[1]

On top of all this, comes another debility. Ever so often, the judges have stated the general principle in ringing prose, but refrained from applying it to the case before them. Determined to strike, but afraid to wound! That in the end, the Judiciary will exercise this judicious restraint has not been lost on the politicians. On occasion, the judges have been even more helpful—detecting distinctions that would have eluded the less learned politicians. A single example will do. As more and more laws were being shoved into Schedule IX, it was pointed out to the Court that, apart from the motivations behind many of those laws being put in Schedule IX and the consequence—for instance, the axe it put to Fundamental Rights—this practice was curtailing a basic feature of the Constitution, namely, judicial review. Indeed, even if one proceeds on that distinction between ordinary laws and constitutional amendments, it so happens that the Constitution had been amended and Articles 31A and 31B inserted. These put a slew of laws beyond the reach of courts, it was pointed out, by providing that they just cannot be called in question for being inconsistent with or taking away Fundamental Rights. The Supreme Court did Jesuitism proud! It is not correct to say that the powers of courts to issue writs and hear appeals for the enforcement of Fundamental Rights in such cases have been curtailed, it said. 'They remain just the same as they were before: only a certain class of cases has been excluded from the purview of Part III and the courts could no longer interfere, *not because their powers were curtailed in any manner or to any extent, but because, there would be no occasion*

---

[1]H.M. Seervai, *Constitutional Law of India*, Tripathi, Bombay, 1996, Volume III, pp.3150–51.

for the exercise of their power in such cases.[1] This line of 'reasoning' was often invoked by governments, and naturally so—after all, it was reiterated several times by the Supreme Court itself. Do we not read in *Sajjan Singh*, '...The fact that the courts could not exercise their powers in respect of the said class of cases, did not show that the powers of the courts were curtailed in any way or to any extent. It only meant that certain area of cases in which the said powers could have been exercised, had been withdrawn...'[2]

How serviceable such fine distinctions have been to the Executive will be evident from the very sequence that we have considered earlier. Compare the passages cited in the preceding paragraph with the justifications that were advanced for trampling upon the Judiciary in the 42nd Amendment. 'How?,' Gokhale demanded, how has the Judiciary been affected? 'No provision in the present amendment has affected the status, the position, the dignity, the independence of the Judiciary,' Gokhale declared. 'The mere fact that by a provision you re-allocate or distribute matters in which jurisdiction or powers will be exercised certainly does not take away the independence of the Judiciary or its dignity or status.' And again, 'We know... the power of the court, the jurisdiction of the court, is not taken away *in matters which really, truly, belong to* the sphere of a judicial decision... on all basic and important matters and *in matters which can legitimately be said to belong to their area*, on all those matters, the Judiciary is yet entitled to adjudicate as against an Executive action or against judicial or quasi-judicial action...'[3]

Such examples can be multiplied. But for our present concern, two attitudes are even more consequential. The peril they put the country to is what we should burn into our minds: the very judgements we have encountered illustrate these.

Perilous trust

Viewed narrowly, the question in *Kesavananda* concerned the right to property. At the time, the right to property was also among the Fundamental Rights that had been guaranteed in Part III of the

---

[1] *Sankari Prasad Singh Deo v. Union of India*, 1952 SCR 89.
[2] *Sajjan Singh v. State of Rajasthan*, (1965) 1 SCR 933.
[3] In the Lok Sabha, 25 and 28 October, 1976.

party with a two-third majority in Parliament for a [period of] four years could so amend the Constitution as to debar any other party from functioning, establish totalitarianism, enslave the people, and, after having effected those purposes, make the Constitution unamendable or extremely rigid.'[1]

It could scrap Article 32, take away the right of the people to turn to the courts for enforcement of their rights, and thus destroy what Dr. Ambedkar had characterized as the very heart and soul of the Constitution.[2]

Parliament could so amend the Constitution as to do away with Part III or IV, scrapping or rendering toothless Fundamental Rights and Directive Principles. It could snatch away powers that have been given to states, and thereby destroy the federal structure that the Constitution has set up, the Judges said.[3]

Parliament could appropriate judicial functions to itself, destroying the separation of functions and powers that is enshrined in the Constitution, the Judges said.[4] Does that sound too far-fetched? But, as we have seen, that is exactly what the Parliament did in the 39th Amendment by appropriating for Parliament the power to decide on the validity of the election of the one in whose grip it was, namely the Prime Minister, and it did so *within just two years* of the Judges

---

[1] *Kesavananda Bharati v. State of Kerala,* (1973) 4 SCC 225, at 365, para 285.

[2] Ambedkar had made light of the fact that the Objectives Resolution had enumerated rights, saying that these had already become 'part and parcel of the mental make up of modern man in every civilized part of the world.' The problem is that the Resolution does not list remedies, he said. 'All of us are aware of the fact that rights are nothing unless remedies are provided whereby people can seek to obtain redress when rights are invaded.' That is why when he was commending what is today Article 32, he told the Constituent Assembly that it was 'an Article without which this Constitution would be a nullity...' If he were asked to name just one Article which was the most important, he said, 'I could not refer to any other Article except this one. It is the very soul of the Constitution and the very heart of it, and I am glad the House has realized its importance... It is remedy that makes a right real. If there is no remedy, there is no right at all...' If only leaders who trade in Ambedkar's name day in and day out, among them the very ones who crushed this and other remedies during the Emergency, read what he had said and written! *Constituent Assembly Debates,* Volume VII, p. 953. See also, *Kesavananda Bharati v. State of Kerala,* (1973) 4 SCC 225, at 639–40, para 1161.

[3] *Ibid,* at 406, para 481.

[4] *Ibid,* at 415, para 499.

having apprehended that claims to unlimited powers to amend the Constitution could result in such changes.[1]

Parliament could outlaw the practice of any religion, and make that of another religion mandatory.[2]

Parliament could amend Articles 85 and 172 of the Constitution decreeing that its life shall not be five years but fifty,[3] something it soon did, mercifully to six not fifty years!

The ruling party or combination could have Parliament legislate that the election of candidates belonging to parties opposed to it shall be void, and that the election of its own candidates, or that of its leader, would never be called in question.[4]

A typical passage in these judgements alerts us to what was already being claimed on behalf of Government. It records for us the sort of 'arguments' on which absolute power was being claimed. At this distance in time, it shows how prescient the Judges were. Even more important, it reminds us how necessary it is to look far ahead. Recording what the Attorney-General and Advocates General had submitted before them, and spelling out what these submissions portended, Justices K.S. Hegde and A.K. Mukherjea observed,

> According to the Union and the States that power *inter alia*, includes the power to: (1) destroy the sovereignty of this country and make this country a satellite of any other country; (2) substitute the democratic form of Government by monarchical or authoritarian form of Government; (3) break up the unity of this country and form various independent States; (4) destroy the secular character of this country and substitute the same by a theocratic form of Government; (5) abrogate completely the various rights conferred on the citizens as well as on the minorities; (6) revoke the mandate given to the State to build a Welfare State; (7) extend the life of the two Houses of Parliament indefinitely; and (8) amend the amending power in such a way as to make the Constitution legally or at any rate practically unamendable.

---

[1]This appropriation of judicial power was one of the main grounds on which the Constitution Bench that heard Mrs. Gandhi's election case—it consisted of the five senior-most Judges of the Court, including the hand-picked Chief Justice A.N. Ray—unanimously struck down the 39th Amendment. *c.f., Indira Nehru Gandhi v. Raj Narain*, (1975) Supp SCC 1.

[2]*Kesavananda Bharati v. State of Kerala, op. cit.*, at 430, para 535.

[3]*Ibid*, 766, para 1423.

[4]*Indira Nehru Gandhi v. Raj Narain*, (1975) Supp SCC 1, at 36, para 22.

'In fact, their contention was that *the legal sovereignty, in the ultimate analysis rests only in the amending power,*' the Judges noted— exactly the sort of assertion which the sovereign parliamentarians advanced during the debates on the 39th and 42nd Amendments. 'At one stage, Counsel for the Union and the States had grudgingly conceded that the power conferred under Article 368 cannot be used to abrogate the Constitution,' the Judges noted, adding, 'but later under pressure of questioning by some of us they changed their position and said that by "abrogation" they meant repeal of the Constitution as a whole. When they were asked as to what they meant by saying that the power conferred under Article 368 cannot be used to repeal the Constitution, all that they said was that while amending the Constitution, *at least one clause in the Constitution must be retained* though every other clause or part of the Constitution including the Preamble can be deleted and some other provisions substituted. Their submission in short was this that so long as the expression the "Constitution of India" is retained, every other Article or part of it can be replaced.'

The Judges were then given the practical argument, one that we shall soon encounter when we turn to another lesson that such sequences throw up. 'They [the Attorney-General and Advocates General appearing for the Government of India and the states] tried to tone down the effect of their claim by saying that, though legally, there is no limitation on the amending power, there are bound to be political compulsions which make it impermissible for Parliament to exercise its amending power in a manner unacceptable to the people at large'—in which direction did the 'political compulsions' push Parliament within just two years of such advocacy? How perceptive the Judges were when, in making short shrift of such argumentation, they remarked, 'The strength of political reaction is uncertain. It depends upon various factors such as the political consciousness of the people, their level of education, strength of the various political organizations in the country, the manner in which the mass media is used and finally the capacity of the Government to suppress agitations. Hence the peoples' will to resist an unwanted amendment cannot be taken into consideration in interpreting the ambit of the amending power. Extra legal forces work in a different plane altogether.'[1]

Adverting to the submissions that had been made by Mr. N.A. Palkhivala against the claims advanced by the Government, Justices J.M. Shelat and A.N. Grover put the matter in words that deserve to be memorized. They wrote, 'According to Mr. Palkhivala, the test of the true width of a power is not how probable it is that it may be exercised but what can possibly be done under it; that the abuse or misuse of power is entirely irrelevant; that the question of the extent of the power cannot be mixed up with the question of its exercise and that when the real question is as to the width of the power, expectation that it will never be used is as wholly irrelevant as an imminent danger of its use. The court does not decide what is the best and what is the worst. It merely decides what can possibly be done under a power if the words conferring it are so construed as to have an unbounded and limitless width, as claimed on behalf of the respondents.'[2]

Another assertion nailed

But, as the Preamble itself makes plain, the people have given themselves this Constitution. Therefore, they have the fullest power to alter or replace it. They act through the Parliament. Therefore, Parliament has the fullest power to alter any and every part of it to any and every extent. That was the line of 'reasoning' that was advanced on behalf of the Government—exactly the 'argument' that, as we have seen, was soon to be deployed to ram the 39th and 42nd Amendments through.

Chief Justice Sikri pointed to the Preamble itself, and where it had located that much-flaunted sovereignty. Debunking the inferences that were sought to be drawn from Article 5 of the U.S. Constitution, he gave two reasons on account of which the claim was untenable: 'Where there is a written Constitution which adopts the preamble of sovereignty in the people there is, firstly, no question of the law-making body being a sovereign body, for that body possesses only those powers which are conferred on it. Secondly, however

---

[1]*Kesavananda Bharati v. State of Kerala,* (1973) 4 SCC 225, at 479–80, para 650.
[2]*Kesavananda Bharati v. State of Kerala,* (1973) 4 SCC 225, at 427, para 531.

representative it may be, it cannot be equated with the people. This is especially so where the Constitution contains a Bill of Rights, for such a bill imposes restraints on that body, i.e. it negates the equation of that body with the people.'[1]

'We find it difficult to accept the contention that our Constitution-makers after making immense sacrifices for achieving certain ideals made provision in the Constitution itself for the destruction of those ideals,' Justices K.S. Hegde and A.K. Mukherjea pointed out; '...one cannot legally use the Constitution to destroy itself.' In a passage that has a direct bearing on the question that concerns us—that is, whether transiting to a somewhat different constitutional System will run into the Basic Structure dyke—they spelled out the contours within which the Constitution may be changed: 'Under Article 368 the amended Constitution must remain "the Constitution" which means the original Constitution,' they wrote. 'When we speak of the "abrogation" or "repeal" of the Constitution, we do not refer to any form but to substance. If one or more of the basic features of the Constitution are taken away to that extent the Constitution is abrogated or repealed. If all the basic features of the Constitution are repealed and some other provisions inconsistent with those features are incorporated, it cannot still remain the Constitution referred to in Article 368. The personality of the Constitution must remain unchanged.'

Making a sharp distinction between the people and Parliament, they emphasized that Article 368 places power to amend the Constitution in Parliament 'a body constituted *under* the Constitution.' 'The people as such are not associated with the amendment of the Constitution.' And this has immediate implications both in law and fact, they showed. First, 'When a power to amend the Constitution is given to the people, its contents can be construed to be larger than when that power is given to a body constituted under that Constitution.' Second, there is the inescapable point of fact: 'Two-thirds of the members of the two Houses of Parliament need not necessarily represent even the majority of the people of this country. Our electoral system is such that even a minority of voters can elect more than two-thirds of the members of the either House of

---

[1]*Kesavananda Bharati v. State of Kerala*, (1973) 4 SCC 225, at 432, para 540.

Parliament. That is seen from our experience in the past.' Third, 'our
Constitution was framed on the basis of consensus and not on the
basis of majority votes. It provides for the protection of the
minorities. If the majority opinion is taken as the guiding factor then
the guarantees given to the minorities may become valueless...
Therefore the contention on behalf of the Union and the states that
the two-thirds of the members in the two Houses of Parliament are
always authorised to speak on behalf of the entire people of this
country is unacceptable.'[1]

Indeed, were amendments to be passed that emasculated the
Basic Structure of the Constitution, and the President were to sign his
approval of those amendments, he would be violating the oath he
took upon entering office, the Judges reminded all concerned. For
when he enters office, the President takes the oath to 'preserve,
protect and defend the Constitution.' 'Does the oath merely mean
that he is to defend the amending power of Parliament?' the Judges
asked. 'Can the amending power of Parliament be considered as the
Constitution?'

The distance between the people and the Parliament is stretched
further by the nature of our political system, the Judges pointed out.
First there are the elections: parties go to the electorate with a
complex bundle of messages and promises. Even if a party were to
win two-thirds of the seats, it cannot claim that it has been given a
mandate by the people to alter the Constitution out of shape.
Furthermore, parliamentary democracy functions on the basis of the
party system. 'The mechanics of operation of the party system as
well as the system of Cabinet Government are such that the people
as a whole can have little control in the matter of detailed law-
making' the Judges remarked.

They had already stressed that a party or combination could get a
two-thirds majority in Parliament with a minority of votes and how
this fact by itself demonstrated that Parliament could scarcely be
equated with the people. They noted that in fact the distance was
greater: 'Indeed, it may be possible for the ruling party to carry
through important constitutional amendments even after it has lost

---

[1] *Kesavananda Bharati v. State of Kerala*, (1973) 4 SCC 225, at 480–81, paras
651–54.

the confidence of the electorate. The members of Lok Sabha are elected for a term of five years. The ruling party or its members may or may not enjoy the confidence of the electorate throughout their term of office. Therefore, it will not be correct to say that whenever Parliament amends the Constitution, it must be held to have done it as desired by the people.'

'There is a further fallacy in the contention that whenever Constitution is amended, we should presume that the amendment in question was made in order to adapt the Constitution to respond to the growing needs of the people,' they pointed out. Parliament is said to derive its authority from the people. But by using its amending power, it can prolong its life and thereby postpone having to go back to the people: '...it is theoretically possible for Parliament to extend its own life indefinitely and also, to amend the Constitution in such a manner as to make it either legally or practically unamendable ever afterwards. A power which is capable of being used against the people themselves cannot be considered as a power exercised on behalf of the people or in their interest.'[1] A mere two years had not to pass, and we were reminded how perceptive this apprehension had been. Under Mrs. Gandhi's thumb, Parliament in fact extended its life, and, during that after-life existence, passed the 42nd Amendment.

A vital limitation

By such reasoning, the Supreme Court has repeatedly held

❏ Parliament has the power to amend provisions of the Constitution;
❏ But it cannot emasculate its Basic Structure;
❏ Among the elements that constitute the Basic Structure is the fact that the power which is conferred by Article 368 to amend the Constitution is a limited power.

The last element has an immediate corollary. It had to be spelt out by the Supreme Court in relation to the provision that had been included in the 42nd Amendment in order to circumvent what had been laid

---

[1]*Kesavananda Bharati v. State of Kerala,* (1973) 4 SCC 225, at 485–86, paras 663–65.

down in *Kesavananda*. In subsequent cases, the Court has specified that the power to amend the Constitution which Article 368 confers cannot be used to make that power an unlimited one. Justice Y.V. Chandrachud put the point precisely in *Minerva Mills* when he specified, 'Since the Constitution had conferred a limited amending power on the Parliament, the Parliament cannot under the exercise of that limited power enlarge that very power into an absolute power. Indeed, a limited amending power is one of the basic features of our Constitution and, therefore, the limitations on that power cannot be destroyed. In other words, Parliament cannot, under Article 368, expand its amending power so as to acquire for itself the right to repeal or abrogate the Constitution or to destroy its basic and essential features. The donee of a limited power cannot by the exercise of that power convert the limited power into an unlimited one.' Even as he delivered a judgement many passages in which could be used, and were in fact sought to be used to cast doubt on aspects of *Kesavananda*, and thus demand yet again that it be reviewed, Justice P.N. Bhagwati also emphasized that the feature of having a power to amend which was limited was one of the Basic Features of the Constitution. And he gave an additional reason for the proposition. He said, 'Now, if by constitutional amendment, Parliament were granted unlimited power of amendment, it would cease to be an authority under the Constitution, but would become supreme over it, because it would have power to alter the entire Constitution including its basic structure and even to put an end to it by totally changing its identity. It will, therefore, be seen that the limited amending power of Parliament is itself an essential feature of the Constitution, a part of its basic structure, for if the limited power of amendment were enlarged into an unlimited power, the entire character of the Constitution would be changed. It must follow as a necessary corollary that any amendment of the Constitution which seeks, directly or indirectly, to enlarge the amending power of Parliament by freeing it from the limitation of unamendability of the basic structure would be violative of the basic structure and hence outside the amendatory power of Parliament.'[1]

---

[1]*Minerva Mills Ltd. v. Union of India,* (1980) 3 SCC 625, at 643, para 17; at 676–77, para 86.

What then are the Basic Features of the Constitution against which the proposals urged in a book of this sort must be assessed?

Basic Features

After a detailed exposition of the evolution of the salient provisions of the Constitution, and dealing at length with the citations that had been offered on behalf of the Government, Chief Justice Sikri observed,

> The learned Attorney-General said that every provision of the Constitution is essential; otherwise it would not have been put in the Constitution. This is true. But this does not place every provision of the Constitution in the same position. The true position is that every provision of the Constitution can be amended provided in the result the basic foundation and structure of the Constitution remains the same. The basic structure may be said to consist of the following features:
> (1) Supremacy of the Constitution;
> (2) Republican and Democratic form of Government;
> (3) Secular character of the Constitution;
> (4) Separation of powers between the Legislature, the Executive and the Judiciary;
> (5) Federal character of the Constitution.
> The above structure is built on the basic foundation, i.e. the dignity and freedom of the individual. This is of supreme importance. This cannot by any form of amendment be destroyed.
> The above foundation and the above basic features are easily discernible not only from the Preamble but the whole scheme of the Constitution...[1]

The features that Justices Shelat and Grover set out were more or less the same. Pointing to the historical background that had preceded the drafting of the Constitution, to the Preamble, to the entire scheme by which the provisions of the Constitution aim at realizing the noble objectives set out in the Preamble, including Article 368, and, while stating that they could not be catalogued, only illustrated, Justices Shelat and Grover listed the basic elements as follows:

(1) The supremacy of the Constitution.
(2) Republican and Democratic form of government and sovereignty of the country.
(3) Secular and federal character of the Constitution.

---

[1] *Kesavananda Bharati v. State of Kerala*, (1973) 4 SCC 225, at 366, paras 292–94.

(4) Demarcation of power between the Legislature, the Executive and the Judiciary.

(5) The dignity of the individual secured by the various freedoms and basic rights in Part III and the mandate to build a Welfare State contained in Part IV.

(6) The unity and the integrity of the Nation.[1]

Justices Hegde and Mukherjea placed emphasis on the Preamble, and the goals it had set. Reproducing the Preamble, recalling the Objectives Resolution that had preceded it, and the provisions in Parts III and IV of the Constitution, they held that the basic features were that India shall be a sovereign country; that our polity shall be democratic; that we will remain one, united country; that the freedoms which have been guaranteed to us as citizens shall remain in tact; and that the State shall strive to ensure the benefits of freedom to all as prescribed in the Directive Principles of State Policy.[2]

Justice A.N. Ray did not give any specific list of items that in his opinion constituted the Basic Structure. However, he reproduced the list of twelve items that Mr. N.A. Palkhivala had submitted during the course of arguments. This list was as follows:

Mr. Palkhivala enumerated 12 essential features. These were as follows: (1) The supremacy of the Constitution. (2) The sovereignty of India. (3) The integrity of the country. (4) The democratic way of life. (5) The republican form of Government. (6) The guarantee of basic human rights elaborated in Part III of the Constitution. (7) Secular State. (8) A free and independent Judiciary (9) The dual structure of the Union and the States. (10) The balance between the Legislature, the Executive and the Judiciary. (11) A Parliamentary form of Government as distinct from the Presidential form of Government. (12) Article 368 can be amended but cannot be amended to empower Parliament to alter or destroy any of the essential features of the Constitution, make the Constitution literally or practically unamendable, make it generally amendable by a bare majority in Parliament, confer the power of amendment either expressly or in effect on the State Legislatures and delete the proviso and deprive the States of the power of ratification which is today available to them in certain broad areas.[3]

---

[1]*Ibid*, at 454, para 582.
[2]*Ibid*, at 479, paras 647–48.
[3]*Ibid*, at 545, para 876.

It is in this list that we encounter 'a Parliamentary form of Government as distinct from a Presidential form of Government.'

Justice P. Jaganmohan Reddy addressed the question with greater specificity. Refuting the assertions of the Government's advocates that nothing in the Constitution was beyond the reach of the amendment power given by Article 368, and that what the basic elements or features were could not be determined with any certainty, he observed, 'The elements of the basic structure are indicated in the Preamble and translated in the various provisions of the Constitution. The edifice of our Constitution is built upon and stands on several props, remove any of them, the Constitution collapses. These are: (1) Sovereign Democratic Republic; (2) Justice, social, economic and political; (3) Liberty of thought, expression, belief, faith and worship; (4) Equality of status and of opportunity.' He proceeded to emphasize that 'Each one of these is important and collectively they assure a way of life to the people of India which the Constitution guarantees. To withdraw any of the above elements, the structure will not survive and it will not be the same Constitution, or this Constitution, nor can it maintain its identity if something quite different is substituted in its place, which the sovereign will of the people alone can do.' He gave telling illustrations: 'There can be a democratic republic in the sense that people may be given the right to vote for one party or only one candidate either affirmatively or negatively, and are not given the choice to choose another opposed to it or him. Such a republic is not what has been assured to our people and is unthinkable by any one foresworn to uphold, defend, protect or preserve or work the Constitution. A democratic republic that is envisaged is the one based on a representative system in which people holding opposing views to one another can be candidates and invite the electorate to vote for them. If this is the system which is the foundation of a democratic republic, it is unthinkable that it can exist without elements (2) to (4) above either collectively or separately. What is democracy without social, economic and political justice, or what value will it have, where its citizens have no liberty of thought, belief, faith or worship or where there is no equality of status and of opportunity?'

He said that what the essential features or the basic elements comprising the structure of our Constitution are, need not be considered in detail as these would fall for consideration in any concrete case where they are said to have been abrogated and made non-existent. But this does not invalidate the dyke, Justice Reddy pointed out: 'The fact that a complete list of these essential elements constituting the basic structure are [*sic.*] not enumerated, is no ground for denying that these exist. Are all the elements which make a law void and unconstitutional ever required to be concatenated for the recognition of the validity or invalidity of laws judged on the anvil of the Constitution?' And then comes the sentence that bears on our proposals: 'A sovereign democratic republic, parliamentary democracy, the three organs of the State, certainly in my view constitute the basic structure...' The passage proceeds to consider whether Fundamental Rights and the Directive Principles can be jettisoned and the Constitution be considered to remain the same.[1]

Justice H.R. Khanna did not give any particular list. But his exposition did emphasize the democratic form of government, the secular character of the State, access to courts and the power of the Judiciary to review laws, amendments to the Constitution, as well as Executive action.

We must now follow the two instances in which 'parliamentary democracy' gets mentioned: in Justice Ray's recounting of the list furnished by Mr. Palkhivala, and in Justice Reddys's enumeration. Do these come in the way of the sorts of proposals that have been mentioned above?

In the years that followed, emphasis came to vary from judgement to judgement as the focus of the case brought different particulars into prominence. On occasion, the expressions were a bit different from the ones that the Judges had used in *Kesavananda*, but just the expressions. There were, of course, disagreements over some aspects. Which Fundamental Rights can be curtailed? To what extent? Are ordinary laws also to be held to the test that they do not violate the Basic Structure or are only Constitutional Amendments to be held to this test? Are the objectives that are set out in the Preamble part of the Basic Structure, or are only the specific provisions of the Constitution, which aim at particularising those objectives, elements of the Basic Structure? Controversies have been endless, as Justice

---

[1] *Kesavananda Bharati v. State of Kerala,* (1973) 4 SCC 225, at 638, para 1159.

Chandrachud remarked in another context, and many a case has turned on the view that a judge has taken on these questions.

One reason the question will have to be settled

While the doctrine of the Basic Structure has gone through several vicissitudes, and has sometimes just about escaped being overturned, its architecture has remained intact. This has remained:

❑ The ideals and aims set out in the Preamble, as well as the elements that permeate different parts of the Constitution—separation of powers between the three wings of the State, judicial review, independent Judiciary, etc.—constitute the Basic Structure.

❑ The specific provisions are the means by which these ideals and aims are to be realized.

The sorts of changes that have been listed above are in harmony with this architecture. Indeed, they are necessary today for attaining the ideals that have been regarded as constituting the Basic Structure of our Constitution.

But there is one bubble on the surface. Most often, 'democracy' is what has been listed as being a basic feature. And occasionally there has been explicit recognition of the fact that the system that has been adopted is one possible variant of democracy, one possible set of means.[1]

But on occasion, what has been listed as a basic feature is 'parliamentary democracy'. The expression has come to be used in three distinct contexts:

❑ On occasion to affirm that this particular variant is what the Framers adopted—recall Justice V.R. Krishna Iyer's extended exposition in *Shamsher Singh v. State of Punjab* to the effect that

---

[1]Hence, for instance: 'Democracy is a basic feature of the Constitution. Whether any particular brand or system of government by itself, has this attribute of a basic feature, as long as the essential characteristics that entitle a system of government to be called democratic are otherwise satisfied is not necessary to be gone into...' *In the Matter of Special Reference Number 1 of 2002, (Gujarat Assembly Election Matter)*, (2002) 8 SCC 237, at 315, para 128.

'Not the Potomac, but the Thames, fertilizes the flow of the Yamuna...'[1]

❏ Most often as a synonym of 'democracy'.

❏ In considering the specific institution or function or power that was at issue.

Thus while holding that, for instance,

❏ The powers of the Governor are strictly limited;[2]

❏ Multi-party system is vital; hence, free and fair elections are vital; hence, secrecy of vote is vital; hence, the evil of cross-voting is to be curbed;[3]

❏ Free and fair elections are vital; hence, the rule of law and a system for resolution of election disputes are essential;[4]

❏ Legislators are immune from having the courts examine what they say or do in pursuance of their parliamentary duties within the Legislature;[5]

❏ An attack on Parliament House is an act of war against India;[6]

❏ As/free and fair elections are vital, voters have a right to know the antecedents of the candidates who are competing for their vote;[7]

❏ A person appointed minister cannot continue as minister unless he is elected to the legislature within six months;[8]

❏ The Legislature should have been consulted while settling reservations in the lower judiciary;[9]

❏ Defections must be curbed; in this context, the powers of the Speaker are...

while emphasizing these particular conclusions, the Court has in passing remarked that 'parliamentary democracy' is a basic feature.

---

[1](1974) 2 SCC 831.

[2]*Rameshwar Prasad (VI) v. Union of India*, (2006) 2 SCC 1.

[3]*Kuldip Nayar v. Union of India*, (2006) 7 SCC 1.

[4]*Kihoto Hollohan v. Zachilhu*, (1992) 1 SCC 309.

[5]*P.V. Narasimha Rao v. State* (1998) 4 SCC 626.

[6]*State (NCT of Delhi) v. Navjot Sandhu* (2005) 11 SCC 600.

[7]*People's Union for Civil Liberties v. Union of India*, (2003) 4 SCC 399.

[8]*S.R. Chaudhuri v. State of Punjab*, (2001) 7 SCC 126.

[9]*State of Bihar v. Bal Mukund Sah*, (2000) 4 SCC 640.

It is possible, of course, to argue that 'parliamentary democracy' came to be mentioned in such judgements incidentally—in the sense that, while arriving at one conclusion rather than the other in regard to the issue that was up for decision, the Court mentioned as a reason that ours is a 'parliamentary democracy'. But as the Court *has* mentioned on occasion that 'parliamentary democracy' is a basic feature, when changes of the kind that have been proposed are thought of, the question will have to be settled that

❏ Democracy is the basic feature;
❏ The system which the Constitution sets out is one possible variant of democracy;
❏ This particular variant has run aground;
❏ The one way to preserve the Basic Structure of the Constitution is to enact the kinds of changes that have been suggested.

Even a cursory glance at the sorts of changes which have been proposed shows that in no way do they fall afoul of the Basic Structure as it has been enunciated by the Court. Most of them do not transgress even 'parliamentary democracy' as it is set out in the Constitution. Two round elections so that whoever is elected has been endorsed by more than 50 per cent of the electorate? Compulsory voting? Larger, multi-member constituencies? Biometric software for Electronic Voting Machines? Simultaneous elections for all levels of government? Sharper qualifications and disqualifications for candidates? Automatic de-recognition of parties that nominate persons with criminal background as candidates? Strict enforcement of rules during proceedings of legislatures? Day-to-day hearings of cases involving persons in public life?... None of these in any way conflicts with the 'parliamentary system' as we know it today. Indeed, one and all of them can only fortify it.

Three proposals alone will require to be considered—direct election of the head of the Executive; permission to her or him to select ministers who are not members of the Legislature; and greater powers to the Judiciary than are envisaged at present to keep both the Executive and the Legislature accountable. These do fall outside the present arrangement, and, as 'parliamentary democracy' has been mentioned in the sorts of judgements we have been considering, the courts will indeed have to assess whether they violate the Basic Structure, or they are instead the one way to salvage that Structure.

But there are things even more basic than structures that we must heed: structures can be set at naught, the sturdiest dykes undermined by the attitudes of guardians. And the very judgements that we have been considering help pinpoint the lessons that are vital.[1]

---

[1] A brief note is in order about Mr. N.A. Palkhivala's list of basic features that Justice A.N. Ray reproduced, and which included 'parliamentary form of government'. Mr. Palkhivala's opposition at the time to the changes that were being sought to be made in the Constitution was not because the Parliamentary System was being replaced by a Presidential System, but because, under the guise of advancing the interests of the poor, etc. an authoritarian system was being smuggled in. Courts were to be made appendages of the Executive, for instance. Fundamental Rights were to be snuffed out forever. The changes had nothing to do with a Presidential System, and everything to do with institutionalizing a dictatorship. In subsequent years, Mr. Palkhivala himself had occasion to revisit the question of the constitutional structure by which we are best governed. He spelt out the advantages that a switch over to a Presidential System could secure for the country, adding the all-important caveat that there were many types of Presidential Systems, and that the one we adopt must necessarily be one that preserves our freedoms and the democratic way of life. See, *We, the People,* Strand Bookstall, Bombay, 1984, in particular Chapters 9, 10 and 13.

Constitution. Stripped of the many vital strands of which it consisted, the argument was:

❑ The right to property is a Fundamental Right;
❑ Fundamental Rights cannot be trampled upon;
❑ Hence, the right to property cannot be trampled upon.

In a sense, Justice H.R. Khanna was reacting to this line of argument. As is well known, he has been one of the most sagacious of the judges who have adorned the Supreme Court. The country will always be in his debt for the singular courage with which he stood up for the citizen and for liberty in the *habeas corpus* case during the Emergency. His judgement in *Kesavananda* holds an important lesson precisely for that reason: it shows how the liberal, how a good man can misplace trust.

Justice Khanna's basic view was that an individual's claims to property cannot be allowed to impede social justice and economic progress. And the ratio of his judgement was carefully circumscribed—Parliament has the power to amend every Article of the Constitution, including every Article dealing with Fundamental Rights, he ruled, but, while doing so, it must not emasculate the Basic Structure of the Constitution.[1] In that sense, his judgement helped fortify the dyke. But his formulations along the way gave perilous latitude to the sovereignty-mongers, and that is why they hold a vital lesson.

Had Fundamental Rights been unamendable, the Framers would have stated so explicitly through a proviso to Article 368, the Judge held.[2] The notion that there are implied restrictions cannot stand.[3] Nor can natural rights come in the way, even though they may be embodied in international treaties to which the country is a signatory.[4] These statements did not affect the pith of Justice Khanna's judgement, namely, that, while Parliament can amend every provision of the Constitution, including those relating to Fundamental Rights, it cannot violate the Constitution's Basic

---

[1]See, for instance, *Kesavananda Bharati v. State of Kerala*, (1973) 4 SCC 225, at 767, para 1426; 768, para 1430; 769, para 1434; 806, para 1508; 824, para 1537.

[2]*Ibid*, at 750, para 1383.

[3]*Ibid*, at 776–77, paras 1447–48

[4]*Ibid*, at 781, para 1456.

Structure. But the sovereignty-mongers began to put such constructions on passages in Justice Khanna's text that later he had to clarify what he had said; for instance, in *Indira Nehru Gandhi v. Raj Narain*. Others had to do so yet again in subsequent judgements—for instance, Justice Chandrachud in *Waman Rao v. Union of India*.[1]

But it was the trust that this good-hearted man placed in the Executive and the Legislature that holds an even sharper lesson. Writing in 1973, that is just two years before the country was to be plunged into the Emergency, Justice Khanna pointed to the special majorities that had to be mustered for amending the Constitution—two-thirds of members present and voting in each House separately; ratification by a majority of state Assemblies—and said that, 'Apart from the fact that the possibility of abuse of power is no ground for the denial of power if it is found to have been legally vested, I find that the power of amendment under Article 368 has been vested not in one individual but in the majority of the representatives of the people in Parliament...' But, as was soon to become evident, that majority may be at the beck and call of an individual. 'The fact that a prescribed majority of the people's representatives is required for bringing about the amendment is normally itself a guarantee that the power would not be abused,' the Judge reasoned. In any case, he said, 'The best safeguard against the abuse or extravagant use of power is public opinion and not a fetter on the right of people's representatives to change the Constitution by following the procedure laid down in the Constitution itself. It would not be a correct approach to start with a distrust in the people's representatives in the Parliament and to assume that majority of them would have an aversion for the liberties of the people and would act against the public interest.'

'Assuming that under the sway of some overwhelming impulse, a climate is creat꜠d wherein cherished values like liberty and freedom lose their significance in the eyes of the people and their representatives and they choose to do away with all fundamental rights by amendment of the Constitution, a restricted interpretation of Article 368 would not be of much avail,' Justice Khanna said. 'The

---

[1](1981) 2 SCC 362, at 381, para 16.

people in such an event would forfeit the claim to have fundamental rights'. But what of the situation when the people are nowhere in the reckoning, what of the situation when all this is done in their name by usurpers? The Judge did not pause to consider. Instead, continuing in that cadence of faith, he said, 'and in any case fundamental rights would not in such an event save the people from political enslavement, social stagnation or mental servitude,' and proceeded to rely on a quotation of Learned Hand...[1]

When the time came to summarize his verdict, Justice Khanna placed his reason in the lap of faith again: 'The possibility that power of amendment may be abused furnishes no ground for denial of its existence,' he declared. 'The best safeguard against abuse of power is public opinion and the good sense of the majority of the Members of Parliament. It is also not correct to assume that if Parliament is held entitled to amend Part III of the Constitution, it would automatically and necessarily result in abrogation of all fundamental rights.'[2] Do 'not automatically', and 'not necessarily' mean that it will not?

The Executive has been entrusted with a far greater power, the power to declare war, Justice Khanna noted. Exercise of that power can spell death for citizens, especially for those who are in the country's armed forces. If the Executive and Legislature can be entrusted with such an extreme power in the faith that the power will not be abused, why can we not entrust the much lesser power—to amend the Constitution—in the faith that this power will also not be misused? 'It is axiomatic that the involvement of a nation in war by a declaration of war against another country can change the entire course of history of the nation,' Justice Khanna wrote. 'A wrong decision in this respect can cause untold suffering, result in national humiliation, take toll of thousands of lives and cripple the economy of the nation for decades to come. If the Government and the Parliament can be entrusted with power of such far reaching magnitude on the assumption that such a power would not be abused but would be exercised reasonably in the national interest, it would seem rather anomalous to have an approach of distrust in those very organs of the State and to deny to the Parliament the power of

---

[1] *Ibid*, at 763, paras 1418–19.
[2] *Ibid*, at 823, para 1537.vi.

amendment of fundamental rights because of the supposed possibility of the abuse of such power.'[1] How stretched the analogy and the inference were soon to sound!

And then came the extrapolation from what had gone before. For seventeen years—till the Supreme Court's judgement in *Golak Nath*—the notion that Parliament has unlimited power to amend the Constitution held the field, Justice Khanna noted. That power was not misused. Why should we not trust that it will not be misused in the future? 'It is not, in my opinion, a correct approach to assume that if Parliament is held entitled to amend Part III of the Constitution so as to take away or abridge fundamental rights, it would automatically or necessarily result in the abrogation of all fundamental rights'— again, that reasoning: because we cannot assume that Parliament will 'automatically or necessarily' abrogate Fundamental Rights, therefore, we must assume that it will not. 'I may mention in this context that for seventeen years, from 1950 till 1967 when *Golak Nath case* was decided, the accepted position was that the Parliament had the power to amend Part III of the Constitution so as to take away or abridge fundamental rights. Despite the possession of that power by the Parliament, no attempt was made by it to take away or abridge fundamental rights relating to cherished values like liberty of person and freedom of expression. If it was not done in the past, why should we assume that the majority of members of the Parliament in future would acquire sudden aversion and dislike for these values and show an anxiety to remove them from the Constitution?'[2] How persuasive that must have sounded in 1973! How trusting it sounded in 1975!

To the good Judge it was just inconceivable that Parliament could ever do the sorts of things that his colleagues had listed: 'We have been told that Parliament may extend its life if it is given unlimited powers to amend the Constitution,' he recalled. 'It may, *but that it will is inconceivable...*' He returned to this apprehension, only to cast it aside: 'Even if Part III may be left intact, a mockery of the entire parliamentary system can be made by amending Articles 85 and 172 which are not in Part III and according to which the life of the Lok

---

[1] *Ibid*, at 764, para 1420.
[2] *Ibid*, at 765, para 1421.

Sabha and Vidhan Sabhas of the States, unless sooner dissolved, would be five years, and by providing that the life of existing Lok Sabha and Vidhan Sabhas shall be fifty years,' Justice Khanna noted. 'This would be a flagrant abuse of the power of amendment and *I refuse to believe that* public opinion in our country would reach such abysmal depths and the standard of political and constitutional morality would sink so low that *such an amendment would ever be passed*. I need express no opinion for the purpose of this case as to whether this Court would also not quash such an amendment. In any case, such an amendment would be an open invitation for and be a precursor of revolution.'[1]

Yes, there are provisions in the Constitution that empower the Executive to declare an Emergency. But it is inconceivable that the party in power will misuse them, said the Judge: 'Even without amending any Article, the emergency provisions of the Constitution contained in Articles 358 and 359 can theoretically be used in such a manner as may make a farce of the democratic set up by prolonging the rule of the party in power beyond the period of five years since the last general election after the party in power has lost public support,' Justice Khanna recorded summarizing the apprehension that had been expressed. 'As the Government and Parliament play a vital part in the Proclamation and continuation of emergency, the emergency provisions can theoretically be used for avoiding the election and continuing a party in power even though it has lost popular support by extending the life of the House of the People in accordance with Article 83(2),' Justice Khanna noted. But he was unfazed: 'The effective check against such unabashed abuse of power is the sense of political responsibility, the pressure of public opinion and the fear of popular uprising. We need not go into the question as to whether the court would also intervene in such an event. *It is, in my opinion, inconceivable that a party would dare to so abuse the powers granted by the emergency provisions*. The grant of the above power under Article 83(2) is necessarily on the assumption that such a power would not be abused.'[2] Just a few months, and the country was to see the inconceivable materialize.

---

[1] *Ibid*, at 766, para 1423.
[2] *Ibid*, at 767, para 1424.

Hence,

❏ It is a fatal fault of the liberal and the good that they assume that everyone else is like them;
❏ The good should also be skeptical;
❏ They should be specially skeptical when someone claims or grabs power in the name of the poor and disadvantaged;
❏ In examining the claim to a power one must see, as Justice Sikri had noted, the possible width of what is being claimed, not the likelihood or otherwise of its being used to the farthest extent;
❏ The time to institute checks and to fortify them is before power is abused; when it is abused, there is little that institutions within the system can do.

To shut one's eyes

Mrs. Indira Gandhi had been held guilty of corrupt electoral practices on two grounds. Election laws were overturned on the very eve of hearings in the Supreme Court: those two practices are not, and shall be deemed never to have been corrupt practices, the sovereign Parliament decreed. The Constitution was amended: no court, the Supreme Court included, shall have any jurisdiction at all to hear election cases against the person who is elected President, Vice President, Prime Minister, Speaker...

As we have seen, the five Judge Bench that heard the matter struck down the 39th Amendment unanimously. Parliament cannot assume judicial powers... The new clauses fly against the right to equality... Democracy is a basic feature; free and fair elections are central to democracy...

But in the same judgement, the same Judges exhibited one of the disabling traits of liberals: to temporize in the face of an assault on the rationalization that we should not push the aggressor too far, lest she...; to shut one's eyes in the hope that, if only we leave bad-enough alone, the evil will go away; to play for time in the hope that something will turn up.

Can one believe today that a Judge of the Supreme Court approved the changes and upheld Mrs. Gandhi's election proclaiming, 'There is no merit in the contention that the constitutional amendment is bad because it was passed when some members of the Parliament were in detention. The legality of the detention orders cannot be canvassed in these appeals collaterally. And from a practical point of view, the presence of 21 members of the Lok Sabha and 10 members of the Rajya Sabha who were in detention could not have made a difference to the passing of the amendment'?[1] And yet one did.

Can one believe today that, even though *Kesavananda* was law, a Judge of the Supreme Court approved the changes and upheld Mrs. Gandhi's election proclaiming, 'The theory of basic structures or basic features is *an exercise in imponderables.* Basic structures or basic features are *indefinable...*'?[2] And yet one did.

Can one believe today that, even though *Kesavananda* was law, a Judge of the Supreme Court approved the changes and upheld Mrs. Gandhi's election proclaiming that changes such as those that had been made in the election laws 'are liable to be tested by Part III of the Constitution or any other provision of the Constitution; but it is difficult to see how these laws could be challenged on the ground that they do not conform to *some ideal notions of free and fair elections to be evolved by the court from out of airy nothing'?* That *'The concept of a basic structure as brooding omnipresence in the sky apart from the specific provisions of the Constitution constituting it is too vague and indefinite* to provide a yardstick to determine the validity of an ordinary law'?[3] But one of the prominent progressives did.

Can one believe today that a Judge of the Supreme Court approved the changes and upheld Mrs. Gandhi's election proclaiming, 'The provisions of Act 40 of 1975 with which we are concerned *have not been shown to impinge upon the process of free and fair elections* and thereby to strike at the basic structure of the Constitution'?[4] And yet one did.

Can one today believe that a Judge of the Supreme Court approved the changes and upheld Mrs. Gandhi's election proclaiming that the Basic Structure test would apply only to constitutional amendments and not to ordinary laws? That 'The norms

[1] *Indira Nehru Gandhi v. Raj Narain*, 1975 Supp SCC 1, at 262, para 695.
[2] *Ibid*, at 61, para 135.
[3] *Ibid*, at 140–41, paras 349, 357.
[4] *Ibid*, at 108, para 239.

of election set out by Parliament or State Legislatures tested in the light of the provisions of the Constitution or necessary implications therefrom constitute the law of the land. *That law cannot be subject to any other test, like the test of free and fair elections in an ideal democracy'?* That 'An ordinary law cannot be declared invalid for the reason that it goes against the *vague concepts of democracy; justice— political, economic and social; liberty of thought, belief and expression; or equality of status and opportunity, or some invisible radiation from them'?* That 'One cannot test the validity of an ordinary law with reference to the essential elements of an ideal democracy. It can be tested only with reference to the principles of democracy actually incorporated in the Constitution. Nor can it be tested on the touchstone of justice'? That 'Liberty of thought, expression, belief, faith and worship are not absolute concepts. *They are emotive words.* They mean different things to different people. Equality of status and of opportunity are concepts *laden with emotional overtones.* In their absoluteness they are incapable of actual realisation. The enacting provisions in the body of the Constitution alone give concrete shape to these ideas and it is on the basis of these provisions that the validity of ordinary law should be tested'?...[1] And yet one of the leading progressive Judges did—all this and much more.

How very understanding the Chief Justice was! He left no one in any doubt about the side on which he stood: 'The amendments made to the 1951 Act by the Amendment Acts, 1974 and 1975 are to give effect to certain views expressed by the Supreme Court in preference to certain views departed from or otherwise to clarify the original intention. It is within the powers of Parliament to frame laws with regard to elections. Parliament has power to enumerate and define election expenses. Parliament has power to lay down limits on election expenses. Parliament has power to state whether certain expenses can be included or may be excluded from election expenses. Parliament has power to adopt conclusive proof with regard to matters of appointment, resignation or termination of service. Parliament has power to state what can be considered to be office of profit. Parliament has power to state as to what will and

---

[1] *Ibid*, at 131, 138-39, paras 315, 345-47.

what will not constitute corrupt practice. Parliament has power to enact what will be the ground for disqualification. Parliament has power to define "candidate". Parliament has power to state what symbols will be allotted to candidates at election. These are all legislative policies.'[1]

Can one believe today how supinely the Court acquiesced in these tailor-made alterations in the law to overcome the Allahabad High Court judgement? But this is what we read from a Judge: 'There is a well-known pattern of all validation Acts by which the basis of judgements or crders of competent courts and tribunals is changed and the judgements and orders are made ineffective.'[2]

And no offence taken! For the same Judge tells us, 'The rendering of a judgement ineffective by changing the basis by legislative enactment is not encroachment on judicial power because the legislation is within the competence of the Legislature.'[3]

Have the election laws not been changed to benefit one person? Is that not discrimination? Does that not fly in the face of the equality which the Court keeps proclaiming is inviolable? Not in this case! For the Judge declares, 'The changes effected by the Amendment Acts, 1974 and 1975 apply to all and there is no discrimination. Retrospective legislation is not by itself discrimination. The changes introduced to the 1951 Act apply to all.'[4]

But isn't the fact of making the changes effective retrospectively a patent maneuver to help Mrs. Gandhi get over the judgement? The Judge is solemn detachment: 'Any law that can be made prospectively can be made with retrospective operation. Giving retrospective effect to legislative amendment is accepted to be valid exercise of legislative power. The power of the Legislature to pass a law includes a power to pass it retrospectively.'[5]

But a judgement has been delivered. The law on the basis of which that case was decided is now being overturned precisely in regard to the practices in regard to which one candidate has been held guilty. No matter, declares a Judge: 'It is also permissible to

[1] *Ibid*, at 62, para 137.
[2] *Ibid*, at 62, para 138.
[3] *Ibid*, at 62, para 138.
[4] *Ibid*, at 45, para 61.
[5] *Ibid*, at 62, paras 138 and 139.

amend a law which is basis of the decision of a court with retrospective effect and rely upon the provisions of the amended law in appeal against the above decision of the court. The court of appeal in such an event gives full effect to the amended law even though such amendment has been made after the decision of the original court.'[1]

But is that not a patent infraction of free and fair elections, of the very basis of democratic government? Not at all: 'The retrospective operation of the relevant provisions of Act 40 of 1975 does not affect free and fair elections. The said provisions of Act 40 of 1975 are general in terms and would apply to all election disputes which may be pending either in the High Court or in appeal before the Supreme Court or which may arise in future. It is no doubt true that the retrospective operation of an amending Act has the effect of placing one of the parties to the dispute in a more advantageous position compared to others but that is inevitable in most of the amendments with retrospective operation.'[2] As good as the dialecticians—Indrajit Gupta and Bhupesh Gupta—in Parliament, in fact a literal echo of their perorations!

Did the time at which these changes had been made; did the precipitate hurry with which they had been affected; did the fact that they had been done precisely to affect the outcome of the case that the Supreme Court was considering not indicate the collateral purpose for which all this had been done? No problem, said the Judge: 'Whenever a Legislature makes a law or amends a law, it has to indicate the time from which it would come into effect. This is essentially a matter for the Legislature and the Court cannot substitute its own opinior. for that of the Legislature. The fact that the change in law is made applicable to pending cases and the classification treats the decided cases as belonging to one category and pending cases as belonging to another category is not offensive to Article 14. Nor can the Court interfere on the score of the propriety of giving retrospective effect to an amendment made in an election law. Indeed, the question of propriety is a matter which is entirely for the

---

[1] *Ibid*, at 100, para 227.
[2] *Ibid*, at 142, para 360.

Legislature to think of and decide. It cannot affect the validity of the law.'[1]

Such examples of shutting one's eyes to the obvious can be multiplied a hundredfold. And judgements of the Supreme Court are just one arena in which we encounter them. The lessons of this brief review for our present concern are:

❏ The Basic Structure doctrine, apart from being perhaps the most important Indian contribution to jurisprudence, is an essential bulwark against the authoritarian claims of politicians;

❏ The less principled our politicians become, the more indispensable is this safeguard;

❏ Hence, the *sine qua non* in contemplating changes in the Constitution of the kind that we are discussing is that the Basic Structure of the Constitution must be preserved;

❏ The proposed changes are completely compatible with the features that the Supreme Court has enumerated as being basic to the structure of our Constitution; indeed, one can argue that, given what we have made of the 'Parliamentary System', switching to an altered System is the one way to preserve those basic features;

❏ A key element of the alternative System must be a sturdy and independent Judiciary;

❏ In addition to other features—the method of appointing judges, of transferring them, of assessing their integrity; ensuring access to the courts, etc.—independence requires that those who are entrusted with such independence must act independently. Freedom is as freedom does.

❏ One way to have them be independent is to keep their rulings under minute and unremitting scrutiny—an example of the task we, whose calling is to read and write, neglect.

---

[1] *Ibid*, at 104-105, para 232.

11

Romanticizing 'the people'

Beyond the specific perversions that have crept in as a result of what we have made of 'democracy', lie myths on which the Parliamentary System rests. They have become so synonymous with freedom, with democracy that to even ask a question about their validity is to be denounced as an enemy of freedom and everything good.

Foremost among these are myths about the individual: that he acts as an individual; that he is well informed, and he acts after weighing alternatives; furthermore, either that he will opt for the course which promotes the general weal, or that, though he will pursue only his own interest, the general weal shall be advanced by 'the invisible hand'

Facts are to the contrary. Save in extreme situations—for instance, when the country is attacked by overt force—the individual looks to his own advantage. He looks to his own advantage here and now. Not to the advantage of the country, all too often not even for what will be to his own advantage in the long run. He is all too easily swept by false promises and visions; by simple slogans; oftener by envy, hatred, fear, greed, blind faith. He is swayed by charlatans. By outright falsehood. Of course, he will learn eventually that the person was a charlatan, that the promise was a false one. But by then it is too late to undo the harm that those whom he had put in office would have inflicted. When the leader has some good in her or him, the realization comes even later: Pandit Nehru and 'secularism'; Pandit Nehru and his stopping our troops before they had thrown the Pakistanis out of Jammu and Kashmir altogether; Pandit Nehru and his unilateral decision to refer the invasion of Jammu and Kashmir by Pakistan to the United Nations; Pandit Nehru and his trusting the Chinese in spite of the warnings of the Sardar... Mrs. Gandhi and the Emergency; Mrs. Gandhi and the ruinous socialist economics;

Mrs. Gandhi and the disastrous crushing of the students of Assam as they sought to save the country from her subalterns who were packing Bangladeshi infiltrators on to electoral lists; Mrs. Gandhi and the training of LTTE cadre in the Nilgiris; Mrs. Gandhi and the patronizing of Bhindranwale; Mrs. Gandhi and the dismissal of the National Conference Government ... which individual would not have learnt the error that lay in reposing so much hope in her? But the harm had been done by then, not the least, to the leader.

As individuals and, perhaps with even greater ease, as a collective, the people can be flattered. Their expectations can be ever so easily enflamed. As these high expectations cannot be fulfilled, the people can, with even greater ease, be made to lunge to pull others down. That used to be the standard fuel for socialist economics and today we see the same fuel being stoked to push reservations. Just as the fact that journalists are free to write what they want has to be set against the ease with which stories can be planted through them so also, that the system gives voters the power to decide must, as has been well said, be set against the ease with which they can be misled. Aware of the latter, some rulers become brazen, confident that they will be able to lead the people into believing anything for a sufficiently elongated moment. Others are frozen in apprehension, not doing the right thing, fearful that their adversaries will mislead the people and oust them.

And the premise that the individual is well-informed about public affairs, that he will exert to inform himself about them before he takes a position, before he votes—this premise is an even greater myth. Forget the dumbing down of the media; forget the absence even of basic literacy. Mancur Olson rightly shows that, even in the ideal setting, the voter who chooses to remain ignorant of public affairs, about specific policies, even about the leaders in whose hands he is placing power, is acting *rationally*. He is being rational both because what he does will have a minuscule effect on who wins, or on which policy gets adopted, and also because the gains that will accrue to him from one outcome rather than another are so minuscule a proportion of the whole. 'Knowledge about the public's business is a public good...,' Olson observes. 'The typical voter is, accordingly, "rationally ignorant" about what choices would best serve the interest of the electorate or any majority in it. This point is most dramatically evident in national elections. The gain to a voter from studying issues and candidates until it is clear what vote is truly in his or her interest is given by the difference between the value to the individual only (rather than the society) of the "right" and the "wrong" election outcomes, multiplied by the probability that a change in the individual's vote will alter the outcome of the election. Since the probability that a typical voter will change the outcome of the election is vanishingly small, the typical citizen, whether he or she is a physician or a taxi driver, is usually rationally ignorant about public affairs...'[1]

The only titbits of information for which the voter spares a moment are ones that are salacious—a scandal: money pilfered, sex, murder; or when he sees an exceptional gain from knowing—some inside dope about what is going to happen in the stock market. Even in such cases, as we see in India, his is but a fleeting glance. The glance is made all the more momentary by the nature of our media today. Every channel is in a race to find some new 'breaking news' every two hours, each image erased by the previous one. This lesson has sunk into politicians, and is of great comfort to them. 'Why are you so upset about what the papers have printed about you this morning?' I heard a much-experienced politician tell another one in my presence. 'Just remain out of sight for two/three days. They will be running after someone else...'

Today, the reader's and the viewer's attention can scarcely be held even by the gravest disclosures. The more commonplace scandals become, for instance, the less the new one excites him. Even in the rare event that some information registers, it leads to little. As getting through the day is so difficult, he is not able to spare the effort that is required to follow up the revelation. Furthermore,

---

[1]Mancur Olson, *Power and Prosperity, op. cit.*, pp.93–94. And as evidence, we have the verdict of one of the great judges of the last century, Learned Hand! He remarked, 'My vote is one of the most unimportant acts of my life; if I were to acquaint myself with the matters on which it ought really to depend, if I were to try to get a judgement on which I was willing to risk affairs of even the smallest moment, I should be doing nothing else, and that seems a fatuous conclusion to a fatuous understanding.' Learned Hand, 'Democracy: Its presumptions and realities,' 1932, in *The Spirit of Liberty, Papers and Addresses of Learned Hand*, Legal Classics Library, Birmingham, 1989, p.93.

the rulers are so often able to mislead him through plants; eventually, they are able to not just raise doubts about the specific disclosure that has been made about them, they are able to undermine his faith in the source itself, that is the media.

As a result, only when things break down, and only when that breakdown affects him personally, does the individual—the romanticized, all-powerful, all-knowing, ever-so-concerned, vigilant citizen—take the trouble to follow up the information. But even then, even when he gets the full facts, even when the complicity of the rulers is clear, he is liable to merely hurl a curse at them. He is least likely to spare time for and take on the costs of that long and patient strife which alone will help bring them to heel.

And then there is many a leader who is actually able to convince his or her followers that, even though they are losing, the group is gaining by his or her making money or violating the law. 'Our self-pride has been restored,' the followers are bamboozled into believing.

Therefore, majorities remain ignorant of their true interests; even when they know, they do not act on them. Against this, special interests are extremely well informed. In their case, the group consists of a small number: each member will gain substantially from a change in, say, an import regulation. The better-off, better organized, better equipped in the group having set themselves up as the leaders and spokesmen of the group, are able to bamboozle others in it that the measure will benefit all of them, when, in fact, they will be appropriating all the benefits. The way reservations are being grabbed by the better-off within the Scheduled Castes and Tribes and the OBCs, and the way these very sections are able, in the face of repeated rulings of the Supreme Court, to prevent even the slightest move to hive-off the 'creamy layer' are current and ready examples.

Hence, as against the diffuse and inert 'people', these few actually strive to get the changes made. Surreptitiously, if that will do—to get their item moved from one part of the commodity classification in the Import Policy Schedule to another. By 'convincing' people at large, if that becomes necessary—that the policy that is actually helping them alone is in the interest of the people at large. This has been the story on fertilizer subsidies, on retention prices for tobacco. By stoking guilt and fear, if that is the only way—look at the specious rhetoric by which reservations have been rammed. While we are taught to romanticize the 'people' and to go on chanting that power lies with the people, Olson points to the inherent asymmetry, an asymmetry that makes all the difference. 'The profits and even the value added in a typical industry and the wages in a typical craft or occupation,' he points out, 'are a small fraction of gross domestic product (GDP). Suppose, for ease of calculation, that a given organised interest obtains exactly 1 percent of the GDP. Then it will pay this organized interest to press for both governmental and cartelistic redistributions to itself up to the point where the social losses are 100 times as great as the amount it obtains! Only then will its marginal share of these social losses be as great as its gain at the margin from further redistribution. Thus, the typical special-interest group has a very narrow rather than an encompassing interest. It faces incentives that are by no means as wholesome as those facing majorities. Unfortunately, they are much more detrimental to society than those facing the secure stationary bandit, often also worse than those that face the gang with a protection racket, and not much better than those facing the individual criminal...'[1] And among the 'special interests' we must reckon not just business and trade unions, but also groups such as Muslims/Christians/SCs/STs/OBCs and their controllers. Corrupt politicians are as special an interest group as any, except that they are subliminally organized, so to say! On the one side are these special interests, and on the other the mythical 'people', too distant and unconcerned to keep abreast of what is being done and what will result from it; too diffuse and scattered to act... Consider a simple but fatal contrast. We can break the hold of special economic interests through external and internal competition. But what can one do to lessen the force of groups that have been stoked to see themselves not as individuals; not as Indians; but as 'Muslims', as 'SCs', as 'OBCs'? The only way would be to galvanize Hindus *qua* Hindus. And this possibility is foreclosed by the detritus of secularist discourse that has piled up over half a century.

---

[1]*C.f.*, Mancur Olson, *Power and Prosperity, op. cit.* pp.95–96.

The commonplace as the touchstone

'You are the *janata janaardhan*,' the politicians tell the people. 'You are the *panch parmeshwar*. You are sovereign.'

They are not just telling the people, 'You have the rights of a sovereign.' 'You are *janaardhan*,' the politicians are telling them. 'Hence, you can accomplish anything and everything.'

'You are the *panch parmeshwar*. Therefore you *know*.' But, as Ortega y Gasset pointed out long ago, there is a special reason why the people are said to know, why the common man's judgement is held aloft as the one that must prevail. His judgement is proclaimed to be correct, he wrote, precisely because it is common— not in the sense that the judgement is 'commonly held' but in the sense that it is held by persons *who have no special qualifications on the issue at hand*. In other words, whatever the issue, the common man's judgement is correct precisely because he is *not* a specialist on the issue. In fact, it must prevail not in spite of, but precisely because he has made no special effort to inform himself about that issue.

Exactly as Ortega y Gasset had forecast, this proposition—that you are the *janata janaardhan*—is supplemented by the further proposition, 'You are the *janaardhan* exactly as you are.' You don't have to be better in any way, you don't have to make any effort to be better in any way. The lawlessness in Bihar reached unbearable depths. Critics began to characterize it as *jungle raj*. Lalu Yadav was quick to appropriate the description: '*Haan, hum jungli hain*,' he declaimed. His critics were the ones who were thrown into the defensive. I remember well a meeting of those who were struggling to end his misrule. A spokesman from Bihar advised, 'Do not use the phrase *"jungle raj"* to describe Lalu's Government because that phrase has acquired political connotation in Bihar and Lalu is using it against us.' Ortega y Gasset put the result precisely—he called it 'the characteristic of our time'—'not that the vulgar believes itself super-excellent and not vulgar, but that the vulgar proclaims and imposes the rights of vulgarity, or vulgarity as a right.'[1]

The people are fed incessant talk of rights. Politicians tell them day and night, it is your right not just to have 'Whatever I need'; nor is

---

[1] Jose Ortega y Gasset, *The Revolt of the Masses*, W.W. Norton & Company, New York, 1957, p.70.

it your right just to have, 'Whatever I desire'; it is your right to have all that and more, and to get all of it right here and now. And do you know, why you are not getting it? Only because the others are taking away what is yours.

The fact is that in no society, and certainly not in a society like India today, can all get, here and now, everything they want or even need. Indeed, the notion that rights are peremptory prerogatives itself diverts such societies from the effort that is required for the country's construction and security.

By sowing these notions in the people, by leading them to believe that they have a right to get everything they want or need here and now, leaders and parties foment frustration; thence bitterness; thence rage; thence either violence or chronic instability, as the people throw one party out only to have to throw its replacement out in the next round.

That they can throw out parties successively gives them the illusion that the system is giving them not just a choice; it is giving them the power to enforce that choice. But, in fact, as we saw earlier, there is progressive homogenization. Parties and their controllers become more and more like each other. Each is subject to the same pressures. Each is subject to the same temptations. Each adopts the same means. Each hones the same skills. In each, the same sort floats to the top.

Politicians see that sooner than the people. One of the things that has surprised me the most since I joined Parliament is how understanding politicians are of each other's predicaments! And, therefore, how *considerate*. This is one reason why no politician is caught, in addition, of course, to the fact that the criminal justice system, including the investigative machinery, are so clogged: those who come to power denouncing the corruption of their opponents soon come to *understand*, 'The poor fellow did it so clumsily. But, *bhai sahib*, many feel that if they don't do all this, then what was the point of becoming a minister?'

This mutual understanding is the strength of the politician. It is the weakness of the system. It saves the politician, but undermines the system. For the people are drained of all respect for authority. Soon, they too believe in nothing, they obey no one.

This dumbing down swiftly encompasses standards and, next, Law itself. As the one thing that matters is *your* interest, as *you* know what is in your interest, as you are *sovereign*, you have the right to sweep aside whatever is standing in your way. The law, the principle which you find inconvenient is by definition immoral, it is a conspiracy of those who are out to deny you your due. The elected representatives do not just keep telling you that you are the sovereign, and, therefore, it is your right to sweep away whatever is standing in your way; they give you vivid examples by doing it themselves: look at the 'law' they recently passed to save their own seats in Parliament by declaring that what is an Office of Profit till this moment is not an Office of Profit the next.

When those *you* have sent to Parliament do this, why can't *you?* Why *don't* you? You are the *janaardhan*, you have the power to disregard law, indeed to sweep it all aside if you want. The individual, therefore, comes to believe that *all* restrictions can and should be removed. But a river, all of whose banks have been breached, cannot remain a river.

This 'rights talk' foments insatiable appetite on the one side, and, on the other, it leads people to believe that there is absolutely no reason for them to exert. When everybody keeps telling them, 'You are sovereign,' why should all privileges not be theirs? Why should every privilege not be theirs *without their putting in any effort?* In this way, the 'rights talk', removes from sight the vital fact—that rights can exist and be realized only if obligations are discharged; that the things they want, like material prosperity, can be acquired and retained only if a new work culture is imbibed, the culture of discipline, of hard and sustained work.

Institutionalized rights-mongering

Of course, activists and politicians trying to work up a following are not the only ones pushing rights. Others are not far behind. Each Commission, to take just example, feels compelled to outdo the ones that have preceded it. The report of the Commission to Review the Working of the Constitution which we have encountered earlier is a ready example—a compendium of clichés on poverty, inequality, globalization... and most of all on rights. In addition to the

Fundamental Rights that Part III of the Constitution already contains, the Commission urged that the Constitution be amended to also include

❑ The freedom of the press and other media, the right to hold opinions, and seek, receive and impart information;

❑ The right against torture, and inhuman, degrading and cruel treatment and punishment;

❑ The right to compensation for being illegally deprived of one's right to life and liberty;

❑ The right to travel abroad and return to one's country;

❑ The right to privacy;

❑ The right to work, specifically the right to rural wage employment for 80 days;

❑ The right to 'Access to Courts and Tribunals and speedy justice' which shall include 'a right to have any dispute that can be resolved by the application of law decided in a fair public hearing before an independent court or, where appropriate, another independent and impartial tribunal or forum' as well as 'the right to reasonably speedy and effective justice in all matters before the courts, tribunals or other fora and the State shall take all reasonable steps to achieve the said object,' and free legal aid.

❑ The right to property, ensuring that no one shall be deprived of his property arbitrarily and without processes prescribed by law and for any purpose other than a public purpose, and, in case the property belongs to a member of a Scheduled Caste or tribe, not until a scheme of rehabilitation is instituted;

❑ The right to free and compulsory education till the age of fourteen—in the case of Scheduled Castes and Tribes and of girls, up to the age of eighteen;

❑ The rights of children: 'Every child shall have the right to care and assistance in basic needs and protection from all forms of neglect, harm and exploitation';

❑ 'The right to safe drinking water, prevention of pollution, conservation of ecology and sustainable development:
   Every person shall have the right
   (a) to safe drinking water;
   (b) to an environment that is not harmful to one's health or well-being; and

(c) to have the environment protected, for the benefit of present and future generations so as to
  (i) prevent pollution and ecological degradation;
  (ii) promote conservation; and
  (iii) secure ecologically sustainable development and use of natural resources while promoting justifiable economic and social development';
❏ The right to social security and to work;
❏ The right to health;
❏ The right to food and freedom from hunger;
❏ The right to clothing and housing or shelter;
❏ The right to culture...

And the beauty of it is that in piling these rights on to the ones that the Constitution already assures us, the Commission was not exactly doing something of its own. In most cases, it was merely recommending rights that the activist judges had already urged from the Benches of the Supreme Court!

The Commission was, of course, all for reservations and, even as it was against excessive use of Schedule IX, it advocated that laws mandating a 'reasonable' degree of reservations should all be put in Schedule IX beyond the purview of courts. The Commission was more than generous in regard to extending reservation to minorities declaring that this would require no amendment of the Constitution, and that the State could institute the enlargement if it felt there is a need for such reservation!

In addition to all these, the Commission urged a slew of schemes for generating employment from afforestation, horticulture, animal husbandry, intensive aquaculture, soil and water conservation, tank rehabilitation, vermiculture, production of organic foods—all this in a review of the working of the Constitution. And why not? After all, the Directive Principles advocate equality, employment...

The Commission was emphatic: these rights must be enforceable. Though it isn't clear against whom the right to culture, for instance, or the right of every child 'to care and assistance in basic needs and protection from all forms of neglect, harm and exploitation' would be enforced. To ensure that the rights were enforceable over the widest ambit, the Commission urged that the definition of 'the State' be expanded to include 'any person in relation to such of its functions which are of a public nature'. That would mean every doctor, every pilot, every bus driver, every teacher, every employer, every journalist, every stockbroker indeed every parent... each and every one of them would henceforth be the State of India! For aspects of the function of each are of 'a public nature'.

The Directive Principles too must result in actual action, the Commission emphasized. Hence, to start with, they must be rechristened, 'The Directive Principles of State Policy *and Action*,' it prescribed. And there must be annual reports by the Planning Commission, by each ministry, about what the government has done to further each Directive Principle. And each of the reports must be deliberated upon by Parliament's Standing Committees... Including reports on impiementing Article 47 which prescribes prohibition? The Commission didn't say! Including reports on implementing Article 48 which prescribes prohibition of cow slaughter? The Commission didn't say! Including reports on implementing Article 44 which prescribes that the State endeavour to enact a Common Civil Code? The Commission didn't say!

And this pattern is repeated down the line. The citizen is at a disadvantage *vis a vis* the State. Hence, these rights. The poor are at a disadvantage *vis a vis* citizens in general. Hence, these rights. From that it is but a small step, 'Among the poor, Muslims are at a disadvantage. Hence...' We thus have the familiar sequence in the Sachar Committee and its *non sequiturs.*

The Committee is set up by Government to rationalize what the ruling coalition feels compelled to do so as to win back what it looks upon as a vote bank. Accordingly, the Committee goes looking for evidence that would establish that the Muslims are badly off. It shuts its eyes tight to the data in its own tables that point in the opposite direction—that the Muslims are indeed doing better than others in several parts of the country. It assiduously refuses to awaken Muslims to how what *they* are doing or neglecting to do is responsible for such disadvantages they say they suffer from in other parts of the country. As all such discourse does, it pastes the responsibility on *the other.*

The net result is predictable: another slew of concessions that must be made to this group *as a group separate and distinct from the rest of the country.*

The Task Force on Border Management, one of the four set up in the wake of the Kargil War, reported with alarm about the way *madrasas* had mushroomed along India's borders. On the basis of information it received from intelligence agencies, it expressed grave concern at the amount of money these *madrasas* were receiving from foreign sources. It reported that large numbers were being 'educated' in these institutions in subjects that did not equip them at all for jobs—other than to become preachers and teachers producing the same type of unemployables. It expressed the gravest concern at the way the *madrasas* were reinforcing separateness in their wards—through the curriculum, through the medium of instruction, through the entire orientation of learning—towards Arabia, towards the 'golden ages' of Islamic rule. It pointed to the consequences that were certain to flow from 'the Talibanization' of the *madrasas*.[1]

And what does the Sachar Committee recommend? 'Recognition of the degrees from *madrasas* for eligibility in competitive examinations such as the Civil Services, Banks, Defence Services and other such examinations'! It recommends that Government use public funds to encourage formation of Muslim NGOs and their activities. It recommends that Government provide financial and other support to occupations and areas in which Muslims predominate. It recommends that Muslims be in selection committees, interview panels and Boards for public services. It recommends that a higher proportion of Muslims be inducted in offices that deal with the public—'the teaching community, health workers, police personnel, bank employees and so on.' It recommends 'provision of "equivalence" to *madrasa* certificates/ degrees for subsequent admissions into institutions of higher level of education.' It recommends that banks be required to collect and maintain information about their transactions—deposits, advances— separately for Muslims, and that they be required to submit this to the Reserve Bank of India! It recommends that advances be made to Muslims as part of the obligation imposed on banks to give advances to Priority Sectors. It recommends that Government give banks

---

[1]For a summary of its observations, *Will the Iron Fence Save a Tree Hollowed by Termites?, Defence imperatives beyond the military*, ASA, Delhi, 2005.

incentives to open branches in Muslim concentration areas. It recommends that, instead of being required to report merely 'Amount Outstanding', banks be told to report 'Sanctions or Disbursements to Minorities'. It recommends that financial institutions be required to set up separate funds for training Muslim entrepreneurs, that they be required to set up special micro-credit schemes for Muslims. It recommends that all districts more than a quarter of whose population is Muslim be brought in the Prime Minister's 15-point programme. 'There should be transparency in information about minorities in all activities,' the Committee declares. 'It should be made mandatory to publish/furnish information in a prescribed format once in three months and also to post the same on the website of the departments and state governments...' It recommends that for each programme of Government, data be maintained separately about the extent to which Muslims and other minorities are benefiting from it. It recommends that special and separate Centrally Sponsored Schemes and Central Plan Schemes be launched for 'minorities with an equitable provision for Muslims.' It recommends special measures for the promotion and spread of Urdu. It recommends the adoption of 'alternate admission criteria' in universities and autonomous colleges: assessment of merit should not be assigned more than 60 per cent out of the total—the remaining 40 per cent should be assigned in accordance with the income of the household, the backwardness of the district, and the backwardness of the caste and occupation of the family. It recommends that grants by the University Grants Commission be linked to 'the diversity of the student population.' It recommends that pre-entry qualification for admission to ITIs be scaled down, that 'eligibility for such programmes should also be extended to the *madrasa* educated children.' It recommends that 'high quality Government schools should be set up in all areas of Muslim concentration.' It recommends that resources and Government land be made available for 'common public spaces' for adults of—its euphemism—'Socio-Religious Categories' to 'interact'. It recommends that incentives to builders, private sector employers, educational institutions be linked to 'diversity' of the populations in their sites and enterprises. For this purpose it wants a 'diversity index' to be developed for each such activity. It recommends changes in the way constituencies are delimited. It recommends that where Muslims are elected or selected in numbers less than adequate, 'a carefully conceived "nomination" procedure' be worked out 'to increase the participation of minorities at the grass roots.' It notes that there already are the Human Rights Commission and the Minorities Commission 'to look into complaints by the minorities with respect to State action.' But these are not adequate as the Muslims still feel that they are not getting a fair share. The solution? Here is its recommendation, and a typical passage:

> It is imperative that *if the minorities have certain perceptions of being aggrieved,*

Notice the touchstone—'*if the minorities have certain perceptions of being aggrieved'*

> all efforts should be made by the State to find a mechanism by which these complaints could be attended to expeditiously. This mechanism should operate in a manner *which gives full satisfaction to the minorities*

Notice again the touchstone—not any external criterion, but *'full satisfaction to the minorities'*

> that any denial of equal opportunities or bias or discrimination in dealing with them, either by a public functionary or any private individual, will immediately be attended to and redress given. Such a mechanism should be accessible to all individuals and institutions desirous to complain that they have received less favourable treatment from any employer or any person on the basis of his/her SRC [Socio-Religious Category] background and gender.

The responsibility is entirely that of the other. The other must function to the full satisfaction of the Muslims. As long as the Muslims 'have certain perceptions of being aggrieved,' the other is at fault...

And for all this it recommends that a National Data Bank be created and it be mandatory for all departments and agencies to supply information to it to document how their activities are impacting Muslims and other minorities. On top of all this, Government should set up an Assessment and Monitoring Authority to evaluate the benefits that are accruing to the minorities from each programme and activity...

The unvarying sequence:

❑ Rights mongering, leads to
❑ Grievance mongering, which in turn leads to
❑ Looking for grievances, which in turn leads to
❑ Inventing grievances, which in turn leads to
❑ Making the 'perception of being aggrieved' as the touchstone, which in turn leads to
❑ The 'leaders' of that group drilling even deeper into the group that it remains discriminated against, which in turn leads
❑ Rulers and would-be rulers to go on pandering more and more to the group *as a group*, which in turn leads to
❑ Splintering the society into ever smaller fragments...

What splendid evolution! Not long ago, unless you saw a Muslim as a human being, and *not* as a Muslim, you were not secular. Now, if you see a Muslim as a human being and not as a Muslim, you are not secular!

The results

The results of such rights-mongering are all round us. It is not that the people are happy about corruption. But they are not prepared to confront the authorities to stop it. Quite the contrary. 'You see, I just have to pay, and somehow get the question paper. You see, it is a question of my son's whole future,' they say. 'But I tell you one thing: unless you chaps in the press expose these fellows, and put an end to corruption, this country is doomed.' The exact same pattern is repeated in regard to the gravest matter—national security. Why is it that even as he betrays our trust again and again, we make it almost an article of faith to trust Musharraf? Because if we were to allow the evidence of his betrayals to seep in, we would have to *change our conduct*, we would have to actually sacrifice something for national security. And *that* we are not prepared to do. Why is it that the Assamese, even as they wail about Bangladeshi infiltrators robbing them of their land, employ the infiltrators as domestic servants? It is the same syndrome: 'We have no alternative but to act as we are doing, but *you* must...'—catch these fellows and end corruption/ identify the infiltrators and throw them out/mop up after Musharraf has done his worst by us.

'Everyone has rights' becomes, 'Everyone has *capabilities*.' Similarly, 'Everyone has equal rights', becomes, 'Everyone is *equally capable*.' To hearken to standards is to be elitist. As 'Everyone is equally capable,' standards and tests that suggest otherwise are a conspiracy of the elite to keep down the under-privileged. Standards thus become illegitimate—'elitist'. Mediocrity becomes the norm. The result?

'Merit and efficiency is [*sic.*] a pure Aryan invention, aimed at maintaining their monopoly,' the Supreme Court judgement quotes—that should be 'approvingly quotes'—from a typical write-up by one V.T. Rajshekhar. The title of the write-up is, 'Merit, my foot. A reply to Anti-Reservation Racists.'[1] 'Nowhere in the world,' the Supreme Court says on the authority of this person, 'are "merit and efficiency" given so much importance as in India which is now pushed to the 120th position—virtually the last among different countries in the world.' 'Upper caste rulers of India,' it continues on the same person's authority, 'keep the country's vast original inhabitants—Untouchables, Tribals, Backward Castes and "religious minorities"—permanently as slaves with the help of this "merit" *mantra*. By "merit and efficiency" they mean the birth. Merit goes with the highborn—the blue blood. This is pure and simple racism. That birth and skin-colour have nothing to do with "merit and efficiency" (brain) is a scientifically proved fact. But the ruling class nowhere in the world is concerned with science because science stands for progress. And those interested in progress will have to be human. That is not so in India. If one has to see man's inhumanity to man in its most naked form he must come to India, the original home of racism and inequality. So, the merit theory beautifully suits its ruling class or caste...'[2]

The author of the passage is a propagandist of an extreme kind. He is given to hurling the vilest abuse. For years and years he and his venomous rag of a journal have lauded the British rulers and British rule. They have hailed those who helped conquer India for the British, they have advocated violence. And here we have the Supreme Court of India elevating the asinine assertions of such a man—by citing them with manifest approval in its judgement!

---

[1]*Dalit Sahitya Academy*, 1996, Bangalore.
[2]*Ashok Kumar Gupta v. State of U.P.*, (1997) 5 SCC 201, at 231, para 35.

This having become the reigning ideology, the norm now is the 'common man'. He has no special qualifications for the job that needs to be done: legislators have no special skills for legislation; officers have no special skills to run ministries; exactly as reservationists do not for the job that has to be done.

The one way to stem this descent would be discourse. But here too the same deification of the 'common man' works the same consequences. Just as no special qualification is required for being an M.P. or a minister or an official, so also neither special effort, nor specialization is required for having an opinion—on China, on Pakistan, on the budget. As Ortega y Gasset put it, 'Today,... the average man has the most mathematical "ideas" on all that happens or ought to happen in the universe. Hence he has lost the use of his hearing. Why should he listen if he has within him all that is necessary? There is no reason now for listening, but rather for judging, pronouncing, deciding. There is no question concerning public life, in which he does not intervene, blind and deaf as he is, imposing his "opinions".'[1]

And there is an all-important auxiliary to this possessing of 'ideas'. Ortega y Gasset continues: 'The average man finds himself with "ideas" in his head, but he lacks the faculty of ideation. He has no conception even of the rare atmosphere in which ideas live. He wishes to have opinions, but is unwilling to accept the conditions and presuppositions that underlie all opinion. Hence his ideas are in effect nothing more than *appetites in words*, something like musical romanzas.'[2]

And it is the 'common man's opinion' which is then obtained and broadcast as the measure. Look at the programmes in which an assortment of 'common men' is asked to pronounce. Look at the comments SMSed to studios which are shown streaming across the TV screen. Look at the instant 'polls' of TV channels—'83% say we cannot trust Musharraf,' simultaneously, '78% say we must respond positively to his formula'! It isn't just that they never tell you 83% *of how many?* Of 10 or of 10,000? Here are 'common men' with no special knowledge of the subject; here are 'common men' whose

---

[1]Ortega y Gasset, *op. cit.*, p.71.
[2]*Ibid*, p.73.

number even we do not know. But you must take seriously their opinion—on every issue: from whether Sachin Tendulkar should retire to what we should do in regard to China!

One can put in this very class—of persons who have opinions without having put in any particular effort—persons in the media itself, say today's TV reporter: fresh out of college, mike in hand, he pronounces on everything. The many discussants in TV programmes are little different: they are there merely because they hold an office or because they are from a political party. In the alternate, because they are not even these, but are stand-ins for the 'common man.' In the rare instance when an expert is invited, he is asked to simplify his opinion and state it in the common man's manner so that, though it is grounded in expert knowledge, his opinion is *just another opinion*, one more among the many differing opinions that are held by different persons. Each of whom deserves as much weight as any one else.

Many of these discussants do not establish their point by logic or by evidence. They do so by assertion backed by the force of the mob. The unwritten message is, if you do not bend to what they are saying, you will face calumny—'he is anti-poor, anti-*dalit*'—and eventually the violent mob.

The sequence is self-referential. And so it feeds on itself. A TV programme is assessed by 'TRP ratings'. A higher score on such ratings, determines, for instance, the quantum of advertising revenue the programme rakes in. The worth of a film is its box-office take. That is, by the extent to which 'masses' view it. As the number of readers increases, the content of the paper becomes shallower. And not by accident The paper has to aim at 'the average reader,' in fact at the least able, *marginal* reader or viewer. If it aims higher, it will lose him to the baser paper or rival TV channel.

The standards of papers fall. Especially when profit depends on the number of readers and when 'masses' have been sanctified as the ones by whose measure standards should be set. This latter proposition was ironically pushed by persons like Lenin who despised the masses, and by persons like Mao who put the masses, and of course the sorts of persons here in India who regurgitate their quotations—that is, our progressive intellectuals—in their place!

Dumbing down on the one hand and profit as the sole objective on the other; rather, dumbing down as the device for profits, have now been elevated into an ideology—the ideology, as far as content goes, of superciliousness. The paper is just a 'product', it is now proclaimed. The next step has been as predictable as it has been inevitable. Today some papers openly charge money for publishing photographs, features, even what appears as 'news': I got the surprise of my life when, to my saying that I just did not believe this would be happening, an entrepreneur of the book world in Kolkata sent me a printed 'Rate Card' specifying what amounts would have to be paid for what type of coverage.

The 'cult of the common man' is itself soon supplanted. As we have seen, the competitive breast-beating for the plight of the 'common man' naturally graduates to even more fervent pounding of breasts for the weak among the common men. Academics and activists as much as politicians go around discovering segments that are even worse off than the last lot on whom they had focused their rhetoric. They go around discovering facets of these segments which others had missed. They inflame grievances. Soon, like full-time politicians, they are inventing grievances. So much has the cult of the 'common man' taken hold by now, that, apart from other things, charging ahead in this progression makes many feel progressive.

The 'people's representative'

The cult of the 'common man' reaches its apogee in the ones who set themselves up as the representatives of the 'common man'. The legislator claims that he is the common man's representative as the latter has elected him. We have already seen how little substance there is in this claim, what with 98.8 per cent of the members of even the Lok Sabha having been elected by a minority of the electorate. But there is another claim that the legislator and even more so the leaders advance in even stronger terms. They represent the common man because they *are most like him.* They adopt the *dehati* vocabulary and diction; they dress 'like the people'; they parade their vulgarity and uncouthness as 'authenticity'. Having appropriated the sole right to speak for the 'common man', they denounce every proposal that may alter the system—the system they have mastered, and become masters of.

In a word, we must shift the emphasis from representativeness to effectiveness.

A counter-example

Remember Edmund Burke. You will recall how angry his constituents had become at the positions he had been advocating on issue after issue. When time came for his re-election, they conveyed to Burke their anger at the fact that, during the time he represented them, he strove to advance not their interests—they were mainly traders—but what he concluded were the interests of the country. His letter to his constituents in Bristol, his speeches on the question whether a member of Parliament must obey instructions of his constituents state precisely the lessons that we should learn.

We look for the man who will pander to us, for the one who will cater to our locality, to our caste. 'I certainly have very warm good wishes for the place of my birth,' Burke tells his constituents frankly. 'But the sphere of my duties is my true country.'

We look for the man who will do as we want, who will be the Tulmohan Ram, with the difference that he will be so on our behalf also and not just on his own. And each politician out-does the other, telling us how he will be a better Tulmohan Ram on our behalf than his rival. And Burke? 'Depend upon it,' he tells his constituents,

>...that the lovers of freedom will be free. None will violate their conscience to please us, in order afterwards to discharge that conscience, which they have violated, by doing us faithful and affectionate service. If we degrade and deprave their minds by servility, it will be absurd to expect that they who are creeping and abject towards us, will ever be bold and incorruptible assertors of our freedom against the most seducing and the most formidable of all powers. No! Human nature is not so formed; nor shall we improve the faculties or better the morals of public men by our possession of the most infallible receipt in the world for making cheats and hypocrites.
>
>Let me say, with plainness, I who am no longer in a public character, that if by a fair, by an indulgent, by a gentlemanly behaviour to our representatives, we do not give confidence to their minds, and a liberal scope to their understandings; if we do not permit our members to act upon a very enlarged view of things, we shall at length infallibly degrade our national representation into a confused and scuffling bustle of local agency. When the popular member is narrowed in his ideas, and rendered timid in his proceedings, the service of the Crown will be the sole nursery of statesmen. Among the frolics

of the court it may at length take that of attending to its business. Then the monopoly of mental power will be added to the power of all other kinds it possesses. On the side of the people there will be nothing but impotence; for ignorance is impotence; narrowness of mind is impotence; timidity is itself impotence, and makes all other qualities that go along with it impotent and useless.

At present it is the plan of our court to make its servants insignificant. If the people should fall into the same humour, and should choose their servants on the same principles of mere obsequiousness, and flexibility, and total vacancy or indifference of opinion in all public matters, then no part of the state will be sound; and it will be in vain to think of saving it.

A rival told the constituents that he would always proceed by their instructions. Burke repudiated the proposition wholeheartedly, knowing full well the cost he may have to pay for his opinion. He told his electors,

> Certainly, gentlemen, it ought to be the happiness and glory of a representative to live in the strictest union, the closest correspondence, and the most unreserved communication with his constituents. Their wishes ought to have great weight with him; their opinion, high respect; their business, unremitted attention. It is his duty to sacrifice his repose, his pleasures, his satisfactions, to theirs; and above all, ever, and in all cases, to prefer their interest to his own. But his unbiased opinion, his mature judgement, his enlightened conscience, he ought not to sacrifice to you, to any man, or to any set of men living. These he does not derive from your pleasure; no, nor from the law and the constitution. They are a trust from Providence, for the abuse of which he is deeply answerable. Your representative owes you, not his industry only, but his judgement; and he betrays, instead of serving you, if he sacrifices it to your opinion.

Burke's opponent had said that he would subordinate his will to the opinion and instructions of those he sought to represent. Burke turned the argument on its head, telling them candidly that, while they may have opinions and inclinations, 'government and legislation are matters of reason and judgement, and not of inclination...' He told the constituents,

> My worthy colleague says, his will ought to be subservient to yours. If that be' all, the thing is innocent. If government were a matter of will upon any side, yours, without question, ought to be superior. But government and legislation

are matters of reason and judgement, and not of inclination; and what sort of reason is that, in which the determination precedes the discussion; in which one set of men deliberate, and another decide; and where those who form the conclusion are perhaps three hundred miles distant from those who hear the arguments?

To deliver an opinion, is the right of all men; that of constituents is a weighty and respectable opinion, which a representative ought always to rejoice to hear; and which he ought always most seriously to consider. But authoritative instructions; mandates issued, which the member is bound blindly and implicitly to obey, to vote, and to argue for, though contrary to the clearest conviction of his judgement and conscience,—these are things utterly unknown to the laws of this land, and which arise from a fundamental mistake of the whole order and tenor of our constitution.

And then he described the true nature and function of a legislature. If only our legislators and commentators were to bear the words in mind! Burke said,

Parliament is not a congress of ambassadors from different and hostile interests; which interests each must maintain, as an agent and advocate, against other agents and advocates; but parliament is a deliberative assembly of one nation, with one interest, that of the whole; where, not local purposes, not local prejudices, ought to guide, but the general good, resulting from the general reason of the whole. You choose a member indeed; but when you have chosen him, he is not a member of Bristol, but he is a member of parliament. If the local constituent should have an interest, or should form an hasty opinion, evidently opposite to the real good of the rest of the community, the member for that place ought to be as far, as any other, from any endeavour to give it effect. I beg pardon for saying so much on this subject...

Today, not only do members of political parties hesitate to express their opinions, but parties also dare not let them do so; the condition of public discourse is such that the media as much as rival parties are certain to pounce on that expression and shout, 'Differences rock Party.' And Burke? Accused of being an Irishman on the Irish question, of being an American on the American question rather than a Britisher—for he defied popular sentiment on both occasions, he stood up to popular indignation and urged that the just demands of these peoples be conceded—he tells his constituents point-blank how he had foreseen the disasters they have invited upon themselves; he had warned them, he reminds them, and they had scorned him. 'What! Gentlemen,' he asks,

> was I not to foresee, or, foreseeing, was I not to endeavour to save you from all these multiplied mischiefs and disgraces? Would the little, silly, canvass prattle of obeying instructions, and having no opinions but yours, and such idle senseless tales, which amuse the vacant ears of unthinking men, have saved you from, 'the pelting of that pitiless storm,' to which the loose improvidence, the cowardly rashness, of those who dare not look danger in the face, so as to provide against it in time, and therefore throw themselves headlong into the midst of it, have exposed this degraded nation, beaten down and prostrate on the earth, unsheltered, unarmed, unresisting? Or on the day that I hung down my head and wept in shame and silence over the humiliation of Great Britain? I became unpopular in England for the one, and in Ireland for the other. What then? What obligation lay on me to be popular? I was bound to serve both kingdoms. To be pleased with my service was their affair, not mine.
>
> I was an Irishn.an in the Irish business, just as much as I was an American, when, on the same principles, I wished you to concede to America, at a time when she prayed concession at our feet. Just as much was I an American, when I wished parliament to offer terms in victory, and not to wait the well-chosen hour of defeat, for making good for weakness, and by supplication a claim of prerogative, pre-eminence, and authority...

Thus, competence, sturdy independence, and commitment—the last not to us and our group but to the whole...

And, as Burke taught, by his example as much as by his words, a person deserves to be elected not because he is '*like the people*'—as little literate as they are, as unaware of the world as they are, as little able to weigh complex legislative proposals and choose between alternative policies as they are. He is to be elected because he is best equipped to weigh which among competing proposals and options is best for them. And not for them in particular, but for the country as a whole.

We have seen how a departure from these basics sets the stage for betraying the people wholesale. The people are sovereign. The legislator is like the people. Hence, he is their representative. He acts in their interest. Therefore, he exercises power on their behalf. Hence, as their collective, Parliament is sovereign... The sequence serves not the people, but the so-called representative. Look at the individual legislator as he disobeys the Chair, as he violates the rules of conduct of the House. He is the people, he is the sovereign. What are rules but his creation? As he created them, he can 'interpret' them, he can disregard them. The conclusion, 'Therefore, Parliament is sovereign,' is of even greater service to the leader, as we have seen. For, while before you and me the legislator—a perfect believer, as a senior civil servant explained to me once, in dialectics, 'Strong to the weak. Weak to the strong'—struts as 'sovereign', before his leader he is obsequiousness itself.

In a word, when we deify 'the people', we clear the way for the usurper, we legitimize the myriad self-serving things that their 'representatives' will do in their name. The people are *not* sovereign. They are *not* all-knowing. They can be swept off into wrong choices by charlatans.

Therefore, just as we must shift the emphasis from representativeness to effectiveness, we must awaken people to their responsibilities. They must be made aware of the limits within which alone they may function.

Rule-abidingness

It was a glittering ceremony. Members of Parliament had assembled in the Central Hall, the very Hall in which the Constitution was adopted. They were there to celebrate the Golden Jubilee of Independence. The President, Prime Minister, and the rest were there. Other, equally glittering events were enacted. On 'this historic occasion', as they called it, members of the Lok Sabha adopted a Resolution unanimously. They proclaimed it to be 'our Agenda for India,' no less.

They resolved, *inter alia*, that 'meaningful electoral reforms be carried out so that our Parliament and other legislative bodies be balanced and effective instruments of democracy; and further that political life and processes be free of the adverse impact on governance of undesirable extraneous factors including criminalization.' Not satisfied, they repeated and elaborated the resolve in the ensuing paragraph! They resolved that 'continuous and proactive efforts be launched for ensuring greater transparency, probity and accountability in public life so that freedom, authority and dignity of the Parliament and other legislative bodies are ensured and enhanced; that more especially, all political parties shall undertake all such steps as will attain the objective of ridding our polity of criminalization or its influence.'

The parliamentarians further resolved that 'the prestige of the Parliament is preserved and enhanced also by conscious and dignified conformity to the entire regime of Rules of Procedure and Conduct of Business of the Houses and Directions of the Presiding Officers relating to orderly conduct of business, more especially by

❑ Maintaining the inviolability of the Question Hour,
❑ Refraining from transgressing into the official areas of the House, or from any shouting of slogans, and
❑ Invariably desisting from any efforts at interruption or interference with the Address of the President of India.'

Now that the proceedings are televised, you must be seeing how scrupulously they are adhering to their solemn resolve!

'But we are sovereign. What are Rules of Procedure and Conduct of Business of the Houses? Who made them? *We* made them. Therefore, we can alter them, we can interpret them, we can disregard them. The question is, "Who is sovereign?" We or the Rules we made?'—that is the premise, rather the presumption. And it follows from that deification of the 'people' and the appropriation of the 'people'.

But this way our country will become what our legislatures have become. We need the opposite premise.

I still remember a vivid lesson I learnt when I first went to the U.S. for doctoral studies. In those days for just a hundred dollars one could buy a ticket and travel anywhere in the U.S. on a Greyhound bus for several months. I decided to use the first vacation to go from Syracuse to Seattle to San Francisco to San Jose to..., all the way back to Syracuse, a complete circle. At the last minute a Professor told me that I could travel for a part of the journey more comfortably than in a bus, that he was driving across to his home in Seattle and I was welcome to ride in his car.

It was a sports car. We were racing across the mid-western states. You couldn't see anyone for miles and miles. The Professor drove at unnerving speed. But every now and then he would slow down, come to a complete stop, and then take off again. At last I asked him why he was doing that. 'But there was a "Stop" sign there,' he explained. Here we were on a vast plateau with no one around as far as the horizon. But just because there was a sign, he would bring the car to a complete stop...

In our case, the status of a person is known by the number of rules he can disregard. That is a major reason why ministers and legislators figure so high on the status ladder!

But sturdy banks enable water to flow faster. Rules *enlarge* my freedom as they bind others to limits that *they* cannot cross. Indeed, a collection of people is a community in as much as its members obey a common set of rules, in as much as they abide by a common set of values. For our structures to function, we have to instill this habit, of rule abidingness—in our legislators as much as in our children.

We have, of course, to devise ways and conventions by which appropriate persons are appointed to institutions. But placing the best persons in jobs is only the first step. Institutions are strengthened or destroyed by the way they function every day in ordinary cases. Just as in our dusty summers we bathe twice a day, we need to nurture institutions twice a day.

Throughout the day.

Every day.

As long as we live.

Nor is there a switch which, once it is turned on, will ensure that the institution shall function well thereafter, there is no alteration in the structure that will ensure that it will subserve the general good forever thereafter.

What the *Dhammapada* counsels us as individuals is also the way institutions are to be tended:

As the silversmith removes impurities from silver, so the wise man from himself: one by one, little by little, again and again.

The individual

In the end, of course, everything turns on the individual, and on how he conducts himself.

Recall the warning of Joseph Story that the Provisional Chairman, Dr. Sachchidananda Sinha recounted in his Inaugural Address to the Constituent Assembly. Story had said,

Let the American youth never forget that they possess (in their Constitution) a noble inheritance, bought by the toils, and sufferings, and blood of their ancestors; and capable, if wisely improved, and faithfully guarded, of transmitting to their latest posterity all the substantial blessings of life, the peaceful enjoyment of liberty, property, religion, and independence. The structure has been erected by architects of consummate skill and fidelity; its foundations are solid; its compartments are beautiful, as well as useful; its arrangements are full of wisdom and order; and its defences are impregnable from without. It has been reared for immortality, if the work of man may justly aspire to such a title. It may nevertheless perish in an hour by the folly, or corruption, or negligence of its only keepers, the people. Republics are created [and here Dr. Sinha paused, and told the assembled members, 'these are the words which I commend to you for your consideration'] by the virtue, public spirit, and intelligence of the citizens. They fall, when the wise are banished from the public councils, because they dare to be honest, and the profligate are rewarded, because they flatter the people, in order to betray them.[1]

Pause at the last few words for a moment: 'They fall, when the wise are banished from the public councils, because they dare to be honest, and the profligate are rewarded, because they flatter the people, in order to betray them.' Can there be a better description of what has been made of Dr. Sinha's state, Bihar? The precise condition having been brought about, can the consequence Story foretold be escaped? And is U.P. not being made a Bihar of? What freedom will survive the wreckage? How will any development that takes place be sustained?

Three years later, the President, Dr. Rajendra Prasad, returned to this very point as he concluded the deliberations of the Constituent Assembly. You will recall his words,

Whatever the Constitution may or may not provide, the welfare of the country will depend upon the way in which the country is administered. That will depend upon the men who administer it. It is a trite saying that a country can have only the Government it deserves. Our Constitution has provisions in it which appear to some to be objectionable from one point or another. We must admit that the defects are inherent in the situation in the country and the people at large. If the people who are elected are capable and men of character and integrity, they would be able to make the best even of a defective Constitution. If they are lacking in these, the Constitution cannot

---

[1] *Constituent Assembly of India, Debates,* 9 December 1946, Book I, Volume I, p.5.

help the country. After all, a Constitution like a machine is a lifeless thing. It acquires life because of the men who control it and operate it, and India needs today nothing more than a set of honest men who will have the interest of the country before them. There is a fissiparous tendency arising out of various elements in our life. We have communal differences, caste differences, language differences, provincial differences and so forth. It requires men of strong character, men of vision, men who will not sacrifice the interests of the country at large for the sake of smaller groups and areas and who will rise over the prejudices which are born of these differences...

Given the occasion, he too expressed hope:

We can only hope that the country will throw up such men in abundance.

And faith:

I can say this from the experience of the struggle that we have had during the period of the freedom movement that new occasions throw up new men; not once but almost on every occasion when all leading men in the Congress were clapped into prison suddenly without having the time to leave instructions to others and even to make plans for carrying on their campaigns, people arose from amongst the masses who were able to continue and conduct the campaigns with intelligence, with initiative, with capacity for organization which nobody suspected they possessed. I have no doubt that when the country needs men of character, they will be coming up and the masses will throw them up.

Of course, he was not—no one in that generation was—the resigning kind. He did not want, not one of those assembled in the Central Hall would have wanted affairs of State to be left to events and chance. And so, in spite of the decades of suffering that those assembled before him had endured for the country, he counselled them,

Let not those who have served in the past therefore rest on their oars, saying that they have done their part and now has come the time for them to enjoy the fruits of their labours. No such time comes to anyone who is really earnest about his work. In India today I feel that the work that confronts us is even more difficult than the work which we had when we were engaged in the struggle. We did not have then any conflicting claims to reconcile, no loaves and fishes to distribute, no powers to share. We have all these now, and the temptations are really great. Would to God that we shall have the wisdom and the strength to rise above them, and to serve the country which we have succeeded in liberating.[1]

---

[1] *Ibid*, 26 November, 1949, Book VI, Volume X, pp.993–94.

Has his prayer been answered? Has his faith in events and chance been vindicated? Has our political class been exerting itself to reconcile those conflicting claims or fanning claims—so many of them, contrived—to foment conflict so as to cement its own following? Has it escaped the snare of those temptations, the loaves and fishes to distribute, the power to share?

But I am on two other points. That the hour of crisis will throw up men and women—the Emergency a JP—is not enough. For governance has to be of a standard from day to humdrum day. So, the questions we must face are: are the Parliamentary System, and what lies at its foundation, the electoral system that were adopted under the Constitution; rather, more accurately, is *what we have made of* the systems that were adopted under the Constitution throwing up, 'a set of honest men who will have the interest of the country before them'? Are they bringing to the fore 'men of strong character, men of vision, men who will not sacrifice the interests of the country at large for the sake of smaller groups and areas and who will rise above the prejudices which are born of those differences'? Are elections throwing up persons who have the ability to run governments?

Hence:

❑ In the end, everything turns on the individual.
❑ Events and chance, sudden crises, even prolonged and painful decline do not automatically throw up the individuals that society so desperately needs. More precisely, events and crises and decline do not automatically put such persons in positions from which they can stem the drift.
❑ Nor should a country rest content just because on occasion such individuals have indeed arrived at those positions. Policies—for development; even more so, for security—have to be sustained, they have to be pursued with unwavering effort for decades. The occasional fluke is not enough.
❑ Nor is it enough that competition is forcing the best persons into positions of authority in spheres outside the State apparatus. The role of the State in our lives must be reduced. But there are minimal functions that only the State can perform—and an inadequate person in *any* of its limbs will weaken the entire structure.

❑ In a word, we must devise such systems as will induce, enable, sustain such persons in public office.

Utopian?

Is all this just *aranyarodan*, a cry in the wilderness? Is it so unrealistic as to be utopian?

I remember the same sorts of reaction when a person like me wrote against the license-quota *raj* in the mid-1960s. I remember the reactions when a few of us argued then that 'socialism' and the economic policies that were being forced in its name were disastrous; that they would cost the country a generation; that they must be replaced. We were not just labeled unrealistic and utopian, our voice was sought to be buried in a mountain of denunciation. A generation of economic progress having been lost, what is the position now? The very persons who were writing those socialist speeches for the rulers now strut around as the champions of reform!

What needed to be done was obvious then. But a weak political class—a class in disarray, a class prisoner of slogans and clichés, unable to think for itself—needed the compulsion of a breakdown to do the obvious thing. Thus documenting the adage in psychoanalysis—'A breakdown is a breakthrough'!

In many ways, the situation in regard to general governance is reaching the same point. The consequences of deterioration are now being visited upon the influentials also—the fear of dengue doesn't spare the families of the high-ups in Delhi; the children of the rich and well-connected also get kidnapped; crime, terrorism affect all. The consequences of pandering to caste-groups impede access to good education for meritorious children, of the well-to-do as much as of the poor. The backlash that will sweep the country as the pandering to Muslims continues will engulf all.

Therefore, I have little doubt that people are being prepared. It is not long before they will look around for alternatives. But we also have a duty; as Lenin would have said, we must give history a helping hand. We must work out alternatives, and make them a part of general discourse so that, when the breakdown comes, and people flap around for some better arrangement, the alternatives would have not just been worked out, they would be familiar.

Who is to provide that helping hand? As we noticed at the beginning, two races are going on in India today. The race between a creative society that displays much energy and innovativeness on the one side, and on the other a scaffolding of the State that is being hollowed by termites. And the race between those who are forging the new India—the middle class professionals and the entrepreneurs—and the political class that is stoking the old India to keep itself in office. The answer to the question—'Who is to help steer the country to the alternative system?'—lies in these races: the ones who are forging the new India are the ones who have to do so.

Legitimacy, authority, even power have shifted from the political class to them. They have to seize these, and put them to work for the country's good. Of course, many of them, for instance, several business houses, are doing exemplary work beyond their professions and businesses. They are promoting education, they are furthering research, they are giving indispensable aid to individuals and to groups that in turn are assisting the needy. This work is indeed commendable. It is indispensable. But it is not enough. Public life is the central ailment that needs to be cured today, public institutions are the ones that most need resurrection and rehabilitation. It is to this task that the ones who are forging the new India have to devote their efforts and resources. One argument is of necessity. Unless they do so, all the good work they are doing will be swamped by the collapse of institutions. When the whole cloth burns, howsoever exquisite the embroidery that they would have done in some corner of the cloth, that too shall burn up. The other is of culpability: after all, to take one instance, they have a major hand in keeping the political class going; that class could not survive without the finances it receives from, say, the business class. Why not use the enormous clout that the money you give out gives you to say, 'If you field a single candidate who has a criminal record, we will cut off all finances to you'?

Activist groups

There is another group that could do a lot, those who are doing what Gandhiji used to call constructive work. There are thousands and thousands of such groups and individuals today, persons and organizations who, in the face of great odds and obstacles, are serving others. Indeed, it is possible that, in large part because of his example and teaching, a larger number of such persons are at work today than in Gandhiji's time. Their work brings succour to countless numbers. Often, it spells the difference between life and death for the latter. But that enormous work is not having the sort of effect that constructive work had in Gandhiji's time; not on the general direction in which the country is moving, certainly not on public life or institutions. That contrast bears some reflection, as well as strong correction.

Gandhiji used constructive work often as the training nursery to nurture and season persons who he would eventually induct into public life. Second, he made that work, whether spinning or attending on leprosy patients, a part of the general movement for emancipation. That all such efforts were ultimately linked to him and that he was pre-eminently linked to the great cause of our Freedom Struggle linked them to that struggle axiomatically. But there was more. Gandhiji consciously linked them to each other and to the Freedom Movement. He made sure that each of them became, and was seen to be a tributary contributing to the great Brahmaputra. The various efforts that are being made today are not linked to any single cause.

But there is another difference. One of Gandhiji's great skills was that he had a programme for everyone. If you could sacrifice your life, he had a programme for you. If you could not give up your life but could go to jail, he had a programme for you. If you could not spend time in jail but could join a demonstration, he had a programme for you. If you could not join a demonstration but could wear *khadi*, he had a programme for you. If you could not wear *khadi* in public but could spin in the privacy of your home, he had a programme for you. If you could not spin but could recite the *Ram-dhun*, he linked that chanting to the national movement. Today, if you don't join the cause 'body and soul', indeed, if you don't join that particular cause body and soul which that group or individual has picked, you are in for censure and derision.

Apart from other consequences, this 'single-issue fundamentalism' prevents our constructive workers from valuing sufficiently the equally exemplary work of others. You may be risking your all to save the country from being inundated by Bangladeshis, but unless you are working to save forests, you are taken to be doing nothing on 'the real issue'. And that is putting it mildly.

And then there is the flaw in means. Gandhiji placed the greatest emphasis on purity of means. But today, and I have personally run into examples of this, enthusiasm, devotion, commitment to a cause have often been taken to condone exaggeration, even untruth, and certainly violence and obstruction. *Bandhs, morchas,* strikes, fasts-unto-death-between-meals, anger and screaming and denouncing are standard instruments. This has turned people off.

It is true, of course, that the obstacles that are put in the way of doing even good work are atrocious. But when those trying to do that act of service react in anger, they end up justifying the oppression. They defeat the cause they want to advance: with that avalanche of angry letters to the American President during the Vietnam War in mind, Thich Nhat Hanh wondered whether the President would read beyond the first few, angry lines... And then there is the question of what such anger, and what resort to such means does to oneself. The question that Thich Nhat Hanh asked the peace activists is indeed apposite: 'But can you write a love-letter? A letter he would read...'[1] What a contrast between the high-voltage denunciations and 'evidence' of our activists and the Buddha's description of the one devoted to right-speech: 'He dwells refraining from false speech, a truth-speaker, one to be relied on, trustworthy, dependable, not a deceiver of the world. Abandoning malicious speech, he does not repeat there what he has heard here to the detriment of these, or repeat here what he has heard there to the detriment of those. Thus he is a reconciler of those at variance...'[2]

The most important consequence goes beyond the effect on activists, beyond the particular cause they have taken up and which is harmed. Resort to such means, the hurling of so much anger harms public life. And that in several ways, direct and indirect:

❏ The good work that is being done gets associated in the public mind with obstruction and denunciation. And thereby loses the power it would have as an example.

---

[1] Thich Nhat Hanh, *Being Peace*, Parallax Press, Berekley, Calif., 1987, pp.79-80.
[2] The well-known discourse forms the subject of Ayya Khema's *Who is My Self?*, Wisdom Publications, Boston, 1997, from which the translation is taken.

❑ It piles even more negativity on to the heap that has already accumulated in public discourse in our country.
❑ It intensifies the adversarial atmosphere that, as we have seen, our political system foments.
❑ The good work becomes a specialization in itself: it does not contribute to the rehabilitation of institutions of governance, nor to reconstructing public discourse.

Thus, activism has to change its stripes, and shed its frown. And the groups have to be independent of the State. Indeed, they have to be an alternate government. But how can one be an alternate to the government, how can one be countervailing power if one is dependent on the State, if one is a limb of some political party?

Here then is an enormous army that could do more. To do so, constructive workers and activists need to:

❑ Lower the decibel level.
❑ Scrupulously stick to means that are pure.
❑ Be of a generous heart towards each other.
❑ Gather their separate beams and bring them to bear singularly on rehabilitating public institutions and public discourse.

Our duty

In any event, whether those making the new India—the entrepreneurs and professionals—and those doing good in specific spheres redirect their efforts or not, each of us must, as a mere individual, do his bit. Even as single, isolated individuals we can help: 'Desist from evil,' the *Dhammapada* counsels, 'Learn to do good.' We can do more. We can keep drawing attention to the fact that there *is* a better way. We must do so, and do so with the faith that the one Gandhiji called his political *guru*, Gopal Krishna Gokhale, expressed in those memorable words.

March 1911: Gokhale has moved a Bill that requires Government to spread elementary education. There has been intense debate for two full days. Gokhale is responding to the discussion. As he comes to the end of his response, he says:

My Lord I know that my Bill will be thrown out before the day closes. I make no complaint. I shall not even feel depressed. I know too well the story of the preliminary efforts that were required even in England, before the Act of 1870 was passed, either to complain or to feel depressed. Moreover, I have always felt and have often said that we, of the present generation of India, can only hope to serve our country by our failures. The men and women who will be privileged to serve her by their successes will come later. We must be content to accept cheerfully the place that has been allotted to us in our onward march. This Bill, thrown out today, will come back again and again, till on the stepping-stones of its dead selves, a measure ultimately rises which will spread the light of knowledge throughout the land. It may be that our efforts may not conduce even indirectly to the promotion of the great cause which we all have at heart and that they may turn out after all to be nothing better than the mere ploughing of the sands of the seashore. But, my Lord, whatever fate awaits our labours, one thing is clear. We shall be entitled to feel that we have done our duty, and where the call of the duty is clear, it is better even to labour and fail than not to labour at all...

We can be more hopeful. Legitimacy and authority and power have been taken out of the hands of the class that has been the main agent of perverting the constitutional system that the Framers had devised. They have passed into hands that are building the new India. Furthermore, notable successes have been achieved—even by individuals labouring alone. And, finally, the disarray that has resulted from the doings of the political class has now reached a pitch that the people are indeed in mind for change.

In any event, even if none of these helpful factors was present, we have the example of the generations that brought us Independence. We must labour out of devotion to them, and in the faith they had.

A few readings

A: *Our Constitution*
Constitution of India.

B: *The way our Constitution came into being*
Constituent Assembly Debates, Volumes I to XII, Lok Sabha Secretariat, New Delhi, 1985.

The Framing of India's Constitution, B. Shiva Rao, ed., Volumes I to IV, Indian Institute of Public Administration, New Delhi, 1966-68.

The Framing of India's Constitution, A Study, B. Shiva Rao, and others, Indian Institute of Public Administration, New Delhi, 1968.

Granville Austin, *The Indian Constitution, Cornerstone of a Nation,* Oxford University Press, Delhi, 1966, 9th Impression, 2005.

Arun Shourie, *Worshipping False Gods,* ASA, 1997.

C: *The way our Constitution has been changed*
Constitution Amendment in India, Lok Sabha Secretariat, New Delhi, 1986.

S.C. Kashyap, *Constitution Making Since 1950,* Universal Law Publishing Company, Delhi, 2004.

D: *Our Constitution in practice*
Report of the National Commission to Review the Working of the Constitution, Justice M.N. Venkatachaliah, and others, New Delhi, 2002.

Granville Austin, *Working a Democratic Constitution, The Indian Experience*, Oxford University Press, Delhi, 1999, 5th Impression, 2001.

N.A. Palkhivala, *Our Constitution, Defaced and Defiled*, Macmillan, Delhi, 1974.

E: Proposals for Reform
Jayaprakash Narayan, "A plea for reconstruction of the Indian polity," in *A Revolutionary's Quest*, Bimal Prasad, ed., Oxford University Press, 1980.

B.K. Nehru, "A proposal for constitutional reform," in *Thoughts on Our Present Discontents*, Allied, Delhi, 1986.

N.A. Palkhivala, *We, the People*, Strand Bookstall, Bombay, 1984.

L.P. Singh, *Electoral Reform*, Uppal Publishing House, Delhi, 1986.

F: Electoral systems
Andrew Reynolds, Ben Reilly and Andrew Ellis, *Electoral System Design, The New International Handbook*, International Institute for Democracy and Electoral Assistance, Stockholm, 2005.

Hansard Society, *Report of the Hansard Society Commission on Electoral Reform*, Hansard Society, London, 1976.

C. Jeffery, "Electoral Reform: Learning from Germany," *The Political Quarterly*, 1998.

Refreshing the Parts: Electoral Reform and British Politics, G. Smyth, (ed), Lawrence and Wishart, London, 1992.

R. Blackburn, *The Electoral System in Britain*, Macmillan, London, 1995.

D. Farrell, *Comparing Electoral Systems*, Prentice Hall, 1997.

D. Farrell, *Electoral Systems*, Palgrave, 2001.

A. Reeve and A. Ware, *Electoral Systems: A Comparative and Theoretical Introduction*, Routledge, 1992.

Report of the Royal Commission on the Electoral System, New Zealand, 1986: in particular, pp.11-80, "The voting system."

G: *The cult of the common man and our political class*
Jose Ortega y Gasset, *The Revolt of the Masses,* W.W. Norton & Company, New York, 1957.

Mancur Olson, *Power and Prosperity, Outgrowing Communist and Capitalist Dictatorships,* Basic Books, New York, 2000.

Adversary Politics and Electoral Reform, S.E. Finer (ed.), Anthony Wigram, London, 1975.

H.W.R. Wade, *Constitutional Fundamentals,* The Hamlyn Lectures, Thirty second series, Stevens, London, 1980.

Index

Accountability: myth in parliamentary system of: 25-27; illustrative changes to ensure: 105-11

Activist groups: sterling work of: 250-51; reasons it is not cumulative: 251-52; suggestions: 252-53

Antulay, AR: on why ambit of Judiciary should be curtailed: 167-68

Ambedkar, BR: repudiates authorship of, and Constitution itself: 18; foreboding about political parties: 70-71; men, not Constitution will be at fault: 85-86; reason Article 32 is very soul, heart of Constitution: 177

Andhra: votes polled, seats won in: 50; politicians and uranium mining in: 65-66

Arithmetic: the answer to performance: 58

Asian Age, The: 171-72

Austin, Granville: on effect of 42nd Amendment: 151

Ayya Khema: 252

Bakshi, PM: 108

Bandits: Mancur Olson on stationary and roving: 22-23

Bangladeshi infiltrators: 97-98

Barooah, DK: hails 42nd Amendment, ridicules Basic Structure: 168-69

Basic Structure: evolution of doctrine: 173; vague?: 173-76; rationale for: 176-80; elements of: 183-88; parliamentary form an element of?: 189-92; emergency provisions held to be part of: 195-96; Rule of Law an element of?: 196-97; federalism an element of?: 198-99

Basic Structure, ridiculed: 'imported by judges': 156-57; 'invented by judges': 160; 'cannot even be cremated': 169

Basic Structure, dangers to: doctrine not adhered to consistently by judges themselves: 195-99; using doctrine to push hobby horses: 199-200; two streams of judgements on: 200; scoffed at by some judges themselves: 201; examples of pronouncements that endanger: 200-05; to push agenda, progressives devalue notion of: 205-06; splitting legalisms: 206-07; laying down the principle, then not applying it: 207-08; perilous trust: 208-14; when judges choose not to see: 214-19

Benami Transactions (Prohibition) Bill: 106

Bhagwati, Chief Justice PN: amending power limited: 184; explanatory statement in *Minerva Mills:* 202-04

Buddha, The: on right speech: 252

Burke, Edmund: exemplary
   representative: 239-43

Chandrachud, Chief Justice YV:
   amending power limited: 184;
   explanatory statement in
   Kesavananda: 201-02
Coalition: interest of partners in
   keeping it weak: 36-37
Common Cause v. Union of India:
   a judgement that deserves to be
   reversed: 108-09
Constituent Assembly Debates:
   70-71, 85-86, 245-48
Constitution: proposals for re-
   examination denounced: 18;
   Ambedkar disowns: 18; Nehru on
   changing it as circumstances
   change: 18-20; number of changes
   in: 20; if power to amend is
   unlimited: 176-80
Criminalization: 77-82

Dasmunsi, Priyaranjan: hails 42nd
   Amendment: 154-55, 162-64;
   what incorporating 'socialism' in
   Preamble should entail: 162-63
Dhammapada: 245
Dharia, Mohan: courageous
   opposition to Election Laws
   (Amendment) Bill: 116, 118-19;
   to 39th Amendment: 127, 132,
   135
Delhi: votes polled, seats won in: 51
Discourse: dumbing down of: 236-38
DMK: ministers switch: 28; heed their
   leader, not the PM: 36-37

Election laws: altered to circumvent
   Allahabad High Court judgement:
   116-18; Lok Sabha debate on Bill:
   118-21; Rajya Sabha debate on
   Bill: 121-26

Electorate: splintered: 27-35;
   incentive for politician to go on
   splintering: 35; hence, no 'national
   issue': 35-36; hence, arithmetic
   the answer to performance: 58
Emergency, The: reasons for
   recounting constitutional changes
   during: 11-12
Executive: illustrative changes: 94-96

Finer, SE: 60, 67
Forty-first Amendment Bill:
   provisions: 141; Rajya Sabha
   debate on: 140-48
Forty-second Amendment: salient
   provisions: 149-51; Lok Sabha
   debate on: 152-64; Rajya Sabha
   debate on: 164-70
Freedom of speech, of legislators:
   104-05

Gandhi, Indira: steamroller majority
   with minority votes: 28;
   announces breakthrough in
   uranium discoveries: 65; election
   case: 115; on 42nd Amendment:
   158-60, 169-70; Basic Structure an
   'invention of judges': 159;
   mistakes of: 220-21
Gandhi, Mahatma: reasons
   constructive work under him set
   country's direction: 250-53
Gandhi, Sonia: *vis a vis* Manmohan
   Singh: 58; effect on perceptions
   about Congress: 71
Gasset, Jose Ortega y: the 'common
   man' as standard: 225-26, 236-37
Gokhale, Gopal Krishna: to serve
   through our failures: 253-54
Gokhale, HR: on election law
   alterations: 117-18, 120-21;
   ominous hint: 121; on election
   laws Bill in Rajya Sabha: 121, 126;

on the 39th Amendment: in Lok
Sabha: 127-28, 134-35, in Rajya
Sabha: 135, 139-40; on 41st
Amendment Bill: 141, 147;
reverses position on advice of
Election Commission: 150; on
42nd Amendment: 152-53, 160-
62, 164-67, 170-71; powers of
Judiciary not curtailed: 208

Governments: myth of secure,
decisive: 24, 56-58

Governments: weak: result of
present system: 36-37

Grover, Justice AN: on test of power
claimed: 180; elements of Basic
Structure: 185-86

Gupta, Bhupesh: supports election
law alterations to circumvent
Allahabad High Court judgement:
121-26; supports 39th
Amendment: 135-39

Gupta, Indrajit: supports election law
alterations to circumvent
Allahabad High Court judgement:
119-20; supports 39th
Amendment: 132-33; supports
42nd Amendment: 153-54

Hand, Learned: chooses to remain
'rationally ignorant': 222

Haryana: votes polled, seats won in:
51

Hegde, Justice KS: what Government
claimed it could alter in
Constitution: 178-79; reasons
Parliament is not synonymous with
people: 181-83; elements of Basic
Structure: 186

Hindustan Times, The: 79-80

Hope: grounds for: 13

Incompetence, multi-tiered:
74-78

Independents: candidates who
lost deposits: 32; Jharkhand
governments buffeted by:
37-49

Indian Express, The: 26-27, 58,
80-81

Indiresen, PV: his law: 77

Individuals: everything turns on:
245-49; our duty as: 253-54

Interest groups: contrasted with
inchoate 'people': 223-24

Interests: claim that parliamentary
form harmonizes: 63-64, 66-69

Investigating agency: to investigate
without permission of state
government: 107

Jharkhand: course of governments of:
37-48; exemplifies more than
itself: 48-49

Judiciary: suggested changes: 96-97;
must preserve independence, role
and power of: 175-79, 183-84,
219; builds the vital dyke: 173-88;
castigated for crossing limit:
119-20, 140, 156-61; blamed for
pushing Government to enact
42nd Amendment: 152-53, 170;
denigrated: 145, 147; alleged to be
part of a conspiracy: 122-24;
charged with acting out of political
motives: 159-60, 169; clamour to
curtail role of: 119-20, 121-25,
130-31, 135-37, 166-67; warned:
157, 160-62, 164, 166-67, 169;
laws, Constitution changed to
curtail its powers and ambit:
117-18, 128-29, 141, 149-51;
denunciations and demand to curb
it continue to this day: 171-72;
internal dangers to guard against·
195-219

Kamath, HV: 176
Karunanidhi, M: spikes Cabinet
    decision on Neyveli Lignite
    Corporation: 37; lauds minister for
    belling the judicial-cat: 171-72
Kashyap, Subhash: on what
    Constitution Review Commission
    had decided: 94-97
Kerala: votes polled, seats won in:
    51-52
Khanna, Justice HR: elements of
    Basic Structure: 188; perilous trust
    of the good liberal: 208-14
Khanna, Tarun: 77
Krishna Iyer, Justice VR: exhorts
    'alert and quick acting legislature':
    115-16; Framers adopted
    parliamentary form: 189-90;
    'ghost' of Basic Structure cannot
    be refuge of proprietariat: 205-06

Leaders: contrast between public life
    and industry: 9-10
Lee Kwan Yew: on choosing the best
    for governance: 77
Legislatures: condition of: 26-27;
    votes polled by winners: 28-32;
    illustrative changes: 99-105;
    disqualifications for being
    members of: 101-102;
    proceedings of: 102-05
Lenin, VI: textbook illustration of
    prescription of: 136
Lok Sabha: votes polled by winners:
    28-29, 33-34; debate on election
    law amendment Bill: 115-20; on
    39th Amendment: 125-34; on
    42nd Amendment: 150-62, 207
Lottery: what if legislators were
    selected by: 87-89

Madhukar, CV: on working of
    Parliament: 26-27

Madhya Pradesh: votes polled, seats
    won in: 52-53
Maharashtra: votes polled, seats won
    in: 53
MPLADS: 33
Mukherjea, Justice AK: what
    Government claimed it could alter
    in Constitution: 178-79; reasons
    Parliament is not synonymous with
    people: 181-82; elements of Basic
    Structure: 186
Muslim League: manages to be
    part of successive governments:
    51-52; supports 39th Amendment:
    134

Naidu, Chandrababu: and uranium
    mining: 65-66
Narain, Raj: election case: 115,
    151
Narasimha Rao, PV, v. State: a
    judgement that deserves to be
    reversed: 109-11
National Commission to Review
    Working of the Constitution: on
    Independents: 32; on
    criminalization of politics: 78;
    what it had decided on two-round
    elections, and compulsory voting:
    94-97; on incongruity in electoral
    law on disqualifications: 101;
    recommendations to ensure
    accountability: 106-07; on need to
    reverse judgement in JMM bribery
    case: 110-11; urges series of rights:
    227-30
Nehru, BK: 100
Nehru, Jawaharlal: on changing
    Constitution as need arises: 18-20;
    steamroller majority on minority
    votes: 28; invoked to curb
    Judiciary: 160-62; mistakes for
    which country pays: 220

Olson, Mancur: roving and stationary bandits: 22-23; reasons why individual remains 'rationally ignorant': 221-22; interest groups: 224

Opportunity: for reform: 249-50

Orissa: votes polled, seats won in: 53

Palkhivala, NA: on one profession that requires no qualification: 75; test for power is not likelihood of misuse but width: 180; elements of Basic Structure: 185; whether Presidential form desirable: 192

Pande, Alka S: 80-81

Parliament: not synonymous with people: 180-83

Parliament, members: cannot solve personal problems of constituents: 33; resolve to abide by rules: 243-44

Parliament, sovereignty of: as rationale for overturning election laws: 115-16; for 39th Amendment putting some elections beyond purview of courts: 126-40; for 42nd Amendment hacking jurisdiction of Judiciary: 152-71; continues to be invoked today to put politicians above the law: 171-72

Parliamentary form: whether an element of Basic Structure: 186, 188, 188-92

Parliamentary system: the one we have: 21; justifications for: 22; turn out to be myths: 24-83

People: myths and facts about: 220-27; 'rationally ignorant': 221-22; as the standard and consequences thereof: 225-27, 234-39; participation in governance: 82-83

Policies: inducement to adopt increasingly irresponsible: 58-63; present arrangements ensure swift reversals: 64-66

Political parties: number in Parliament, governments: 36; fight each other and join up: 35-36; condition as organizations: 69-74; what they have made of politics: 67-69; grievance mongering, to manufacturing vote banks, to pandering: 58-63; national parties weaken: 61-62, 69-72; character of regional parties: 73-74

Prasad, Rajendra: on task of every individual: 246-48

Rajasthan: votes polled, seats won in: 54

Rajshekhar, VT: 235

Rajya Sabha: debates: on Bill to change election laws: 121-26; on 39th Amendment: 135-40; on 41st Amendment Bill: 140-47; on 42nd Amendment: 164-71

Ramaswamy, Justice V: impeachment proceedings against: 25

Ray, Chief Justice AN: elements of Basic Structure: 186-87

Reddy, Justice Jaganmohan: elements of Basic Structure: 187-88

Reddy, Justice BP Jeevan: 108-11

Reddy, YS Rajasekhara: and uranium mining: 65-66

Reforms: electoral outcomes and: 61-62; have spurred new leadership in industry: 86-87

Representation of the People Act, Section 8: 101-02

Representative, people's: sense in which he is taken to be: 33, 238-39; sense in which he should be: 239-43

Representativeness, myth of: 27-36,
  50-56
Rights mongering: Constitution
  Review Commission: 227-30;
  Sachar Committee: 230-34
Rules: routinely flouted in
  legislatures: 26-27; MPs resolve to
  adhere to: 243-44; need to abide
  by: 244-45

Sachar Committee: divisive
  recommendations of: 230-34
Shelat, Justice JM: on test of power
  claimed: 180; elements of Basic
  Structure: 185-86
Sikri, Chief Justice SM: if amending
  power is unlimited: 176-78;
  reasons Parliament is not
  synonymous with people:
  180-81; elements of Basic
  Structure: 185
Singh, LP: 99
Singh, Manmohan: Left parties on: 26;
  systemic reasons for perceived
  weakness of: 36-37; Sonia Gandhi
  vis a vis: 58
Singh, Prakash: on sway of criminals:
  79-80
Sinha, Sachchidananda: exhorts
  Constituent Assembly: 245-46
Sinha, Yashwant: on reforms and
  electoral outcomes: 61-62
Singh, Swaran: heads Committee on
  Constitution: 149; on 42nd
  Amendment: 155-57
Socialism: Congressman on what
  incorporation in Preamble should
  entail: 162-63
Spencer, John: 32
States: votes polled by winners in
  legislatures: 29-32
Stephen, CM: on 42nd Amendment:
  157-58

Story, Joseph: on individuals:
  245-46
Structure: impacts conduct: 10-12,
  85-89
System, an alternative: 94-111
System, present: immutable?: 17-18;
  one of many: 89-92; a means: 92;
  criteria for assessing: 92-93

Tamil Nadu: votes polled, seats won
  in: 54-55
Task Force on Border Management:
  on madrasas: 231
Thakkar, Justice MP: 204-05
Thich Nhat Hanh: counsel to activists:
  252
Thirty-ninth Amendment: rushed
  through: 126-27; provisions: 128-
  29; Lok Sabha debate on: 126-35;
  Rajya Sabha debate on: 135-40

United Kingdom: result of first-past-
  the-post system: 32
Uranium mining: politicians reverse
  positions regarding: 65-66
Uttar Pradesh: candidates elected by
  11-20% of electors: 33-34; lesson
  politicians draw from this: 35;
  votes polled, seats won in: 55

Veerasamy, Arcot N: denounces
  judges: 171-72
Vittal, N: 106
Vohra, NN: findings about nexus of
  criminals and politicians: 78; their
  fate: 78-79
Voting: small swings cause major
  dislocations: 50-56; compulsory:
  89; illustrative changes: 97-99

Wade, HWR: 66-67

Acknowledgements

This brief book spells out some of the points I urged in the second *Nani A. Palkhivala Memorial Lecture*. Perhaps we owe the dyke of the Basic Structure more to Mr. Palkhivala than to almost anyone else. For this debt and so many others that we owe him, it was a great honour for me to be asked to speak in his honour. I am most grateful to the Trustees of the Nani A. Palkhivala Memorial Trust for asking me to deliver the lecture.

I remain indebted to my friends, Surendra Malik and Sanjay Kapur of *Supreme Court Cases*, for allowing me to continue to use their splendid software.

I am grateful to the research wing of the Election Commission for the data that have been used while discussing the results of the current first-past-the-post system.

To friends at *Prabhat Khabar* and *Ranchi Express* for helping reconstruct events in Jharkhand.

To Sanjay Kanvinde for the illustration that has been used on the cover.

To Virender Singh of *The Hindustan Times* for the photograph of Parliament House that has been used in the front endpaper. And to Manoj Chhabra of *The Times of India* for photographs of the U.P. Assembly that have been used in the rear endpaper.

WILL THE IRON FENCE SAVE A TREE HOLLOWED BY TERMITES?
Defence imperatives beyond the military

Should we put our trust in Musharraf's *"naya dil"*? Or should we look at the nature of the State and society in Pakistan? What is poured into children in *madrasas*? In "non-religious" schools in Pakistan? What is the relationship of the Islam-*pasand* parties, terrorist groups and the ruling establishment in Pakistan?

Over *sixty thousand* persons have been killed by terrorist-related violence in India in the last twenty years. What transforms a believer into a killing-machine? What lessons have we learnt in fighting terrorism?

Vast tracts of the country are being annexed by Bangladeshi infiltrators. What does this hold for the security of the country? What consequences have already come about for our elections? Who is knitting terrorist and Islamic organizations together in our Northeast? What danger does this spell? What danger does the unrelenting radicalization of Bangladesh itself hold for us?

Will China not translate its economic might into military might? Is it not already doing so? Has it not ringed India? Myanmar has become a dependency of China. Bangladesh has entered into a defence pact with it. The relationship between Pakistan and China is described by them as between lips and teeth. Tibet has been militarized. What does this spell for us? What does China's new strategic doctrine mean for countries that lie on its rim—as India does?

China's strategy—even in regard to territory—has been clear as daylight: "grab; hold; let time pass". Has it not already made us lose Aksai Chin? Does anyone today even suggest that it be returned to India? Why will China's current claim to Arunachal spell less peril?

Will the USA or Russia do our work for us?

Does the way that institutions of the State are being hollowed not constitute the even greater, and immediate threat? Which is the idea that has not been proposed? What happens to recommendations that are "accepted", on which "action is taken"?

But how can even institutions of State be rectified when superciliousness becomes the ideology of the media?

With a wealth of evidence, ARUN SHOURIE spells out imperatives for defence beyond the military.

FALLING OVER BACKWARDS
An essay against Reservations and against Judicial Populism

How is it that what was explicitly forbidden by the Constitution—classification based on caste—has become the rule? How is it that what were *enabling* provisions have become *mandatory minima*? Where does the figure 50 per cent come from? How is it that in practice it is exceeded blatantly? Are the benefits not being 'hogged by a few, the better-off among these castes? Has the "creamy layer" been actually hived off? How is it that what were begun as reservations at entry became reservations in promotions also? How did this become a right to *accelerated* promotions? How did *that* become a right to "accelerated promotions with consequential seniority"? How did *that* become a right to have the prescribed standards diluted—to the point of being waived altogether? Even in educational institutions. Is this any way to become a "knowledge super-power"?

As there has been no caste-wise enumeration and tabulation since the 1931 Census, from where does this mythical figure—"OBCs are 52 per cent of the population" come? And what did the 1931 Census itself say about its caste-wise figures?

The race then was to get one's group recognized as a *higher* caste. How has it become a race to get it anointed as "backward"? Are the "backward castes", the weak ones who need protection and special privileges? Are they not the dominant, and domineering castes? Who is most responsible for atrocities on *harijans?*

How have the Courts come to acquiesce in such wholesale perversion of the Constitution? Is their role to cheer such perversion on? Or is to *conserve*, to protect the Constitution?

Where will this process end? Has it not already enfeebled the State structure? Has it not already riven our society? Has it not subverted parliamentary democracy? Has Pandit Nehru's warning not come true—that "This way lies not only folly, but disaster"?

With trenchant evidence from the Archives of the 1930s and '40s, from Censuses, from judgements of the Supreme Court, with telling facts about the situation that has already come to prevail on the ground, ARUN SHOURIE nails the perversion of the Constitution, and urges a complete reversal. The weaker sections must be helped, but by altogether different methods.

GOVERNANCE
And the sclerosis that has set in

"Can officers use red or green ink on files?" A simple question, you may think. But in Government it is enough to set off meetings, letters, references to other ministries that stretch over a year.... A tree falls on to the house of the Indian High Commissioner in Singapore; memos fly to and fro, and for nine years Government cogitates, and deliberates, and weighs pros and cons, unable to decide who is to repair the house, and how... From such trifles to matters that spell the difference between life and death, the same pattern... Governments shut their eyes to a problem. The problem swells. Governments look the other way. The problem explodes. Governments set up an institution to tackle it. Five years later, exactly what had been forecast comes to pass—the problem is still there, and the institution has become another problem... As the institution has not worked, a law is passed. As the law is not enforced, amendments are decreed that make penalties under the law more frightening. Legislation as a substitute for enforcement. Vision statements, plan documents, strategy papers as a substitute for execution....

Improving governance is the reform we need. But how is reform to be brought about when every proposal has to be put through the same winding, interminable loops? Can the structures be "reformed" at all? Or does what was done with Industrial Licensing, with import and export controls, does what ARUN SHOURIE strove to ensure in the telecom sector show the way? That is, wherever possible, to jettison the function?

In a rare glimpse into what has become of governance, Shourie argues that the only way ahead is to revolutionize the nature of the Indian State—from the principal "Engine of Growth" it was taken to be in the '50 and '60s, from "The Great Monitor" it became in the '70s and '80s, to an enabling State, a State that clears the way so that others may do their best for the country. A leaner State, but one that performs those fewer, and indispensable functions better.